WHERE TO, AUSTRALIA?

WHERE TO, AUSTRALIA?

by
GRAHAM L PATERSON

Strategic Book Publishing and Rights Co.

Strategic Book Publishing & Rights Co., LLC
USA | Singapore
www.sbpra.com

For information about special discounts for bulk purchases, please contact Strategic Book Publishing and Rights Co. Special Sales, at bookorder@sbpra.net.

ISBN: 978-1-948260-43-5

DEDICATION

This book is dedicated to everyone who would like to have a better political system for Australia.

It will take you on a journey down a path seldom travelled in the history of politics. It will explain why politics is so important in all our lives, but it will also show you that you are responsible for whatever political system you choose for your society. People are the fountainhead of all political power – not the politicians and not the lawyers, and definitely not the judges – it is always the people – because, without the people, there is no political power.

This journey offers you the potential for a more honest system; a system less corruptible by money, and one that can give you better control over your elected and appointed representatives. It is not a perfect system because human nature guarantees that perfection is unattainable in the affairs of mankind. However, it provides a foundation for each of us on our journey to a better future. This journey creates a set of rules that a large number of ordinary people would like to see adopted for the betterment of their society.

It's a journey that commenced many years ago, but a journey that has seldom been able to demonstrate why it is, that the people who are ruled are the ones who control the rulers. This is a journey down a path to a democratic and independent nation. A nation established by a philosophy that offers a level of freedom under a set of fundamental rules. Rules that can be understood by any reasonably educated person; rules that are clearly spelt out in a genuine people's Constitution.

Nobody needs a law degree to read and understand this Constitution.

It takes you on a journey towards the type of society that respects the rights and freedoms of everyone willing to live by the rule of law. It is a journey that defines the sort of governmental system that is designed to serve a public purpose for the benefit of our society.

It is a governmental system that is accountable to the people, and it is a governmental system that is there to serve the people and their society.

WHERE TO, AUSTRALIA?

FOREWORD

Before we get started on this book, I need to ask you if you believe Australia is an independent country. From all accounts, a great number of people do believe Australia is independent, and a democratic one at that. But, do you know when and how we are supposed to have become an independent nation? It seems, even the High Court doesn't know, according to the Sue v Hill case of nineteen ninety-nine.

And do you know what a "democracy" really is?

Have you ever thought about how you would define a democracy?

Obviously, there are quite a few ways people can choose to define what they believe to be a democratic country, but what are a few of the basic essentials? What would you consider as an ideal and desirable set of principles for a democratic Australia?

How about these?

1. Do you think the people should have some authority over political decisions?
2. Do you believe the Australian Government should issue and control the nation's money supply?
3. Do you believe our national affairs should be free of external demands and interference?

These would seem to be a fairly good set of principles for a democratic Australia, and if we are to be an independent nation, they would be pretty much essential.

Unfortunately, Australia would fail each one of them.

Of course, there are plenty of other principles people will come up with, such as a Bill of Rights, a vote, free education, free speech, and free health care; just to name a few. Having a vote once every three years, or so, doesn't really constitute authority over political decisions. Voting is just one relatively minor aspect of "democracy", and as it turns out, a rather deceitful and manipulative one at that.

So, are we all happy to leave things as they are, and not bother to question whether we are independent, or even a democratic country? Does it even matter whether or not we are a proper and legally independent nation? I suppose if everybody thinks we are an independent, democratic nation that's all that really matters. But can we just toss the rule of law out the window and not bother whether things are done legally or not? To some people that represents a state of anarchy, which on the one hand can mean total chaos and on the other hand it can mean absolute "freedom". I doubt too many people who would agree to abandon the rule of law and take the risk of living in a state of anarchy.

Many years ago, a British Judge, Sir Edward Coke, stood up to King James I and said to him, *"You only have the power to rule which the law gives you ..."*

In our case, despite the surreal concept of the Queen of England being our "supreme ruler," in fact, we are under the control of whichever political party, or coalition of parties, has the majority of seats in the House of Representatives. Why is that so? What is this law that gives the political parties the power to rule over us? I guess it must be what is known as the Primary Law of the Commonwealth. If Australia does, in fact, have a Primary Law, then I suppose, it has to be what is known as Australia's Constitution. Unfortunately, there is no original mention of political parties in this Primary Law, and certainly, no reference to any such controlling authority.

And what is Australia's Constitution these days?

That's a tricky question because hardly anyone knows what Australia's Constitution is. In fact, very few people even know that Australia doesn't have a Constitution that they can claim to own, not one that's ever been put to the people for their acceptance. And that is contrary to what the Federal Government and the academics have been saying for years. It is a deliberate lie to claim the British Act to form the Commonwealth of Australia was ever approved by the Australian people. That Act has never been put to the vote in Australia.

I bet there are a quite a few legal and Constitutional experts who would dispute that statement, and not the least, the judges on the High Court of Australia. What Australia uses as its Constitution is still, to this day, a nineteenth-century British Act of the British Parliament. An Act that has never been repealed, and is still legally in force. If we continue to use the British Act of nineteen hundred as our Constitution, it must always be the property of the UK Parliament. That Act is titled "The Commonwealth of Australia Constitution Act 1900 (UK)," and despite the fact it was proclaimed on the first of January nineteen hundred and one in Melbourne, Australia, it is still the property of the UK.

Unfortunately, that British Act has many flaws, not the least that it has virtually nothing to do with "democracy." Democracy was a quaint concept in the nineteen hundred's that was shunned by most of the forty-nine ·politicians and lawyers, and one banker, who was responsible for drafting, what far too many people believe, is "our" Constitution. All these fifty men did, was to draft a document to maintain the status quo of the nineteenth century; a document that was subsequently altered by the British Government before being inserted as Clause 9 of the British Act.

Australia doesn't "own" a Constitution. The Federal Government and the legal fraternity are still, deliberately and dishonestly, using the British Act that has never been repealed by the British Parliament. Despite political parties being an established fact in nineteenth-century British politics, the British Parliament didn't see fit to recognise the existence of political parties in their Commonwealth Act, nor did it bother to include the position of a Prime Minister.

These wee small problems don't seem to bother anyone, then or now. Contrary to the historical myths that have been perpetuated over the years, neither the British Act nor the altered draft document that became Clause 9 of the Act, have ever been presented to anybody in Australia, for their approval.

The ultimate conclusion of this little excursion into history tends to show that, by any reasonable logic, Australia cannot be an independent nation. Until the British Act is repealed, Australia must continue to be tied to Britain's apron strings, despite the farcical nineteen ninety-nine decision of the High Court of Australia declaring Britain to be a foreign country. Geographically, Britain is certainly a foreign country, but legally, Australia is still very much tied to the UK as long as their British Act is used as our Constitution.

So, what is the purpose of a book on a new Constitution for an independent Australia? Writing this book is based on the belief that every word must be chosen carefully for a specific reason. Every word in a Constitution has to be carefully thought out and written in a logical and understandable way. The fundamental aim is to write a Constitution that will limit the ability to distort and manipulate the meaning and intent of the words. That, of course, is a tremendously difficult task to achieve in the English language. But even so, the effort must be attempted if we want a Primary Law that can be read and understood by every reasonably educated person.

This book attempts to do that, but it has gone one step further, by providing an explanation and justification for every Chapter of the draft Constitution. The book also uses the unusual approach of creating a discussion between ordinary people. This is to demonstrate that a Constitution isn't just a legal document for the exclusive use of lawyers, politicians, or judges. The Constitution is a philosophical document as much as it is a legal document, and it is up to the people to say what philosophy, and what laws, they want for their society and their nation.

The following book takes the bull by the horns, and even while kicking and snorting, it tries to drag Australia into the realm of a truly independent and democratic nation.

CONTENTS

PART 1

PART 2

PART 1

CHAPTER 1

Introduction

This book has many authors of which I'm just one. But why, you might ask, am I writing this book at all?

I am writing this book because I passionately believe Australia must become a true and proper independent nation.

It is a patent lie that the British Act Australia uses as its Constitution has served "us" well. It hasn't served "us", the people, at all. It was never intended to serve "us"; it was always intended to serve the politicians and the lawyers, and in that, it has been spectacularly successful.

Just ask yourself; if Australia is supposed to be an independent nation, why hasn't the British Act of nineteen hundred been repealed?

Why is the British Act still in force, and why does the British Parliament still consider it a legal document? It is always applied whenever the Australian Government appoints a Governor General. Do you know why? Are any of the supposed constitutional "experts" prepared to admit why this is so? In nineteen ninety-nine, the High Court of Australia, in a split decision, proclaimed Britain to be a foreign country. The eminent judges also asserted that Australia was an independent nation, even though no judge could define how or when this supposed independence occurred. I am very sure many of the politicians, and all the lawyers and Judges know why this antiquated and out of date British Act is still in force. The explanation is fairly obvious to anyone who cares to think about it.

Neither the Australian Government nor the British Government can move to repeal the Act without admitting that Australia is still a colony of the UK.

None of the fraudulent attempts to claim otherwise will stand. Not the nineteen thirty-one Westminster Act, not when the British Parliament amended their Immigration Act in nineteen seventy-three to cancel the status of Australian people as British subjects. Not even the deceitful nineteen eighty-six Australia Act, and certainly not the nineteen ninety-nine High Court split decision in the Sue v Hill case. The repeal of the British Act would be an open admission that Australia remains tied to Britain's apron strings, and we truly are "The Concealed Colony." (The title used for the comprehensively detailed, but ultimately futile, submission to the UN in nineteen ninety-nine. This submission was made on behalf of all Australians by the Institute of Constitutional Education and Research of Victoria, Australia)

Any attempt to repeal the British Act would immediately throw Australia into limbo, unless, there is a replacement Constitution sitting in the wings ready for immediate implementation. Obviously, no such replacement Constitution could be implemented without the approval of the Australian people at a nationwide referendum in Australia. The ramification of this situation has been an ongoing difficulty for the legal fraternity, and the Government, since as far back as nineteen hundred and nineteen.

The inability to repeal the British Act is clear proof of the lies being perpetuated since nineteen hundred and nineteen. Billy Hughes is the only Prime Minister we have ever had who was honest enough to try and do the right thing. Australia was declared a sovereign and independent nation when invited to join the League of Nations as an inaugural Member. The recognition of that status needed formalising in two ways. First, Australia had to create their own Constitution, and secondly, Britain had to repeal their Act forming the Commonwealth of Australia. Billy Hughes tried to introduce a bill into Parliament to start the wheels in motion for creating that new Australian Constitution but had to withdraw it in the face of a hostile reception. Neither the repeal of the British Act, nor Australia creating their own Constitution, ever happened, but every PM since nineteen hundred and nineteen has been aware of the anomalous relationship between Australia and the UK. And so too, with patent dishonesty, has every High Court of Australia. Hence the need to try and address this anomaly. The first attempt was the nineteen hundred and thirty-one Westminster Act, which Australia adopted, in part, in nineteen forty-two, but when that failed, Hawke tried the nineteen eighty-six Australia Act. The obvious illegitimacy of both these attempts is demonstrated by the fact that neither Act was put to a referendum. The deceit surrounding these Acts is further demonstrated by the fact both Acts could only be recognised when passed by the UK Parliament.

This book aims to address that failed attempt by Billy Hughes.

The book describes, in detail, the reasons and purpose for every Chapter included in the draft of a new Constitution for an independent Australia. This project was started back in nineteen ninety-eight when a few hundred people from all around Australia made submissions to Joe Bryant's Alternative Three Movement. They wanted a say in the sort of Constitution that would be needed for Australian to become an independent Republic. Unfortunately, their voice was never heard at the time, and although their names are now mostly lost, their voice is being resurrected.

But, why am I bothering? Let's face it, hardly anyone gives a damn about the Constitution, about any Constitution for that matter, at least, not until a problem arises and somebody goes and checks the rules. I was asked that question the other day. "Why do you bother when nobody else cares about the Constitution, least of all the politicians?" I replied that when people live together with others, whether it's a family, a village, a city, or a nation, there have to be some rules about how the people should relate to each other. Fundamentally, that set of rules is the Constitution. But a problem arises when the rules aren't followed, and that's when the people have to decide what to do about that. Thus, the people have to start talking about what sort of generally accepted system they can create for dealing with people who don't follow the rules. The creation of any such system, by the agreement of the people, forms the basis for creating a "government". When that happens, the system then needs to be incorporated into the set of rules that is the Constitution.

Thus, two important points arise from the above discussion. That the creation of a Constitution, and the development of a governmental system, are both the property of the people. Both are intended for the benefit of the people and their society. Constitutions and Governments should never be considered as the exclusive property of either politicians or lawyers, but unfortunately, in today's world, that is mostly the case. By any logical and democratic reasoning, it should be up to the people to tell the politicians and lawyers what "powers, privileges and immunities" the people are prepared to allow their representatives and public servants, and not the other way around.

So, tell me, why did you want to write a book like this?

That's simple. Because, so far, I've never seen an up to date and practical Constitution for an independent Australia.

Surely, there are versions written by the constitutional experts?

The few versions I've seen have mainly been variations of the existing British Act.

That's fair enough because the existing Constitution has worked pretty well for the last hundred years or more.

It really hasn't worked at all well for the people, but it's been great for the politicians and lawyers.

Is that why you want to change everything?

A lot of things will need to change if we become an independent nation.

That's a heap of crock, we're already independent and have been for a long time.

Is that so? Then, how come the Queen of England is still our head of state?

She's not. We have the Queen of Australia, and she's our head of state.

That's interesting. Did you get an invite to her coronation in Australia?

No; I didn't need one, they just told us it happened, and she's now our boss cocky.

So, you believe everything you're told, do you?

And that, unfortunately, sums up the state of affairs in Australia today. Too many people tend to believe anything they are told rather than trying to work out the facts for themselves. As the Public Relations people like to say, "If it's not on Television it never happened."

So, how do we explain why a great number of people have, over the years, wanted to make Australia an independent nation? In fact, the call for independence can be traced back to the eighteen hundreds with Henry Lawson's Journal, "The Republican," being a notable example.

Our problem is showing the world we really are independent. How can we logically do that when everyone knows the Queen of England is our Head of State? What's involved in making Australia an independent nation? I suppose the first thing is that the people want it to be that way, that they really want to be independent and not have to kowtow to some foreign aristocracy just because they are called a King or a Queen.

Probably, the easiest way to prove our independence is to have our own Australian Constitution. But what sort of Constitution will we choose? Virtually every Constitution used in the world today has been written exclusively by politicians and lawyers. As far as we know, there has never been a Constitution written by the people. The people have been hoodwinked into believing it is too difficult to write their own Constitution, but that's a furphy. Mostly, Constitutions are seen as a legal/political document, but really, all they do is spell out the type of Government the people get and what "powers, privileges and immunities" will apply to the elected representatives of the people. Doesn't it make sense that the people ought to say what sort of Government they want and what sort of "powers, privileges and immunities" they are willing to allow their elected representatives? What's hard about doing that? It's just a matter of common sense.

When one sets about drafting a new Constitution, it is necessary to have a clear concept of what one hopes to achieve. It does help to do a study of Constitutions used around the world to see what they say, but mostly, deep down, everyone has a fair idea of the sort of Government they would like to have.

So, what sort of Government would you like to have?

Well, I certainly don't want a police state where the Government controls everything.

Yes, fair enough, but that's just saying what you don't want. What do you actually want?

Well, I want to be free to do what I want, to go where I want, and to say what I want. How's that for starters?

That is probably the way a lot of people would describe "democracy", but if you want that for yourself, you will have to allow that for everyone else.

So, what's wrong with that?

Just think about it for a while. If everybody could do what they want, go where they want and say what they want, would anybody be safe, or have any privacy?

Ahh, I see what you mean. There's got to be some limits there somewhere, doesn't there?

Yep. There's no such thing as freedom without responsibilities. As soon as you have responsibilities you have to have some way to see they are observed. And then you have to work out what to do about them when they are not.

While the United States Constitution does commence with the statement, "We the people…" it is largely the creation of lawyers and politicians, many of whom were both. Of all the Constitutions studied, the US Constitution did originally come as close as any to being classed as "a people's Constitution". However, over the past couple of centuries, the US Congress has made abundant use of the loophole woven into the document that says, "Until Congress otherwise provides …" or words of a similar nature. The use of this phrase has a direct bearing on Part 9 of the British Act of nineteen hundred, which is the Act that formed the Commonwealth of Australia as a single enlarged colony of Britain.

What, I thought that's when we became independent?

Not a hope. We were always to be a colony of England; Australia was never intended to be independent of the "mother" country.

That's bullshit. That's what all that ruckus was about in nineteen hundred and one. Realistically, the first of January should be celebrated as Australia Day and not when that fleet of Pommie criminals invaded Australia.

Boy oh boy; are you messed up.

I'm an Aussie, and I know whether I'm independent or not.

Well, if you do know, that's more than the High Court judges know. None of them seem to have a clue when we became independent.

But that's crap. We have the Australia Act; we have the Queen of Australia, what more do we want?

A bit of a problem there. The Australia Act had to be approved by the British Parliament, and the Queen of Australia is still the

Queen of the UK. I don't think she has ever been crowned in Australia.

Bugger off. You are just trying to confuse me with facts.

And isn't that the typical Australian response when they come across anyone who contradicts what they believe? "Don't confuse me with the facts. I'll believe what I want to believe."

As for the first draft of an idea for a Constitution, Andrew Inglis Clark is the Tasmanian lawyer who was credited with creating that original version. It went on to form the basis for Part 9 of the British Act. Clark had spent time in the United States and was familiar with the US Constitution. Hence, a lot of the US terminology is used in Clark's draft. That is the reason Australia has finished up with a House of Representatives and a Senate, instead of the British terminology of a House of Commons and the House of Lords. He also plagiarised parts of the US Constitution, word for word, but didn't seem to understand the purpose of the words. It also explains why Part 9 of the British Act includes thirty-nine provisions allowing Parliament to alter this Part 9 without going to the people via a referendum. The words, "Until Parliament otherwise provides…" or similar, are sprinkled liberally throughout the document, thus giving rein to the wholesale manipulation of the Constitution at the whim of any political party that happens to be in power at any time. Of course, the constitutional "experts" say these loopholes are necessary to allow flexibility in the document. That is justified, but only if the loopholes are specific for updating certain sections and restricted in altering the intent and purpose of the meaning.

On another note defining how we read the Constitution are the opening words, "Whereas the people…have agreed….." This is totally different to the clear and definitive statement, "We the People…." This latter statement clearly defines the "people' as the owners of the document, whereas the former statement says the "people" have agreed to what has been presented to them. It does not imply "ownership", and in fact, the claim of "Whereas the people… have agreed…" is not even the truth.

Don't give me that. The history books tell us we had all those referendums before the Constitution could be passed.

Is that right? Do you honestly know what the referendums were about and what the few eligible men were asked and allowed to vote on?

Whether they wanted Australia to be independent or not?

Tough luck mate. That was never the question. All they were asked was whether they wanted unity of the colonies or not. The actual wording was "unity or disunity." The draft for what was to go into the British Act as Part 9, and titled "Constitution", was never in question, the politicians and lawyers had already decided that.

But that Constitution was part and parcel of the referendums?

That's what a lot of academics, and others, want you to believe, but when the British Government made a lot of changes before they would let the draft for Part 9 go to their Parliament, there was never another referendum in Australia to agree to the changes.

So, what you are saying is, those opening words, "Whereas the people … have agreed…" are not true?

Exactly, it's a lie that's been perpetuated since nineteen hundred and one.

Although a certain number of suitably qualified men were given the opportunity to vote in the referendums of eighteen ninety-eight, eighteen ninety-nine and nineteen hundred, what they were asked was whether they wanted unity of the colonies or disunity. The acceptance of Part 9 of the British Act was a fait accompli. The acceptance of the Act was automatically assumed if those few eligible men voted for unity. According to the available statistics, the final "Yes" vote for unity amounted to approximately eleven percent of the then population in Australia, excluding, of course, the aborigine population and all the female population.

It so happens that when the final draft was taken to the UK for insertion into the British Act, the British Government demanded and got amendments to the draft before they would allow it to be presented to their Parliament. That amended draft, or for that matter, the British Act as a whole, was never presented to the few eligible male voters in Australia for their acceptance. Hence it is a deliberate lie to claim the Australian Constitution in its final form was ever presented to the "people" before it was enacted by the British Parliament.

As we all know, change is about the only real constant in our world. Hence it is important that any Constitution created by the people has to be subject to some form of periodic review. That's the best way to make sure the rules remain relevant, and the system is kept up to date. This draft of a new Constitution includes a provision for just such a review process, but one that is open to any interested person, or organisation, and a process conducted independently of the Government.

CHAPTER 2

Background Notes for
Developing the Draft Constitution

The following notes represent the background relating to the development of this draft for a new Constitution, but they are not part of the Constitution itself. As mentioned in Chapter One, it is necessary to have a clear concept of what one hopes to achieve, and when we are dealing with certain philosophic concepts, it is useful to record the ideas as they occur. It is also useful to record the reasons and motivation supporting the aims of the exercise. Hence, the purpose for including these notes in this book is to give the reader the background to the thinking behind the written words.

NOTES

This series of notes has been progressively compiled by the author during the process of writing a new Constitution for an independent Australia. They are not part of the actual Constitution, but are random comments, in no particular order, to help clarify the concepts and thoughts behind what is written. Part of the fundamental aim of writing this Constitution is to write it a way that the words can be read to make the intention clearly understood. Hopefully, this will leave little opportunity for the lawyers to manipulate, misinterpret and deliberately distort the intent.

This Constitution follows a rare and unique approach in the annals of Constitutional law and theory. It is intended to be a philosophical document as much as it is a legal document. Also, it is compiled, virtually entirely, by hundreds of ordinary Australian people. Joe Bryant established the Alternative Three Movement in nineteen ninety-eight and convened a series of public conventions in the various Australian States. He invited people to make submissions for what they would like to see in a Republican Constitution. The responses received from those conventions came from the common sense of hundreds of interested people, some with experience in politics and law. The Alternative 3 Movement did produce its own draft Constitution, and this new version incorporates part of that work. This draft is also based on the author's recently published book, "The Australian Constitution as it is Actually Written." That book analysed the current British Act from today's perspective and in the light of the many significant events that have occurred over the past one hundred and seventeen years. It is also the first time in a hundred and sixteen years that such a clause by clause, section by section, detailed analysis has been done for that now antiquated and out of date Act, Australia uses as its Constitution.

You're telling me nobody has done that for a hundred and sixteen years?

That's right. That's not to say there haven't been dozens of books written about the Constitution, but none of them have recently gone through it Chapter by Chapter and Section by Section.

Why a hundred and sixteen years? Did someone do it back then?

Yeah. Two lawyers did it when they wrote, "The Annotated Constitution of the Commonwealth of Australia."

Who were these guys, and why did they do it?

Their names were Robert Garran and John Quick, and they did it to explain how the Constitution should be understood.

Well, that was pretty decent of them. I guess they wanted to make it easy for ordinary people to understand?

You gotta be joking! It took them a thousand and eight pages to try and explain the thirty-six pages that represents the British Act.

That's bloody ridiculous. Nobody is going to read a thousand and eight pages to find out what the Constitution says.

It is always necessary to recognise the fundamentals of an issue if one is to understand what one hopes to achieve. When the issues concern a Constitution and Government, those fundamentals are crucial if we are to arrive at a logical approach. It is obvious that the people are the originators of both a Constitution and a Governmental system. It is axiomatic that any group of people who wish to live together, whether it's as a family, a village, a city or a society, there must be a set of rules defining how people should relate to each other. In essence, that set of rules is the Constitution, and if we are talking about a democratic concept, it is the people who should decide what rules they wish to live by, not the "rulers". However, when a set of rules are agreed there needs to be a way of ensuring the rules are followed, and when they are not, there needs to be some system in place to decide what to do about that. So, essentially, when the people create a system to see that the rules laid down in the people's Constitution are followed, what they do is to create a governmental system. The creation of any such system must then become an additional subject to be dealt with in the Constitution.

In an ideal world, it is obvious that both a Constitution and the governmental system are a direct creation of the people. In effect, both these things are or should be, the property of the people, and it should never be reversed to the extent a Government becomes the authority over the people and tells the people what rules they can or cannot have in their Constitution.

Unfortunately, today's world is far from ideal, and the reversal has happened, and in virtually every country, it is the Government that decides what sort of Constitution the nation can have. But that does not always need to be the case; changes are possible if the people choose to make it happen.

You're not kidding. That's what I've read in the papers. It's always the Government that wants to change the Constitution. They all think they own it.

That's happening in Turkey today. The PM is changing their Constitution to give himself more power.

Yeah, I read that. What's this "power" they all seem to want so much?

Political "power" always come down to the same thing. Control of the people; to do whatever the leaders want irrespective of what the people want.

That's pretty rude. How do they get away with it?

The same way they do in Australia. Keep the people in ignorance about the Constitution.

That can't be right. The Constitution is available to anyone to read.

That's true enough, but how many people do you think could understand it, even if they were to read it?

I don't know. I suppose you'd have to be a lawyer to understand it?

Do you reckon that's why the Constitution has never been taught in our schools?

Come off it. There are plenty of lessons about how the Government works.

Ahh, but that's different. The way the Government works isn't the way it is described in the Constitution.

That's crap. How can the Government be different to what's in the Constitution?

Well, there's no such position as a Prime Minister in the Constitution and nothing about political parties.

But the Prime Minister runs the country, or his party does so, they have to be there.

There you are. That's why the Constitution is never taught in our schools.

To correct this reversal that has taken place, the whole focus of this new Constitution is from the perspective of "the people." The intent is to define the powers and limitations the people are prepared to delegate to their elected representatives. This approach clearly distinguishes the people's representatives from the political party's representatives. By extension, the powers and limitations apply to every Government instrumentality that is created through this Constitution.

This is a truly unique Constitution concept where a Head of State has specifically limited and identified executive power and no hidden "Reserve" powers. Where an independent Council of eminent people operates without executive power - but is a body of people, who can function as independent adjudicators and also the body of last resort. The Parliament is the principal instrument invested with executive power, but that power is restrained by the Constitution. There is nothing like the thirty-nine provisions in the old Constitution, such as, "Until Parliament otherwise provides...," or similar words. Those provisions are loopholes that allow Parliament to alter the intent and meaning of the Constitution without going to a referendum. The few such provisions in this new Constitution are specifically limited. It is the Council's responsibility to ensure all legislation complies with the Constitution prior to the Head of State giving assent. The Parliament, in turn, is under the control of the people through defined legal processes. These start with elections after each fixed term in office and the swearing of allegiance to the people under Oaths of Office. There is a citizen's recall process and a lawful impeachment process right to the top of the political/bureaucratic chain of command. Finally, there is an independent and public Periodic Constitution Review Process, to keep the Constitution relevant and up to date.

As far as can be discovered, no other accepted Constitution/
Primary Law in modern history has truly been written in this
context and from this perspective, although some may claim to
do so.

*Are you saying there are thirty-nine ways the Parliament can
change the Constitution without having a referendum?*
Yes, that is exactly what happens.
How can they do that?
*The "founding fathers" wanted to make sure they could keep
things exactly as they were in the nineteen hundreds. They wanted
to make sure they could keep control of the Constitution, or more
accurately, that the future politicians could keep control.*
How did they do that?
*As mentioned before; they used words like, "Until Parliament
otherwise provides…" or similar wording and that allowed them to
do what they wanted without going to the people.*
But we've had referendums over the past hundred years?
*Yes, that's true, but they mainly dealt with Sections of the
Constitution where the loophole wasn't included.*
Is that why we had to have referendums? And who decided that?
*Every referendum has been proposed by the Government in
power, but the unwritten convention is that it has to be with the
agreement of the main opposition party.*
Why is that? Don't the people have a say?
*There's nothing about the political parties in the Constitution, and
the only say people have is 'yes' or 'no' to what the Government wants.*
And what does the Government want?
*Almost every referendum has been aimed at giving the Federal
Government more power over the States, or over the people.*
Have they been able to get what they wanted?
*Of the forty-four questions asked in the seventeen referendums
Australia has had since nineteen hundred and six, only eight
questions have been agreed by the people.*

Jeez, are the people that conservative?

On the contrary, the people have an inordinate amount of common sense in denying the Government their grab for even more power than they already have.

The primary issue related to this exercise of writing a new Constitution is whether the people truly want Australia to become an independent nation, free of all the legal, political and constitutional ties with the United Kingdom. That should have happened in nineteen hundred and nineteen when we were admitted, as supposedly, independent members at the formation of the League of Nations. Although there was one attempt in nineteen twenty to formalise our independence, it failed, and ever since we have been tied to Britain's apron strings.

The following statement was made in nineteen twenty by Sir Geoffrey Butler KBE, MA and Fellow, Librarian and Lecturer in International Law and Diplomacy of Corpus Christi College, Cambridge, author of "A Handbook to the League of Nations". He refers to Article I of the Covenant of the League of Nations. *"It is arguable that this Article is the Covenant's most significant single measure. By it, the British Dominions, namely, New Zealand, Australia, South Africa, and Canada, have their independent nationhood established for the first time. There may be friction over small matters in giving effect to this internationally acknowledged fact, but the Dominions will always look to the League of Nations Covenant as their Declaration of Independence."* (Source – Annotated Covenant of the League of Nations - League of Nations archives - Geneva, Switzerland).

The late Professor G. Clements, Eminent UK Queen's Councillor, and Emeritus Professor in Law at Cambridge University is also reputed to have understood the true legal position of the Australian Constitution when he is said to have remarked,

"The continued usage of the Australian Constitution Act (UK) by the Australian Governments and the judiciary is a confidence trick of monstrous proportions played upon the Australian people with the intent of maintaining power. It remains an Act of the United Kingdom. After joining the League of Nations in nineteen hundred and nineteen, Australia became a sovereign nation. It had no further legal power to use, alter or otherwise tamper with another nation's legislation. Authority over the Australian Constitution Act lies not with the Australian government nor with the Australian people; it rests solely with the UK. Only they have the authority to repeal this legislation ..."

These facts remain true to this day – as long as we continue to use the Commonwealth of Australia Constitutional Act as our Constitution, clearly an Act of the British Parliament, we cannot be an independent nation. There are only two ways Australia can become independent of the UK; one is for the British Parliament to repeal that Act, the other requires the Australian people to take unilateral action and declare our independence.

There are no other options.

That's bloody amazing. You mean to say Australia could have become an independent nation back in nineteen hundred and nineteen?

Yes, it's all true.

But why didn't it happen?

Technically, it did happen because we could only sign the covenant for the League of Nations as an independent member nation.

So, what was the problem?

Basically, the problem was, it had to be formalised.

What's that mean?

Well, Britain should have repealed their British Act that formed the Commonwealth of Australia, and Australia should have then written their own Constitution.

So why didn't that happen?

Mainly, because it was a "Clayton's" independence.

You mean it was never real; just make-believe?

Yes, sort of. Billy Hughes, the Prime Minister at the time, did try to introduce a bill into the Australian Parliament in nineteen twenty, to get a new Constitution underway, but he had to withdraw it.

Why?

Well, think about it. Here was Australia that had just come out of a horrendous war on behalf of the "mother country," with thousands of soldiers killed and wounded. And there's Billy Hughes saying, in effect, "Stuff the "mother country", Australia wants to go it alone."

Yeah, I guess I can see the reaction.

There are three basic ways we can choose for writing a new Australian Constitution. The first is to do what was proposed in nineteen ninety-nine; to modify the existing Constitution in the deceitful "minimalist" change, by eliminating references to the monarchy and retaining the antiquated document with all the flaws and inaccuracies in respect to the undefined Westminster system of Government that is used.

The second option is to do a complete rewrite starting from scratch and picking out any relevant bits from any other source and adapt them to the Australian environment.

The third option is to use the existing Constitution as a base, in as far as some parts have been proven viable, but to change the philosophic foundation and re-write the new Constitution from the perspective of the people. This would create a properly relevant Constitution defining the system of Government and the powers and limitations the people are prepared to allow their elected representatives.

While it tends to be taken for granted that the people of Australia want the nation to be considered as a "democracy," there seems to be little understanding of what "democracy" actually means. Probably, the best definition is the one provided by Abraham Lincoln as, "Government of the people, for the people and by the people."

Having a vote does not define a "democracy," but it is part of the definition along with issues, such as, "free speech," the right to life, freedom of choice, and the recognition that the people are the foundation of all political power. The purpose of a democratic Government is to serve the people; the people are not there to serve the Government.

I thought everybody knows what Democracy means. Are you saying they don't?

Yes, that's right. How do you describe Democracy?

It's pretty much just as you wrote above.

But every "freedom" and every "right" that is perceived as part of a Democratic system has to come with responsibilities.

Yes, that's right. I can accept that.

A lot of the problems seem to arise when we start talking about "rights."

Why? It's natural that people should have "rights".

Maybe, but people have to realise if they claim a "right" it automatically imposes an obligation on someone else.

I don't think many people look at it that way?

That's probably true. Even the fundamental "right to life" does that. It obliges everyone else to recognise that we all have a "right" to live.

But how many people actually observe that?

Ahh, that's why all these claims to "human rights" tend to get very messy. It seems so hard to enforce them on a universal basis.

The purpose of a people's Constitution - While a people's Constitution must be about the people's rights and freedoms, it must also deal with their responsibilities, and if the people choose a representative type of system, that system has to include the authority the people are prepared to delegate to their elected representatives. Just as importantly, a people's Constitution needs to focus on the authority of leadership, by stipulating in some detail, how this leadership must be for the benefit of the people, and the nation, and not develop into an authority beyond the control of the people.

It is proposed that there would be a simultaneous referendum held in conjunction with the referendum to adopt this new Constitution. The second referendum is to ask the people what title they prefer for the position of the Head of State, either President or Governor General. If the title President is selected, then the State Governor's title would become Vice President.

Why would you want to do that; ask people to choose the title for the Head of State?

Basically, it's just observing the principles of democracy.

But isn't the title President pretty much universally accepted for a republican system?

That's true, but Australia has a tradition of having a King or Queen as their Head of State, with a Governor General as their representative.

Yeah, I know that, and obviously, we can't keep using the title of King, or Queen, for our Head of State.

Actually, we could if we wanted to, but I don't think that wouldn't go over too well.

I know there is still very significant support for the monarchy, and to a lot of people, the Governor General is seen as our onsite Head of State.

That's true, but it is also a familiar title even though it is closely linked to the monarchy.

There certainly is a link, but under this new Constitution, the Head of State is largely a ceremonial position that doesn't have any of the reserve powers associated with the monarchical traditions.

OK, but isn't that all the more reason to scrap the title?

Maybe, but we still think it is a decision for the people to make; not for us to tell them what they can have.

Fair enough, but aren't you doing that with the Constitution; telling them what they can have?

Not at all. This draft is the creation of a lot of people over a long period of time. It will have been publicly aired, discussed, modified, developed and refined to a point where it has become a practical and workable proposal.

So, you reckon it is about as good as the people can make it?

More or less. We must draw the line somewhere, but because of the periodic review process built into the draft, it will always be open to development and improvement as we learn.

It certainly will be well publicised and discussed as part of the referendum process so, I guess we'll just have to leave it up to the people to decide if they want it, or not.

Exactly, if they choose to accept it the way it is presented, then they can also decide what they want to call their Head of State.

The concept of an Australian Council came up in nineteen ninety-nine as a way to create a non-political supreme body to replace the potential dictatorial powers of a Governor General. It also aims to get the Head of State out of the hands of politics and money. Any election process for a Head of State was seen as inevitably getting entangled in politics and money and degenerating into the farce of the American presidential circus. This modified version of the Australian Council is designed to replace certain functions of the "Crown". One of the Council's other function is to act as an appeal of last resort for the people. In addition, the Council acts as an adjudicating body for vetting legislation to ensure it conforms to the Constitution. If approved, the Council will then authorise the Head of State to give assent. The Council is specifically denied any executive authority, but if any legislation is questioned, the Council shall return the bill to

Parliament, with a public report detailing the Council's concerns. It is then up to Parliament to address those concerns. As the body of last resort, the same process applies to the High Court or any other entity involved. The council shall issue a public report recommending a review, but any subsequent decisions by those bodies concerned shall become final.

Various names were suggested for the Council, but the title, Australian Council, seems the most appropriate. If it were created as an independent body of eminent people, made up from, say, the six Governors/Vice Presidents of the States, it could have the status granted to the Governor General, but deny such total overriding authority in the hands of one person. In addition, the Council could provide the nominal Head of State for all the ceremonial functions related to that position, and thereby remove that position from the political arena. This would avoid an expensive and potentially divisive election process, especially if the political parties are eliminated from the process.

Of course, this all depends on what powers and authority the people are prepared to allow their Head of State. In this Constitution, the Head of State is granted executive authority on only one occasion. As the Commander in Chief of the Armed Forces, the Head of State can declare Australia in a state of war if the nation comes under physical attack from the armed forces of another nation. All other deployments of Australia's Armed Forces come under the executive authority of the Parliament.

The Council could set up a rotational basis for a State Governor/Vice President to become the nominal Head of State for a defined period (three to five years). However, the appointee would only be permitted to act in the legal and political arena with the consent and approval of the full Council. The State would nominate a replacement Governor/Vice President for the person chosen to act as the Head of State.

The non-political association of the Council would be greatly enhanced if the State Governors/Vice Presidents are each appointed by a two-thirds approval of their State Parliaments. That provision is contained in the new Constitution. This would tend to neutralise or diminish, political party associations. As members of the Council, the Governors/Vice Presidents would be taking on a higher duty in representing the whole of Australia in addition to their own State. This concept for a Council of State Governors/Vice Presidents is very much in accord with the concept of federation.

In terms of the Council, all the State Governors/Vice Presidents are of equal standing, and any evenly split decisions must be decided in the negative, as any such split decision would clearly indicate some genuine concerns being involved. Thus, it is reasoned, the chosen Head of State, who would chair the Council meetings, is not given a casting vote in any Council deliberations.

That idea of a Council sounds like a bloody good idea.

Yes, we believe it is.

This recent US election for a President is a glaring example of what happens when an election gets mixed up with politics and money.

It certainly is.

The US president seems to be almost all-powerful. Do we want an Australian President, or Head of State, to be like that?

I don't think so. Why should any Head of State have the power to sack an elected Government?

Somebody should if they do the wrong thing.

Nope, not even then. If a Government breaches the Constitution, this is where an independent Council can step in and ask the High Court to rule on the issue. If the Court confirms the breach, they would suspend the Government and call for new elections.

That sounds pretty logical, but is it ever likely to happen?

It would if the people of Australia approve this draft Constitution at a referendum.

Well, I'd sure love to see that happen.

In the above case, where the Head of State is appointed from the Council, the High Court would convey their decision to the Council, and the Head of State would act on the basis of the Court's decision.

That sounds like a very good democratic process. No power in the hands of any one single person.

Political Parties - While political parties have been a fixture in most countries for the past couple of centuries; it is unrealistic to believe they can be eliminated, but that is not to say they should be ignored in a Constitution. In writing a people's Constitution, a number of facts must be recognised. In modern-day politics, the political party represents the greatest potential threat to the well-being, freedom and independence of a nation's citizenry. The Constitution has a duty to future generations of Australians, and part of that duty is to define the conditions that must apply to the politicians. Very few elected representatives in today's politics are there to represent the people; mostly, their primary responsibility is to represent the political party that contributed to their election. Politicians as a class, have the greatest opportunity to do the most harm to our Nation and our Society. The 'keystone' of any people's Constitution is its ability to control the nation's elected representatives, and that means controlling the way political parties operate in the political system.

No ruling political party is ever in the position to speak for the nation as a whole. The claim of having a mandate is limited to the political arena in allowing the party, with a majority of seats in the House of Representatives, to form a Government. That is the only mandate a ruling political party ever has. It does not give a political party the authority to speak on behalf of all the people, which they never do anyway because the ruling party is always biased toward their party members, the party's policies, and its supporters.

You're going against the grain when you say political parties are the greatest threat to the welfare of the people.

Surely, you have enough examples throughout history of the disasters caused by political parties?

Where do you mean? Germany and Russia for example?

They are two of the most obvious examples, but then a lot of blame can also be sheeted home to the politicians of many other countries, not the least, the more recent history of "regime change" being forced on countries by the Governments of the US and Britain.

Yeah, I see what you mean. But political parties can also work for the good of their society.

Maybe, but usually, it is for the good of their party and supporters rather than the society as a whole.

But a strong political party can bring stability to a country.

And what does "stability" mean if it can only be maintained by force?

In Australia's first Constitution, the "founding father" gave the politicians the authority to set up their own "powers, privileges and immunities" without any input from the people. This is akin to giving the inmates the keys to the asylum. Granting that authority to the politicians is one of the major disasters of the original Constitution, as those "powers, privileges and immunities" are the very crux of what should be entirely in the hands of the people to determine.

That sounds bloody awful. Why should the politicians be allowed to say what privileges and powers they can have, and especially what they can get away with because of immunity?

If the people had been allowed to be involved with this first Constitution, I'm sure they would have put a stop to this obvious rorting of the system.

Why weren't the people involved?

Everything in those early days was a closed shop. Only the fifty politician and lawyers were allowed to attend the last few conventions, and they set it up so the system they were used to would remain in place.

That's not very democratic?

Of course, it isn't. Democracy was never a part of the considerations.

So, how come people got to vote in the referendums?

What "people" are you talking about?

All the people that voted.

You mean the few eligible male voters and some of whom probably had multiple votes. No women were allowed to vote, and the numbers showed that only about eleven percent of the total population in nineteen hundred actually approved the "unity" of the colonies.

That hardly amounts to an endorsement.

Religion and Politics – While it is an accepted myth that religion and politics should not mix, that is to deny the clear historical evidence over the last couple of millennium at least. Politics and religion are completely interwoven with each other, and very much remain so today. This is not something a Constitution can ignore, and it is totally ludicrous to make a statement, as did the original Constitution in Section 116, "The Commonwealth shall not make any law for establishing any religion, or for imposing any religious observance, or for prohibiting the free exercise of any religion……."

The only valid bit of this Section is the last part, which says, "and no religious test shall be required as a qualification for any office or public trust under the Commonwealth".

A lot of people consider this a declaration of religious freedom in the Commonwealth, but surely there have to be some criteria to define what can be classified as a "religion". Unless this is done, virtually any group could call themselves a "religious order" and be free of any government interference. For example, is Scientology, Mormonism, Paganism, Satanism, Buddhism, Atheism and Taoism, or any other type of proclaimed worship, a legitimate religion, and do they come under the wording of "any religion"?

While this prohibition on making laws is in respect to the specified aspects of establishing a religion or imposing any religious observance, the bit about prohibiting the free exercise of any religion would seem to deny anyone the right to bar Sharia law. However, Section 116 is largely ignored because; the Commonwealth does make laws relating to religious issues in a great number of other aspects, e.g. religious education and religious schools, and exempting religious organisations from taxation, and not the least, by endorsing the Christian festivals of Christmas and Easter as official holidays.

You're getting into touchy stuff here when you talk about religion.

Don't I know it? Apart from the bullshit about religion and politics not getting mixed up, the whole issue is a can of worms.

That sure is the case today, especially where Islam is concerned.

Only too true. I've lived and worked for years in Malaya and Indonesia and couldn't have asked for a better relationship with the people.

That's the catch, isn't it? There are exceptions to every rule.

Unfortunately, that's true. You can't tar and feather a whole nation because of a few rebels, or "terrorists" as they are now called.

It seems anyone who is against the Government is now labelled a "terrorist".

That is becoming the norm these days.

When you look back over history, religion has been the cause of so much strife and bloodshed for so long.

Yeah, as I said, a can of worms.

Preamble – Contrary to the current British Act, and also to the various perceptions some people have regarding that Act, it does not have a specifically defined Preamble. The closest equivalent is the three opening sentences before the commencement of the following nine clauses. If those sentences are to be regarded as valid and legitimate parts of the Act, then it effectively binds Australia as an "indissoluble" colony/dominion to the British Crown in perpetuity. This would permanently deny Australia any legal opportunity of gaining their independence from the UK as long as this British Act remains in force.

A Constitutional Preamble is akin to what is today called a "Mission Statement." Its purpose is to set out the basic philosophy, which the people wish to accept in the formulation of their government, and the making of the laws that will control their society. Any such Preamble must always be recognised as an integral part of the Constitution, and only subject to change through the nation-wide referendum process that is included in the Constitution.

I think it is a bloody good idea to have a decent Preamble to set the tone and principles that need to apply in making laws.

That's right. After all, that's what Government seems to be mostly about; making laws to control the society.

It's not so bad if they make the laws so anyone can understand them.

If they did that, there wouldn't be any need for lawyers.

Let's face it, the people who draft the laws are all trained in the profession. They make sure their drafting complies with accepted legal standards of obscurity.

And I'll bet there are very few politicians who really understand the bills their party leaders tell them to vote for.

Yes, another problem with party politics. Do as we say, or you don't get endorsed next time.

Australia's Money Supply - Possibly, one of the most important aspects of the original British Act is the way the authors dealt with the issue of "currency, coinage and legal tender." While these three "things" may have been separate forms of "money" in the nineteen hundreds, they are no longer classed as separate in today's world. "Money" has now become the single most important tool for survival, and hence, the control and issuing of "money" is the foundation that determines the economic standards and quality of life for every nation on Earth, including Australia.

It can be reasonably assumed that Australia's founding fathers, and the British Parliament for that matter, had no understanding that they were granting their newly formed Commonwealth of Australia the status of monetary sovereignty. Not that many people have any understanding of what monetary sovereignty means. By including the two subsections 51(xii) and 51(xiii), they gave the Australian Parliament total control of all banking in Australia, except State banking within the borders of the State, and the creation of all currency, coinage and legal tender.

The Australian Government was actually granted monetary sovereignty from the time the British Act was proclaimed in nineteen hundred and one, by virtue of the two subsections mentioned above.

That status has only been used once in Australia's history to date, through the creation of the original Commonwealth Bank of Australia. That Bank operated as the publicly owned Government bank from nineteen hundred and eleven to nineteen hundred and twenty-three, when it was legislatively destroyed by the Bruce/Page Tory Government. With this new Constitution, Australia will have the authority to create and manage its money supply in the best interests of the people and the nation.

This is incredible. Is it really true the Government can create as much money as they like?

That's what monetary sovereignty means, although it's not without certain conditions.

Like what?

Well, if a Government doesn't want to destroy the economy, they can only create as much money as there are things to buy.

But if they can create as much money as they want they can buy anything from anywhere?

Up to a point. A responsible Government must put their nation ahead of themselves, and that means promoting jobs and the nation's productive capacity.

And not buying overseas, you mean?

Only if it can't be produced internally. The important thing is that a monetary sovereign Government doesn't have to run up any debt.

But if Australia is monetary sovereign, why do we have so much debt?

Ignorance and bad management. Plus the fact the people elect people who have very little experience in running a business as big as the Government.

Ahh, party politics again?

As far as this Constitution is concerned, it is axiomatic that no human being is endowed with infallibility. Hence, it is an accepted tenet that everyone is accountable, irrespective of their station in the society. In particular, this applies to the justices of the High Court of Australia. However, it is an accepted principle that the justice system should be, and should be seen to be, independent, but that is not to say it shouldn't be held accountable if the Court makes a "wrong" decision. The appeals process largely covers this accountability at the lower levels of the justice system, but this draft Constitution has three provisions for addressing accountability of the High Court. In two cases the Australian Council is the body of last resort. If successfully appealed to, the Council has the authority to instruct the High Court to review a decision, but any subsequent review by the High Court becomes final. The other provision given the Council is to instruct the

High Court to hear an issue which they have previously denied a hearing, provided accepted justification is presented to the Council. The third provision is through the Citizen's Recall Process that can be used by any citizen if they have verifiable proof of misconduct.

Jeez, you're getting into deep water here.

Why is that? Do you believe the High Court judges are infallible and shouldn't be held to account?

I mean, after all, we're just ordinary people; what do we know about the law?

God; that's a stupid question.

What do you mean? Why is it stupid?

Who do you think the laws are made for? And don't they always tell you, "Ignorance of the law is no excuse."

Yeah, but that's bullshit. Nobody can know all the laws that are written, not even the lawyers.

Exactly. That's why we have Courts and Judges, and even the judges don't always know the law.

So, are you saying it's the same for the High Court?

Of course, it is, and that's easy to prove.

Oh yeah. How come you're such a smart arse?

You don't have to be a smart arse to know when something is wrong.

You mean the High Court makes wrong decisions?

They sure do. Every split decision they make is a flawed decision. If the seven, supposedly, top legal brains in the country can't come to a unanimous decision, then the decision isn't based on legalese, it's based on personal opinions.

Yeah, but if you get a majority decision that must be right?

Why? Why is a majority of opinions any more correct than the minority, even if it's only one Judge in dissent? They are just opinions, that's all, and opinions based on prejudice, political leanings, upbringing, bias and personal attitudes.

You're saying the judges should decide the issue based on the law as it stands?

That's correct. Seven unelected people have no right, or authority, to make up laws as they see fit, only the Parliament has that authority.

So, if the High Court can't come to a unanimous decision, they should hand the issue back to Parliament?

Exactly.

Impeachment is a process included in the US Constitution as a guarantee that no person is above the law, right to the very top of the political and bureaucratic chain of command. It is a way of demanding accountability from the people's representatives and those people employed to serve the people. This draft Constitution includes specific procedures for both initiating and conducting the impeachment process. Part of the initiating process is the inclusion of a Citizen's Recall provision that is specified and detailed in a Chapter of the draft. This process is distinct from the provisions allowing the Council to intervene with the High Court, but it does not exempt individual Justices from being held accountable on personal grounds.

Impeachment is a pretty drastic step, isn't it?

Yes, it is. It's probably about the worst thing that can happen to any elected, or appointed official whose duty is to serve the public.

I guess you'd have to be pretty careful in the way you use it?

Definitely. That's why there is a very strict process involved to ensure it isn't arbitrarily used.

And any claims must be proven, and anyone accused gets a chance to defend themselves?

Most definitely. Impeachment is the last resort in the process and won't happen lightly.

Even so, it sounds as though it would be a strong inducement for people to do the right thing, especially if they are there to serve the public.

Just having it in the Constitution could be enough to make people think twice about their actions.

A Periodic Constitutional Review Process – shall be a process independent of the Government and the legal profession. The concept is to provide a system that is open to any interested person, group, or organisation, as well as the Local, State and Federal Governments, to submit proposals for amending the Constitution. The aim is to create the opportunity for every interested Australian Citizen to become involved in formulating changes to their Constitution. This concept embraces a fundamental philosophy that must apply in our Democracy – that the Constitution of Australia is the exclusive property of the Citizens of Australia - it is never the property of the Government. It is therefore rejected that the Commonwealth Government has the sole right to propose amendments to 'our' Constitution. The right to alter the Constitutional intent rests solely with the People and not with the Government and certainly not with the High Court.

What is important is that the final outcome of the Process will be translated into definite action through a mandatory referendum of the publicly approved amendment proposals. The details of a suggested process are included as an Appendix to the draft Constitution.

What do you want this for? Most people don't give a stuff about the Constitution, and they wouldn't know what to say anyway.

Well, to start with there is a hell of a lot of people out there who do give a stuff. That's proven from the hundreds of submissions we got in nineteen ninety-eight and nineteen ninety-nine.

Yeah, there might be, but they're not lawyers.

What's that got to do with it?

The Constitution is a legal thing, isn't it?

It is in part, but it also has to be something ordinary people can read and understand.

36

I bet I couldn't read and understand the current Constitution if it took Quick and Garran a thousand and eight pages to explain?

If they are correct, then no one is capable of reading and understanding it.

Are you saying they are wrong?

Yes, that's what I'm saying. What they wrote was how they wanted the Constitution to be, not about the way it is actually written.

I bet there is nobody around who agrees with you?

Probably not, but by all logical reasoning, the Constitution should always be the property of the people; they are the rightful owners, not the politicians or the lawyers.

So, that's why you say it needs to be read and understood by ordinary people.

Exactly. It has to be a common-sense document saying what sort of Government the people want and what limits they want to place on their elected representatives.

And how do you expect that to happen?

Well, to start with, it is a provision of this Constitution that teaching the Constitution shall become a compulsory subject for every High School curriculum.

As simple as that?

Precisely, as simple as that.

CHAPTER 3

Discussing the Contents of the
Draft Constitution and a Preamble

This Chapter starts off with the list of Contents for the draft Constitution and follows with a Preamble that defines the philosophy underpinning the Constitution. It is the parameters contained in the Preamble that must be observed in making laws and determining the interpretation and intent of the words.

It's philosophy that's gotten us into this mess, and it is only philosophy that will get us out.

Yeah, and who says?

Actually, Ayn Rand said that years ago, and it was probably the truest thing she ever said.

Come off it. Since when did philosophy have anything to do with anything?

Actually, it's got everything to do with everything.

That's bullshit. I don't have a philosophy.

Wanna bet? Of course, you have a philosophy. Maybe you don't know it, and maybe you've never thought about it, but you have a philosophy you live by.

Yeah, if that's so, what is it?

Do you agree with all the things the politicians do? Like giving themselves exorbitant superannuation, virtually unlimited expenses, and ripping off the public anyway, they can?

Of course not. They're a bunch of parasites.

Well, what would you do if you had the chance? Would you grab everything you could get your hands on and not give a shit whether it's honest or ethical?

No, I wouldn't. I've got some principles, and I don't steal things just because they're there.

There you are. That's your philosophy, and that's the way you live.

The concept of an official Preamble is not used in the British Act, nor in Part 9 of that Act, the part which represents the Constitution of the Commonwealth.

The British Act starts off with three sentences, which is the nearest thing that could be construed as a Preamble. There seem to be some conflicting views as to how a Preamble is to be used in a Constitution. Some people say it has to be relevant and considered an integral part of the Constitution, while others, such as John Howard, claimed it was not relevant and carried no legal weight. If Howard's contention is to apply, then there is no point in having a Preamble at all.

This conflict also seems to apply to the British Act, as some people claim that, as far as Australia is concerned, only Part 9 of the Act is relevant to Australian law. That of course, is patently ridiculous because no one can pick and choose what parts of a legislative Act they want to use and what they can simply ignore.

It is true that the provision for a Referendum contained in Part 9 of the British Act only applies to that separate part. But, any time the people vote for a change to Part 9 that amendment has to go to the British Parliament for approval before it is adopted.

So, what are you saying? That Australia doesn't have a Constitution, and we are all just, sort of, operating in limbo?

No, that's not what I'm saying. The Commonwealth of Australia is a creation of Britain.

Hang on there. It was all those Aussies back in the late eighteen hundreds that created Australia, not the Poms.

Back in the eighteen hundreds, all those "Aussies" you talk about were British subjects of the Queen.

Yeah, maybe, but they are the ones who created the Commonwealth of Australia.

All they did was to create a document, which after changes by the British Government, became Part nine of the British Act.

But that document was what created Australia.

Not at all. It was only a document that meant nothing until the British Parliament agreed to allow the six colonies to merge into a single bigger colony.

Are you telling me that all the British did was make one big colony out of all the other colonies?

Yep, that's right. We were a colony then, and in fact, still are today, although the status was changed to a Dominion in nineteen hundred and seven.

The real truth of the matter is that the Australian Government has no authority whatsoever to alter or amend or ignore, any of the first eight parts of the British Act, and that would include the three opening sentences. The first of those three sentences states categorically that the Federal Commonwealth of Australia shall be indissoluble under the Crown of the United Kingdom. It should be quite obvious to any rational person that, as long as this British Act remains in force, Australia can never become a sovereign and independent nation.

Wow, you are really screwing me up. How come so many people think we are an independent nation?

I think they think that way because it's what they want it to be. It may also be because it's the way they have been brainwashed to believe.

Hey, come off it. Who's been brainwashing us? You're not saying it's the Government?

Yep, them and the academics too, and not forgetting the lawyers.

God, you're full of it. Are you trying to tell me the Government is deliberately telling porkies and misleading us?

Afraid so mate.

How can that be? Where's your proof?

The proof is easy to come by. It starts with the Westminster Act around nineteen thirty-six, which the Australia Government eventually partly endorsed in nineteen forty-two. When that didn't work so well, Bob Hawke came up with the Australia Act of nineteen eighty-six.

Yeah, so what's wrong with them?

Two things. Both Acts tried to say that Australia was an independent nation, but neither Act could become law until they were passed by the British Parliament.

That doesn't make sense, does it? If we are independent why does the British Parliament have to give us their approval?

Exactly. And don't you think the Australian people ought to have had a say whether they wanted to be independent or not?

Are you saying those Acts should have gone to a referendum?

Yes, of course, that is what should have happened, but all the Governments since nineteen twenty knew we should have become independent when we were allowed to join the League of Nations.

So, right up until nineteen eighty-six, all the Government knew we were still part of the UK and not independent?

Yes, they have been conning us all that time. As Goebbels said, make your lie big enough, and tell it often enough, and the people will eventually believe it.

So, as our first step in learning why Australia needs a new Constitution, we can look at the contents of such a Constitution. This will show us what needs to be included and how we might place some limitations and responsibilities on the people we elect to represent us.

As we said before, it's just a matter of common sense. Those elected representatives are really no different to us, that is until they get into Parliament; then it's a different ball game.

A NEW AUSTRALIAN CONSTITUTION
DRAFT of a
CONSTITUTION FOR AN INDEPENDENT
AUSTRALIAN NATION

CONTENTS

PREAMBLE

We, the people of the Commonwealth of Australia, a Federation which was constituted under the Act of the British Parliament (63 and 64 Victoria, Chapter 12) dated the ninth day of July 1900, have agreed to adopt this new Australian Constitution governing the Federal Commonwealth Parliament, the Government, and all the Federal Courts of our Nation, in accordance with our beliefs, as set out in this Preamble.

As this Constitution also represents the Constitution of our independent Australian nation, any Federal law shall take precedence over State law should conflict arise.

In setting out these fundamental beliefs and principles governing the application of this Constitution, this Preamble must always be treated as an integral part of the Constitution in the formulation of Laws and judicial decisions.

WE hold to the belief that all Australians, including the descendants of the original Aborigine inhabitants, are created equal under the rule of Law, that we are endowed with certain inalienable rights; these include the right to life, liberty within the law, responsible free speech, and ownership of property, self-defence and the pursuit of happiness. It is the responsibility of every elected member of the Parliament to guarantee, under oath, that these Rights are universally sustained within the nation.

All Rights are ordained as the possession of the people, but in the interest of our society and the Commonwealth of Australia, those rights come with the responsibility not to unlawfully encroach on the rights of anyone else.

WE further hold to the belief in the Rule of Law as the only viable option for a Democratic Society. This belief is based upon the universal values contained in our historical Common Law heritage. This heritage is derived from the Great Charters of England, handed down to us through the centuries as part of the development of British Common Law and subsequently incorporated into Australian Common Law. While it is recognised that laws do impact on the unrestrained rights of the people, this Constitution defines good Government as subordinating all laws to maximising the concept of individual freedom for the people legitimately living in this nation.

WE hold these values to be inviolate and that no Parliament, or Court of the Commonwealth of Australia, shall have the right to deny, or rescind, the inherited rights, freedoms and obligations of any Australian citizen as provided by our Common Law heritage.

WE, the people of Australia, hereby declare that we are a sovereign independent Nation made up of Australian States and Territories.

WE, the people of Australia, further declare that our Parliamentary system shall comprise of an Australian Council, a House of Representatives and a House of Senators, each of which shall be formed and function in the manner set down in this Constitution.

WE also declare that the Government of Australia shall be vested and maintained in the four principal, non-political areas covered by the Public Service Departments, the Police Service, all sections of the Judiciary and the Defence Forces of Australia.

All Members of the Australian Council, as well as every Member of the Australian Parliamentary system, and of each of the Government Services designated above, shall at all times, be responsible to the People of Australia and shall, as provided for in this Constitution, swear to such allegiance by the Oath of Office contained herein. Any infringement of this sworn obligation shall be open to challenge through all legitimate means, including the Citizen's Recall procedures as set out in the Constitution, and possible impeachment procedures, if applicable.

WE, the people of Australia, declare that the responsibility for the Government of the Commonwealth of Australia shall be vested in the Members of the House of Representatives whom shall appoint, or elect, from their membership, a Prime Minister, with the powers and authority as specified in this Constitution.

The Prime Minister shall then select Members from either House of Parliament to act as Ministers in charge of the various Government Departments; with the duties and responsibilities, as provided for in this Constitution. No one person shall be a Minister of more than two such Government Departments at any one time.

The Ministers selected by the Prime Minister shall form an Executive Cabinet with the duties and responsibilities as set out in this Constitution.

The High Court of Australia shall be as provided for in this Constitution and any judicial decisions relating to this Constitution must be with the unanimous agreement of all the Judges hearing the case.

In the light of the changes that are taking place in our modern society, a periodic Constitution Review process involving public participation is included in the Constitution to ensure it is kept relevant and up to date,

Every part of the Constitution, as listed in the Contents, shall only be amended by a nation-wide Referendum, unless there is specific provision for either, or both Houses of Parliament, to make changes. The purpose of any such provision is limited to keeping the Constitution up to date and retaining a relevance to the changing society. Every such provision is specific in its application, and cannot be subverted to a wider application unless approved at a Referendum.

The power to set aside this Constitution, or its respective provisions, is not granted under any circumstances, but changes may be made via either a Class 1 or a Class 2 Referendum, except for any Sections designated as permanent.

Page Reference for the Contents and Preamble 195 and197

CHAPTER 4

Discussing the Need for Definitions

One of the major faults with the British Act of nineteen hundred is the total absence of any definitions of the terms and entities used in the Act. While many of the terms may well be commonly understood by the legal profession, the fact is, the Constitution represents the Primary Law of the Commonwealth. As such, it should be possible for any reasonably educated person to read and understand what it says. It is a well-known cliché that ignorance of the law is supposed to be no excuse, but nobody should need a law degree to understand what the law says.

Oh yeah, who says? Half the time the lawyers don't even know the law.

That's probably true for a lot of lawyers because, if it weren't true there wouldn't be so many cases ending up in Court.

How come?

Well, if the lawyers really did know the law they would be able to tell their clients straight away whether they're in the right or wrong.

In which case, there would be no need to go to Court?

Precisely.

So, why doesn't that happen?

Mainly, because the legal system is so stuffed up. Some laws go back centuries, and then we have a heap of untrained politicians incapable of legislating clear and easily understandable laws.

Are you implying all the politicians need to become lawyers?

Not at all. Mostly, the bills are being written by trained people, but the politicians need to make sure they understand what the party tells them to vote for.

You mean the politicians should read what they are asked to vote on?

Yes. They must use their common sense and make sure what they are presented with is clear and understandable.

That's logical; if they don't understand the bill how do they expect ordinary people to understand?

And, unfortunately, when they pass amendment after amendment to laws going back decades, it is virtually impossible for anyone to understand what is meant.

What's the answer? Is there any solution possible?

Not under the present system. There's too much money at stake for the legal profession to clean up the mess.

Many of the problems that arise from this current Constitution stem from the fact that the meanings of the words can be read in different ways. The only logical way to sort this out is to provide a set of definitions at the commencement of the Constitution. That way everyone reading the document will know the meaning and intent of the word or the way the words are used. In the event of new words being introduced into the Constitution, or the meaning of existing words changing in the fullness of time, the Parliament becomes responsible for adding and amending the list of definitions as part of the Constitution.

When you say the Parliament, you mean both Houses, the Reps and the Senate. Is that right?

Yes, of course. The definitions apply to both Houses; hence, it is only logical that both Houses have to agree to any changes or additions.

But won't that get messy if different parties have control of the two Houses?

Only if the politicians are so bloody-minded, they can't agree on how to understand some straight forward English language.

If you are going to put definitions on words won't that destroy the flexibility that goes into writing legislation?

I would bloody well hope so!

Jeez, they are going to hate you.

It is also a responsibility of Parliament to clarify the definition of any words in the Constitution that may not initially be included in the list of definitions. Once clarified, the words would be automatically added to the list. Unless this is done, the interpretation of the Constitution will, by default, be removed from the authority of Parliament and handed over to an unelected body of people in any Court. It seems to be common for Courts to interpret the written law in different ways, and that includes the High Court as well.

Any process that allows individual people to interpret words as they see fit is not a democratic process, and that applies very much to the legal fraternity.

There are many commonly used words that can be interpreted in different ways. Regarding the Constitution, this can become a critical issue. Take the words, "the number of people" for example, as used in Section 24 of Part 9 of the British Act. In the "Constitution" these words are used in the formula for determining the number of politicians who will make up the House of Representatives. They are also used to determine the number of politicians that will come from the respective States and Territories. It, therefore, becomes essential that everyone should know exactly how these words are defined. The commonsense definition of these words have to mean the nation's, or the State's, population – and the definition of population means the number of people living in a specific area. There should be no misunderstanding about this. It should have been quite clear and obvious, but the major political parties must have seen some political advantage in defining the phrase by legislation.

Unfortunately, Section 24 contains the perennial loophole of "until Parliament otherwise provides…" and it appears that at some stage Parliament decided that "the number of people" only referred to the people on the electoral roll. In nineteen seventy-four there was a referendum seeking what they called "Democratic elections". The purpose was to require the electorates to be based on the overall population, and not just the people on the electoral roll, or the geographical size of the electorates. The proposition was obviously confusing, as the referendum was lost in all States except New South Wales. The referendum was also unconstitutional, as "the proposed law" was not publicly and widely presented to the voters, seemingly because, nobody had ever bothered to draft the law to say what was intended.

So, the draft Constitution is at pains to make this definition quite clear, and remove any opportunity for the politicians to manipulate it to their advantage. The definition is as follows: "Australia's Population – As the population figure for Australia, and the respective States, is used in the formula for calculating each State's allocation of Members for the House of Representatives, it is necessary to define what is meant by "population." Although the Parliament has a responsibility for every person living in the Commonwealth of Australia, for the purpose of the formula, only the recognised legitimate citizens of the nation, whether living in Australia, or overseas, or even if incarcerated, shall be included in the term "population." This term shall not be modified to apply only to eligible voters, as Parliament has a wider responsibility to include all the newly born and youths not yet of voting age. This population figure will be determined by the Bureau of Statistics as at the most recent Census."

That is a pretty open-ended definition, isn't it?
What's open-ended about it?
Why should people in jail get counted? That doesn't seem right.

If they are Australian citizens, they have every right to be included. They are as much the responsibility of Government as are law abiding citizens.

Well, doesn't that argument apply to migrants, whether illegal or not?

No, it doesn't, for the same reason, we wouldn't include tourists, or people who overstay their visas. Until a person becomes a citizen, they would have to be viewed as temporary residents.

Yeah, I guess that makes sense.

The point about writing definitions is that they have to be written in a way that can be commonly understood.

And agreed as well?

Yes, and agreed by the public, not just the legal profession and the politicians.

An initial list of definitions is contained in the actual Constitution draft. They are subject to amendment and additions in the fullness of time, but that becomes a responsibility of the Parliament. However, as the Constitution is the Primary Law of the nation, it is only logical that any changes or additions to the list of definitions must be open to public comment before being adopted. The people must be able to understand the way words and phrases are defined so that their use in the Constitution will be consistent with general usage.

That's a bit rude, isn't it, letting the politicians decide the meaning of word, and expressions, and not giving the public a say?

Any changes, or additions, are open to public comment by anyone interested.

Well, I guess that's fair enough. The pollies aren't likely to ignore logical concerns.

We can probably give the politicians a little credit for some degree of common sense.

That might be alright if it were up to the individual politician, but I suspect they would always be under the control of the party.

What are you implying? If there is an ideological benefit to a definition, they will try to use it?

That's obvious, isn't it?

The Constitution provides for a small bipartisan group from each House to liaise and come up with an agreed definition.

That might work. It sounds practical enough.

Do you see what's happening here?

No; what?

You and I are talking about writing a Constitution, and there's not a lawyer in sight.

Bloody amazing!

There are some very common and well-defined words in the English language that seems to be either misunderstood or deliberately misinterpreted when applied to the British Act. Every normal English speaking person clearly understands the distinction between the words "may' and "shall", and we must assume, so did the "founding fathers". If they did not know the difference, then why would they use two different words to mean the same thing? Maybe, it's just one of those unwritten conventions that the lawyers and politicians like to cling to whenever it suits their purpose. However, this new Constitution makes it very clear at the outset that there is a distinction between those two words, and irrespective of any traditional practices of the legal fraternity, the words are not interchangeable.

But, what about the most important definition?

What do you reckon is the most important?

The Head of State, of course.

No need for a definition. Everything to do with that position is dealt with in the Constitution. The powers and responsibilities are all defined.

But surely, he's the boss of everything?

Nope. A democracy does not hand over the control of the nation to any one person, whether it's a man or a woman; that would be a dictatorship.

But every country has a President who sets out the policies and runs the country?

Maybe in the USA and some other countries, but the current Head of State for Australia is the British Queen, and she has virtually no say in what Australia does.

So, our President is going to be the same as the Queen, a figurehead without any power?

Pretty much. Just some well-defined and limited executive power, and certainly no hidden "reserve" powers. All the main executive power rests with the Australian Parliament, and that's as it should be.

Page reference for Definitions 201

CHAPTER 5

Discussing the Reasons and Need for a Transition Period

Obviously, if the nation is to start off with a brand new Constitution and a modified political and governmental system, this will require a period of adjustment. The crucial thing about this transition period is that the nation must be guaranteed a properly planned changeover that avoids any dislocation or interruption with the orderly function of the bureaucracy, both State and Commonwealth. There must also be a continuity in the leadership during this period so that at no time will the nation be left without the recognised leadership of the State Governors or the Governor General. It shall also be necessary to guarantee the funding of the bureaucracy so that all the essential services can continue as normal.

Do you honestly think this is ever going to happen?

I do believe there are going to be fairly big changes when the Queen either dies or abdicates.

Yeah, you are probably right, but will it be any different from last time?

If the Republicans try to pull the same contrick again, they will lose.

What contrick are you talking about?

Trying to maintain the status quo and all the unconstitutional established systems and conventions that aren't in the British Act.

But, aren't they talking about a completely new Republican Constitution?

They weren't last time. All they were talking about was taking out references to the Queen and the monarchy.

You reckon they will try to do the same thing again?

Almost certainly. That's why they are continually focussing on the Head of State, and won't say anything about making Australia an independent nation.

So, if they do that, virtually everything will stay the same?

Pretty much, just some name changes, but all the systems will remain in place.

So, there won't be any need for a transition period?

Yes, that's about it, but if the mood is for change, and genuine independence becomes the issue, a transition period will be necessary.

And if we do go independent with a brand new Constitution that is going to affect the States?

Certainly. And that's the sort of scenario this transition period is trying to address.

The severing of the nation's connection with the British monarchy will mean that the positions of the State Governors and the Governor General will need to be reformed, and this is provided for in the new Constitution. Until this Constitution is approved and accepted by the people of Australia, the existing referendum process, as defined in the British Act, will have to apply. This means the new Constitution can only come into effect if approved by a majority of the people and a majority of the States. If that occurs, then the simultaneous referendum asking the people what title they would prefer for Australia's Head of State, either a Governor General or a President, shall apply. In the case of this simultaneous question, the decision will be made by the majority of the people without the need for a majority of the States to approve.

Is that going to be legal, to have a different sort of referendum than we've had in the past?

Yes, it will be entirely legal if the first referendum is successful.

But that first referendum includes the States and will be run the same as always?

Precisely. Part 9 of the existing British Act will still apply, right up to the point when, and if, a new Constitution is accepted.

So, from the time of that acceptance, the new Constitution comes into effect?

Right; and that's why the second type of referendum can then be used for the second question.

Why are you asking what title the people want for their Head of State?

As you must know, there is a fairly close split between the Monarchists and the Republicans in Australia, and it seems only fair to ask the people which title they would prefer.

So, it's a sop to tradition by keeping a link to the past rather than having a clean break?

You could say that, but the title is irrelevant, it's the powers and authority that go with the position that will matter.

Fair enough. I guess it's only right the people should have a say.

The justification for using a straight majority vote is contained in the new Constitution, which sets up the two classes of referendums. Class 1 involves any changes to the Constitution and any issues that directly affect one or more of the States, e.g. the creation of a new State, and therefore, a majority of the States must also approve the changes. The Class 2 referendum is used for national issues involving treaty arrangement, declarations of war, questions of national planning, and similar issues that are not directly constitutional or State related. A Class 2 Referendum shall be decided by a simple majority of the votes.

Should the simultaneous question be decided in favour of the title President, then the senior position in the States shall be titled Vice President.

How much disruption is this change of title going to cause the States?
Not as much as people might think. Certainly, very little during the transition period.
But what about later?
Largely, the changes will be administrative in respect to the laws. The functioning of the bureaucracy will remain much the same.
Won't that be a big job changing all the thousands of laws to remove reference to the monarchy?
Sort of, but it can be covered by some blanket legislation in the interim. The amendments can be done progressively over time.
So, the States just retain a Republican Governor, or get a Vice-president, and carry on pretty much the same.
Mainly, that's it for the States. The other major changes will be to select a Judge to sit on the High Court of the Commonwealth, and the creation of the Australian Council.
Now, that's going to be interesting.

This transition period provides for the establishment of interim entities until new elections are held and new appointments made. These interim positions are restrained from doing anything outside of the specific functions laid down for the duration of the transition period. It is noted that there is no equivalent Chapter, or provision, in the currently used British Act, although the Act did stipulate that certain functions had to be performed within specified time frames.

So, what's the timeframe for this transition period?
It is provided for by virtue of the various functions that will occur during the transition period.

What functions?

Calling for new elections to start with, then moving on from having an Interim Australian Council to the eventual official Australian Council with the new State Governors or Vice Presidents.

And what comes after that?

Once the official Council is installed the first business on the agenda is to choose a Head of State.

And then what?

The Head of State gets sworn in by the existing Chief Justice of the High Court, and the Head of State can then swear in all the newly elected politicians.

So, effectively, the transition period ends with the first sitting of the new Parliament?

Yep, that's it.

Page reference to Chapter 1 Transition 209

CHAPTER 6

Why a Constitution needs to establish its Foundation

Chapter 1 Part 1 represents the start of the new Constitution by setting out in some detail the foundation principles that have gone into creating this document. It defines the ownership of the Constitution and the historical background related to Australia's Common Law practice. This is derived from British Common Law and the numerous charters on which that is based.

The Chapter further declares Australia's status as a monetary sovereign nation and sets out certain limitations about what the Federal Parliament can and cannot do.

Is this foundation mainly an acceptance of all the existing practices?

Not at all. It sets out some of the cornerstones that do need to be recognised as natural parts of the Australian culture.

Like what, for example?

Well, for one, it recognises Local Government as an established tier in our system of Government.

Oh, so it will be written into the Constitution at last?

Yes, but under the condition that Local Government has to remain under the umbrella of the State Government until the people decide otherwise.

But the people have twice rejected handing over Local Government to the Feds, why risk it now?

It's not risking anything. What it is doing is clarifying the issue to make sure Local Government remains close to the people.

The Chapter establishes the recognition of the three levels of Government applicable to the nation, starting with Local Government, then the State and Territory Governments, with the Federal Government at the pinnacle of the system. Despite the fact that some people question the legitimacy of the Local Government system, it has always been a completely legitimate constitutional provision in each of the original colonial responsibilities. For some strange reason, the Federal Government has tried twice to have Local Government come under Federal jurisdiction, as though they don't already have enough on their plate in trying to manage the Commonwealth. As Local Government isn't dealt with directly in the British Act, the Federal Government had to resort to a referendum to have it included. There was never any honest explanation as to why the Federal Government wanted to control the Local Government sector. It has been said there is a hidden agenda to use Local Government as a way to neutralise the authority of the States. Supposedly, the intention is to eventually regionalise the nation and thereby eliminate the States. That is really the only logic that makes sense in this action. Essentially, that is a long-term Fabian approach where the ultimate aim is achieved through gradualism before the public wake up to what is happening. In terms of this new Constitution, its target is for the here and now, and it accepts that the Commonwealth of Australia is a federation of the six separate States. Whether there is any justification for a change to this status has to be a question for the future. As of now, there would seem to be little motivation for any major radical change to the system the people are familiar with. However, there is perceived to be a genuine demand for definite improvements to the system of governance. Mostly, the demand relates to making the elected representatives more responsive to the needs of the society, and at the same time, make those representatives more accountable.

There certainly is a fairly strong public demand to make the Government more responsive and more accountable. How are you going to do that?

It's a sort of philosophical thing really.

There's nothing philosophical about the way the Government operates. It's just practical politics.

Yes, and that's the problem.

Why? Politics is politics.

Our stupid party political game is just an adversarial contest in trying to score points. The politicians don't represent the nation, or the people, they just represent the party.

So, how are you going to change that? Surely, you're not going to try and eliminate political parties?

No, that would be near impossible. Political parties are a reality, but that doesn't mean they shouldn't be controlled.

How do you reckon you can control them?

The simplest way is to force a two-thirds majority vote in both Houses before any legislation is passed.

That will never happen.

It will if the people agree to adopt this new Constitution.

But no party is going to agree to that.

And that's precisely why we have a people's Constitution and not a political party Constitution.

That's going to be a hard ask, but I can see the point.

Everything in this new Constitution will be explained and available to the people before the referendum.

So, no secret agenda, just let the people decide if they want to control the Government or not?

Yep, that's it on the knocker.

The Foundation Chapter points the way to these changes while retaining links to the past. A degree of flexibility is included to allow the legal and judicial system to evolve and better serve the Australian people. This Foundation provides a direct link to the Preamble concerning the way the Constitution is to be interpreted and what the lawmakers need to take into account when making laws. Possibly, the most important issue in the Foundation is the clear recognition of Australia as a monetary sovereign nation. This provision represents the single most important factor in allowing the nation, and the people, to become a truly economically independent nation.

But, who knows what monetary sovereignty means? I bet there aren't too many people out there?

Yeah, and that's a major problem, very few people know what it means, but all the top bankers do, for sure.

How do you know if that's true?

Because of the myth continually promoted by the banks.

What myth is that?

That the bank only lends out money deposited in its customer's accounts.

Of course, they do that; where else are they going to get the money from?

Well, you explain to me how a bank can lend out money when not one single customer ever has their account reduced because their money has been lent to someone else?

Ahh, I see the problem. So, where does the money come from that the banks lend?

Actually, it comes out of thin air. Under the fractional reserve system, the banks can create "money" by simply punching a few keys on a computer keyboard.

That's bullshit. How can that be legal? Who lets them do that?

It's legal because the Government lets it happen.

That doesn't make sense. If the Banks are allowed to create "money" just like that, why doesn't the Government do the same?

The Government does do the same thing, but only in a tiny little way.

Why, and how?

The Government uses their monetary sovereign status, granted to them by Sections 51(xii) and 51(xiii) of the Constitution part of the British Act, to create all the coins and notes we use as physical money.

Isn't that what money is; all the coins and notes?

Nope, they are less than ten percent of the "money" used in Australia; the ninety percent and more is "money" created by the Banks as interest-bearing loans.

If the Government has control of the money supply, why does it borrow money from people?

Good question. I wish some politician would give us an honest answer to that.

Page reference to Chapter 1 Part 1 The Foundation 214

CHAPTER 7

Discussing the Reasons and Purpose
for an Independent Australian Council

Following on from the Chapter setting out the foundation for creating this Constitution, we now go into the details for the formation and composition of the Australian Council. The concept of an Australian Council is to establish a small practical and workable group of eminent people to act as an independent authority so that the overriding authority is not in the hands of any one person. The "power" and responsibility of the Council is to review and advise; it was not envisaged to have any executive authority. The Chapter also explains how the Council will function and the limits of its responsibilities. As explained above, the concept of a small non-political group of eminent people was seen as an alternative way to create a supreme body without risking a divisive, money oriented and political party dominated appointment of the Head of State. By having the Council made up of the Governors/Vice Presidents from the six States, the Council would choose one of their members to take on the position of Head of State for a designated period. The member so chosen would then become the chairperson of the Council and the State would appoint a replacement Governor/Vice President to fill the vacancy. The chairperson does not have a casting vote, and any evenly split decisions of the Council are to be decided in the negative.

This is a pretty radical idea. Is anyone likely to go along with it?

Well, it is different, but the concept came up in nineteen ninety-nine, although the idea was for a much bigger Council.

What happened to it?

Exactly what was expected? The media was up the arse of the Government and refused to give house room to any alternative ideas.

So, it never had a chance?

As the PR people like to say, "If it ain't on TV it never happened."

Do you think it might have a chance now?

That's hard to say, but the revolting spectacle of the recent US Presidential election might give people a second thought about electing a President for Australia.

Yeah, that could be true, but why was electing a President so popular back in ninety-nine?

Obviously, the people don't trust the Government, and they certainly didn't trust Howard to pick and control the Presidency.

But could a PM control the President?

Under the Westminster system, the PM is certainly supposed to control the Governor General, except when the GG chooses to actually read the British Act.

You mean like Kerr did?

Theoretically, yes, but everyone chose to get on the bandwagon of unwritten "reserve powers," even though the British Act clearly states the GG could do what he did.

You mean he didn't need any "reserve powers" at all?

That's right; it was all part of the mystique cloaking the British Act, in the effort to make it "unknowable" to ordinary people.

But, weren't the powers and authority of the President spelt out for a republican system back in nineteen ninety-nine?

Back then, Howard and Turnbull made sure nothing was ever clearly said about what role the President would have, or what authority would go with the position.

Except for the Prime Minister being able to sack the President?

Yep, that was the punchline Howard used to make sure the Republicans lost the vote.

The Council does not have any executive authority but acts as a body of last resort. It may mediate, and if deemed justified, make a recommendation to the appropriate source for a review of the issue raised. Any such issue would become non-applicable until the recommendations are addressed. The Council will also act as an adjudicating body in the event of a political crisis, but with the ultimate remedy of recommending a new election. That's as provided for in the Constitution. The Council also has the responsibility to ensure that any legislation coming out of the Parliament conforms to the Constitution. If so approved, the Head of State is then authorised to give consent to the legislation.

That's also a radical departure from what I know of the current system.

Apart from the fact that the current system is unconstitutional; the suggested idea follows a very sound and logical process.

What do you mean the current system is unconstitutional?

Well, you do know it is the Westminster system of Government that is used, don't you?

Well, yeah, I suppose I do.

Why the "suppose"? Don't you actually know?

I know how the Government works; the Parliament and the Prime Minister and all that, but I'm not exactly sure what the system was called.

OK then, for your information, the system of Government we use in Australia is called the Westminster system.

So, how is it unconstitutional?

Well, you show me one single mention of the Westminster system in the British Act. And for that matter, show me where a Prime Minister is created.

But that's the system we've used from day one?

Yep, and it has been unconstitutional from that very day.

What has happened under the currently used Westminster system of Government, is that the Prime Minister instructs the

Governor General to give consent to any legislation that is passed by Parliament. Most Governor Generals and I would guess, every politician sitting in Parliament, past and present, have never read the British Act from cover to cover, let alone understood what it says. If they had done so, they would know the system of Government described in that Act is very different to the one that is practiced. They would also know there is nothing in the British Act to say the Governor General must always do what the Prime Minister says, simply because there is no Prime Minister in the Act.

But, how can that be? Australia's always had a Prime Minister.

Yes, we have had a person holding that position even though there is nothing in the British Act that defines its role, its authority or its responsibilities.

But Australia couldn't operate without a Prime Minister?

Maybe so, but that's not the point. Nobody should be allowed to interpret a law anyway that it suits them, and certainly not the Primary Law of the land.

But if, as you say, this is unconstitutional, why hasn't the High Court done something about it?

That is another very good question.

Surely, the High Court knows what the Constitution says?

Maybe, but that's a bit questionable.

How come?

I guess it's the way they are trained. No academics or legal professions ever question the validity of the Government in respect to the Constitution.

But surely the Primary Law has to be read and applied as it is written?

Seems not. The High Court has never allowed anyone to question the legitimacy of the Westminster system, or the position of the Prime Minister.

But that's crazy. Who gave the High Court that sort of authority; to ignore the Constitution?

Oh, they don't ignore it, they just pick and choose what bits to acknowledge, as and when it suits them.

Does that make them a law unto themselves; a bunch of unelected people who are above the Constitution?

I believe most of them think that way.

Under this new Constitution, the functions of the Head of State are largely ceremonial, but as the Commander in Chief of the Armed Forces, the Head of State does have the executive authority to declare war in the event of Australia coming under direct military attack. All other deployments of Australia's military forces come within the executive authority of the Parliament. The concept of the Council has the benefit of taking the overriding authority out of the hands of a single person so that no one person shall ever be in a position to dismiss an elected Government, as was the case with Sir John Kerr. The Council of six eminent people and a Chairperson is seen as a practical and compact group that should be capable of functioning in the best interests of the nation.

When you think about it, it's not very clear how we would go about picking candidates for the job as President.

That's right. If it's only a ceremonial role, it probably doesn't matter too much who gets the job.

You mean it could be anybody; a singer, Crocodile Dundee, Mal Meninga, or even Dawn Fraser?

That's right. They wouldn't have to know anything about politics, or the Constitution. All they do is hand out gongs and open some flower shows.

What's the point of having an election then, if they are not going to have any authority?

No point really, just a big waste of time and money.

But what if they do have some authority? That'll be a different ball game, won't it?

It depends a lot on what sort of authority the people would give their Head of State.

That's a laugh. When have the people ever had any say in what authority they can give anybody, let alone the Head of State?

I admit, it's a quantum leap, but it is exactly the way a proper democratic system is supposed to work.

But, I'm sure the Government is going to control that and make sure any Head of State comes under the control of the politicians.

Well, here's an opportunity to change the system, if the people are willing to take the responsibility.

How? By adopting this Constitution?

Yes. But if they insist on electing a Head of State there'd be no way anyone can keep politics and money out of it.

Page reference to Chapter 1 Part 2 The Australian Council 218

CHAPTER 8

Discussing the Powers and Authority of the Head of State

Since nineteen ninety-nine, the issue of the Head of State has been the deliberate and preferred "primrose path" to lead the "sheeple" to their "eternal bonfire". It remains so today, as it is still the mantra of the Australian Republican Movement, and the Government. What it aims to do is set up a stark contrast between a conventional Republican Presidential system and the hereditary monarchical system. In doing so, it establishes the groundwork for another divisive referendum.

Is that what happened in nineteen ninety-nine? Was it just a contest between Turnbull's republicans and Howard's monarchists?

Yes, that is exactly what happened. And when they gave us a choice between that bloody awful "minimalist" Constitution or keeping the abortion of the British Act we already have; no wonder so many Republicans said, "No way".

I didn't go for the change, but that was more because I didn't really understand what was going on.

I guess that was the same for a lot of other people.

As they said, "If it ain't broke, why fix it?"

That was the classic cliché used by the monarchists because; they knew they were on safe ground. Hardly anyone knows anything about the Constitution.

But, there were a lot of people at those Conventions, wasn't there?

Well, not so much a lot, just a bunch of carefully selected people that included a majority chosen and appointed by the Government. That way, the Government ensured it got the predetermined result it wanted.

Are you saying it was a setup?

It sure was, and the media went along with it, balls and all. It lived up to its name, a monumental "con-con", set up by the Howard Government and their Republican cronies.

What the Republicans haven't been prepared to do is disclose the powers and authority with which they plan to clothe their Presidential Head of State. On the one hand they say, "No more Sir John Kerr's as the top cocky" and on the other hand, they say this will simply be a ceremonial role.

If it is to be a simple ceremonial role why is it so "important"?

Surely, the making of Australia as a truly independent nation is far more important than some powerless figurehead sitting at the top of the table? The catch is, once we start talking about independence we have to start looking at the detail needed to sever all political and legal ties with the UK, and not just the monarchy. England is currently immersed in a similar type of problem with their "Brexit" from the Eurozone.

I can't remember ever hearing any talk about Australia becoming independent.

Of course, you didn't. That's far too a murkier issue to bring out of the closet.

But didn't the High Court say that Britain was a foreign country back in nineteen ninety-nine?

They did say that, but it was a deliberately spurious political decision.

Come off it. The High Court doesn't make wrong decisions?

You wanna bet? How come they made that decision when not one of the Judges could say when Australia supposedly, became independent?

That doesn't make sense.

Of course, it doesn't.

If the High Court judges claim they don't know when and how Australia became independent, who does?

Good question?

Isn't that something the Australian people ought to have a say about?

Not according to the High Court. They seem to think it is entirely in their hands.

But that's bullshit.

Precisely. Why should a small bunch of unelected people have any say about Australia becoming independent?

Putting aside for the moment what should be the real focus of the Republican debate – Australia's independence and sovereignty – we need to look at aspects of how we might go about choosing suitable contestants for the position of Head of State. We then need to look at how one contestant might be selected from what is called, "the popular vote". To date, all the chattering classes, and the media have been pushing the concept of a popularly elected Head of State, but remaining deathly silent on how this might evolve. Nowhere has there been any discussion on the qualifications and experience that might be necessary for the position. The qualifications and experience, of course, would be directly related to the role envisaged. There is talk about the position being apolitical; also about it being purely ceremonial. There is other talk about the position having a modicum of authority, but according to the politicians, the position has to be completely in the pocket of the Prime Minister.

Now, that's a thing, isn't it? What's the Head of State supposed to do?

Really, the question should be, "What do the Australian people want the Head of State to do?"

That's a purely hypothetical question, isn't it?

Not at all, if this new Constitution is adopted.

I reckon that's going to be in the too hard basket, but what do you reckon the role is going to be?

Well, I certainly don't want another dictator like Kerr, who can sack an elected Government on a personal whim.

But there was a political crisis at the time, wasn't there?

Sort of, but not really.

What do you mean, not really?

The Government operates under the unconstitutional Westminster system, which is almost entirely based on unwritten conventions and tradition.

So, what happened?

The opposition had control of the Senate at the time and the opposition leader, one Malcolm Fraser, broke with tradition and refused to allow the Senate to pass the money bills to fund the Government.

So, the Whitlam Government would have run out of money and couldn't pay anyone?

Technically, that's how it was portrayed. In essence, it was dirty politics, but with lots of undercurrent issues that never came to the surface at the time.

Are you getting into some sort of conspiracy theory?

Yeah, maybe. But like all conspiracies, it is usually very hard to come up with concrete evidence.

That's true enough. Most conspiracies are just a lot of talk that can't be verified.

The catch is; where there's smoke, there is often fire.

So, where do the people figure in this debate? Do they have a say in what sort of powers and authority they would like to bequeath to their Head of State? Or are the people just going to be given a choice from what the "establishment" says they can choose from? It has to be patently obvious that if the Head of

State is to be elected by popular vote, there is no way the position can avoid getting embroiled in the ugly swamp of money and politics. Does Australia really want to go down that path of the US type of fiasco? Australia's current electoral process is already mired in the quicksands of corruption. This is demonstrated from Dr Lindy Edward's two thousand and seventeen report on the seventy million dollars of "dark money" that poured into the last election without any semblance of accountability. That the political classes, and the Electoral Commission, allow this to happen is a savage indictment on the corruptibility of all concerned, not to forget the legal system.

What can the legal system do about it?

Probably not much off their own bat. They have to wait until someone comes up with a claim, or a breach of the rules.

Shouldn't the Electoral Commission be responsible for that?

Logically, they should be, but like so much legislation, it is probably riddled with loopholes that any Tom, Dick or Harry can slide through.

Isn't the High Court supposed to uphold the Constitution?

That's what most people are led to believe, but the Court won't do a thing until someone with a lot of money decides to challenge a law as unconstitutional.

If the law is unconstitutional, how did it get passed in the first place?

Oh, that's easy. The Governor General just gives the assent to any law that comes out of Parliament. Theoretically, he does that on the Queen's behalf, but in reality, he always has to do what the Prime Minister tells him.

Even if the law is unconstitutional?

Yep, even then.

That's bloody awful.

Well, nine times out of ten the GG doesn't have a clue what the Constitution says anyway, and it doesn't seem to matter much if they do bother to get a legal opinion.

But, if they wanted a legal opinion, who would they go to; a Government lawyer?

Probably, or a Judge, but what Government lawyer, or Judge, is going to buck the Government?

Page reference to Chapter 1 Part 3 The Head of State 225

CHAPTER 9

Discussing the Executive Authority
of the Parliament

This chapter of the new Constitution deals with the principle political entity that has executive authority in the governance of the Commonwealth. That entity is the Parliament, which consists of the House of Representatives and the Senate. As with the original British Act, any reference to the Parliament always includes both Houses. The Head of State, as the Commander in Chief of the Armed Forces, is the only other position with some specifically defined executive authority. That authority only comes into effect if Australia comes under direct military attack by a foreign nation.

While the accepted practice is followed, by selecting a member of the House of Representatives to be elected as the Prime Minister, the unwritten convention of the Prime Minister being able to dictate to the Head of State is not included.

Surely, the Head of State should have the executive power to override the Parliament if it gets out of hand?

Why? Why should that sort of power be given to any single individual if we are to be a democracy? That's the basis for a dictatorship.

No, I don't mean that. What if the Parliament acts unconstitutionally?

At the bottom line, that's the responsibility of the people.

Come off it. What can the people do?

Well. If they approve this new Constitution, they are approving several measures to address an unconstitutional Parliament.

Such as?

An independent Australian Council to start with; a Council that examines all laws and actions coming out of Parliament.

But what if the Council is corrupt?

Then, we are buggered, but it is hard to imagine the six States couldn't find at least one honest and eminent person to represent Australia on the Council.

Yeah, that sounds fair enough.

Besides, there are two provisions in the Constitution, which serve to address any improper conduct concerning a Council member.

Is that right? What are they?

One is the Citizen's Recall process, where anyone with genuine proof of wrongdoing on the part of a Council member can mount a challenge.

That's a bit risky, isn't it?

Not at all. Only genuine claims with proof would continue to be processed.

And what's the second provision?

That is the impeachment process, which applies to every elected and appointed person with the responsibility to serve the people.

You mean the Head of State as well?

Yes, him or her, as well as the Prime Minister and every High Court Judge.

You'll never get away with that.

It's not me getting away with anything. If the people vote for this new Constitution, they will do so because that's what they want.

What, making the politicians and bureaucrats accountable?

Dead right! It gives the people direct control of the system.

And isn't that how it should always be?

The Speaker of the House of Representatives and the President of the Senate are vested with the constitutional authority to create, publish and maintain a comprehensive Operating Manual for their respective Houses of Parliament. These Manuals shall set out the rules for the conduct of proceedings and the disciplinary action to be applied to any breach of the rules. In effect, this will require codifying any acceptable unwritten convention currently in use, but scrap any out of date and unnecessary conventions based on outmoded tradition. These Manuals will be available to the public, and unwritten conventions will cease to exist.

What's all this about unwritten conventions? I've never heard anything about them.

Naturally, they are unwritten so; no one really knows how many there are or what they are supposed to be used for.

That doesn't make sense.

Well, there are a lot of things that don't make sense when you start to look at how the Parliament functions.

What do you mean?

There is a stack of Pommie traditions that are carried out on a sort of ritual basis. Mostly, they really have no practical use and are just part of a symbolic system in maintaining subservience to the monarchy.

Where do they come from, these symbolic rituals?

It's just part of the earlier century's aristocratic traditions that are practiced in the UK Parliament.

You mean we are just copying the Poms for no real reason other than tradition?

Pretty much the case. After all, most of the early politicians in the colonies were English bred and had no real Australian identity at the time.

The reason for setting out the rules via a Manual is to do away with the unwritten conventions and make the rules and penalties publicly available for all to see. By handing the responsibility to the leader of each House to organise the creation of their respective Manuals, it provides a degree of flexibility in making it easier to keep the rules up to date. The alternative is to create the Manuals by a formal legislative process, but this is seen as being unnecessary and potentially unwieldy. Each House can have their stand-alone rules Manual without needing the approval of the other House. There will be no loss of authority by avoiding the legislative process, as the rules Manual is a specific constitutional requirement. Each Manual is to be made publically available, which will tend to ensure the rules and procedures contained therein conform to acceptable rational and ethical standards of the society.

The Constitution will establish the parameters applying to the powers, privileges and immunities of their elected representatives, and the Manuals will conform to these parameters. The aim is to create a governmental system that is clearly responsible to the people, not the Head of State, not to a Prime Minister, and certainly not to any political party. Should the elected representatives wish to try and manipulate the rules and/or disciplinary actions, there will be ample opportunity for the public to voice their concern and disapproval.

Isn't that a bit risky letting the politicians make up their own rules and penalties?

Not really. Many of the rules are already established, but they are mostly unwritten conventions interwoven with a stack of old traditions.

If they are already established why do they need to put them in a manual?

Because, most people don't know what the rules are, let alone the penalties when the pollies break the rules.

So, you reckon, if the people know the rules it will be easier to ensure the pollies follow them?

The Parliamentary system they use is a pretty elite club, with a heap of special rules that aren't written down anywhere.

Rules, like what?

Well; they have majority leaders, minority leaders, whips, Parliamentary Secretaries, ushers, and all sorts of other positions that don't get a mention anywhere in the Constitution.

Like the Prime Minister?

Yes, exactly like that. A position that is almost all-powerful, but without any Constitutional authority, obligations or responsibilities.

So, that'd go in the Manual, wouldn't it?

No, if we are going to have a Prime Minister, it definitely has to go in the Constitution, along with whatever authority the people are willing to allow him, or her.

Yeah, that makes far better sense.

The chapter also deals with the qualification that will apply to any candidate for political office. There are none of the perennial loopholes in this Chapter that will allow Parliament to alter the meaning and intent of the conditions set down. Any amendment, addition or alteration to this Chapter can only be accomplished through a national Class 1 Referendum. Likewise, the procedure for determining the "powers, privileges and immunities" applicable to the elected representatives is also dealt with in the Constitution. In Part 9 of the original British Act, the "founding fathers" gave the politician the authority to decide what "powers, privileges and immunities" they could give themselves. Clearly, that is a gross miscarriage of responsibility because those "powers privileges and immunities" are the very things that should be entirely in the hands of the people to determine. As has been said, the action of the "founding fathers" is akin to giving the keys of the asylum to the inmates, and over the years those "inmates" have certainly made the most of that generous "gift".

I certainly agree that the powers and privileges of the politicians must come from the people. We can't let those buggers give themselves whatever they want.

Unfortunately, that's the way it's been from the start.

I guess, if fifty politicians and lawyers are going to get together to write a Constitution they are going to make sure they are well looked after.

Yep, that's human nature for you.

Yes, that's pretty close to what human nature is; looking after yourself and bugger anyone else?

Isn't that what politics comes down to? They were the Bunyip Aristocracy of the colonial era so, why shouldn't they have all the power and privileges of the rulers?

Nothing much has changed; has it?

To date, that's true, but the whole system is enmeshed in a web of hypocrisy.

How come? Why do you say that?

Well, on the one hand, we have a bunch of career politicians who place limits on the position of a Governor General, and age limits on Judges, and on the people as well, but refuse to place any limits on themselves.

But isn't it the people who decide how long a politician stays in power?

Up to a point, but it's the political party system that controls the selection of candidates, their funding, and the choice of electorates.

Maybe so, but there is still no guarantee that a party's candidate will be elected.

That's true, there's no guarantee, but the system still results in politicians who keep getting re-elected year after year.

That's good, isn't it? That makes for stable Government?

Nope, it just leads to a stagnation of policies and ideas aimed at maintaining the status quo.

How is the Constitution going to change that?

By limiting the number of consecutive terms, any politician can be a candidate.

That sounds good. Politics should never be a long-term career for anybody.

When it's all boiled down, politics is about power; power over the people; no matter how you want to dress it up.

The Chapter establishes a bipartisan Rules Committee for each House with authority to determine if a representative is in breach of the Rules laid down in the Manual. The Rules Committee shall investigate and report on a breach of the specified constitutional provisions and deliver their findings to the Australian Council for action. What this Constitution is trying to do is place the accountability of the elected representatives squarely in the hands of the people, but in an orderly and responsible manner.

Finally, the Chapter decrees that any issue deemed of national importance to the Commonwealth shall require the approval of a minimum vote of two-thirds of the total membership from each House. Thus, all bills that come before either House can only proceed with the two-thirds approval of the elected members.

Jeez, that's going to be a hard ask, getting the political parties to work together.

They seem to have no problem working together when it is something that is for their mutual benefit.

Like what for example?

Like when there is a pay rise on offer, or changing the Constitution to give the Federal Government more power over the States, or the people.

That's crap. There's an independent body to decide on pay rises.

Yeah, and who appoints this supposedly independent body if it isn't the Government?

I don't know, but I doubt the parties just agree to change the Constitution only if it is going to give them more power.

You wanna bet? Why have only eight out of forty-four referendum proposals been accepted by the people?

It's like everyone says; Australians are conservative.

That's the bullshit excuse the pollies and academics always use.

OK, if you're such a smart arse, why is it so hard to make changes through a referendum?

Because the people have enough common sense to see when the pollies try to make a grab for more power.

Now, that's gotta be a heap of bullshit.

OK. So why do you think every proposal for change is only allowed to come from the politicians?

I don't know. Isn't that's what's in the Constitution.

Nope, it's not. The Constitution does not give the politicians a monopoly on proposing changes.

So, why have they got one then?

Just another one of the unwritten conventions that have never been approved by the people.

Page reference to Chapter 2 Part 1 The Parliament 228

CHAPTER 10

Discussing the House of Representatives under the New Constitution

Despite the fact the Senate is referred to as "the Upper House", it is really just a leftover class distinction from Britain. Their House of Lords, the sort of equivalent of Australia's Senate, was the repository for many of Britain's nobility. Most people know and understand that the House of Representatives of the Australian Parliament is the more important House, even though it is often referred to as "the Lower House". The principle Constitutional distinction between the two Houses is that the House of Representatives has about twice the number of elected representatives as the Senate. The other Constitutional distinction is that money bills for the funding of the Government can only originate in the lower House. Other than those two differences, there is little distinction between the ways the Houses function.

It seems a bit peculiar that Australia's founding fathers chose to follow the American Republican system for naming their Houses of Parliament rather than the traditional English system?

Yes, there does seem to be a bit of an anomaly there.

Do you think it was because we didn't have enough Lords in the colonies at the time?

Possibly, but I think it was more to do with Clark's familiarity with the American system.

Even so, he was only one voice in the fifty politicians and lawyers who made up the final convention.

That's true, but most of the responsibility for deciding the final draft came down to just a few of them, with Griffith as the major influence.

Nevertheless, it is still a bit strange when you think about it.

But, it wasn't just the names of the Houses that were used, there were also sections of the US Constitution that were copied as well.

Isn't that plagiarising?

Sort of, but I don't think the US Constitution comes under copyright laws.

I guess there was good reason for copying parts of their Constitution?

Actually, not so. They only copied some of the wording but left out the important reason why the section was in the US Constitution.

That's a bit stupid, isn't it?

Hard to say. I guess they just didn't understand enough about the US history.

However, under the unconstitutional Westminster system of Government, it is the traditional unwritten convention that the unconstitutional Prime Minister must come from the House of Representatives. It is a quite inexplicable and astounding omission on the part of the "founding fathers" that they did not see fit to specify that the Westminster system of Government shall apply. After all, that was the system they used in their colonial Parliaments, and it was the only system they really knew. Are we simply to assume that it was taken for granted that the Westminster system was to apply automatically? So, why did the "founding fathers" spend so much time in painstakingly documenting a system in their draft, which was fully intended to be ignored? Does that make sense? Was there a hidden agenda for ignoring political parties, the Westminster system, and most importantly of all, the position of a Prime Minister?

It certainly doesn't make sense to me. If they knew the Westminster system was to be used, surely they could have documented it accurately?

That would be the logical assumption.

Even though the system is almost entirely based on unwritten conventions, it would be easy enough to set out the basic principles?

One would have thought so. Instead, the founding fathers came up with a system that puts the Governor General at the apex and with virtual dictatorial authority.

But, the Queen is at the apex, isn't she?

Technically, yes, but in a practical sense, everything revolves around the Governor General down here in the colony.

But, that's not how it happens, is it?

No, it's not, but that's because the politicians and the Courts don't follow the British Act as it is written.

It seems quite preposterous that these, supposedly, learned men were unaware of these crucial omissions, and that they were deliberately establishing a virtual dictatorial system with the Governor General as the real apex of their planning? On reading Part 9 of the British Act as it is written, it is hard to get any other impression. Surely, if anyone is to sit down and draft the primary law for a country, it can't rely on assumptions for the way it is to be read? If the primary law is created on that basis, what does it say for every other law it authorises?

That's a good question. If the Courts and the politicians aren't following the Constitution, how come they are allowed to get away with it?

Ignorance, I suppose, is the real answer.

Ignorance by whom?

Probably by the people mainly, but certainly by the politicians and lawyers.

Is it ignorance or is it deliberate?

Well, the people definitely don't have a clue, as hardly any of them know anything about the British Act.

But, what about the politicians and lawyers?

As far as the politicians are concerned, I doubt there is one politician in the Federal Parliament who has ever read the Constitution. If they had they would know the Government isn't operating the way the Constitution says.

So, what about the lawyers?

I guess we can blame Quick and Garran for that. Their huge epistle they wrote in nineteen hundred and one just accepted that the Westminster system was to be used. It virtually became the "Bible" for the Constitution in Australia's legal fraternity.

The House of Representatives is where all the "action" takes place, but to the casual observer, it really looks like an absurd spectacle taken directly from the Roman era of gladiators pitting themselves against one another in an arena. Instead of the romantic vision of armour cladded gladiators, we have some rather insignificant little men dressed in suits, pathetically trying to score verbal points off an opponent. Mostly, this verbal jousting comes in the form of prepared speeches, usually written by speechwriters and very seldom presented by anyone skilled in public speaking, let alone with genuine oratorical conviction.

That's a pretty good analogy of a couple of protagonists slinging mud at each other in the centre of the arena. There's an audience on each side jeering on their "champions," as "Caesar" watches from his chair at the head of the proceedings.

It really is a stupid system with the two major parties at each other's throats.

Well, that's right. We elect representatives in the hope they will do their best for the nation, but all they do is what is best for their party.

And getting re-elected at the next election.

And not to mention all the perks they pick up along the way?

It really is a pathetic system when you stop to look at it properly.

But what's the alternative? This is the only system we've ever known. How can you change it to something better?

That's a tough ask under the present circumstances. About the only option is to look for ways to make the political parties work together for the benefit of the nation rather than their party ideology.

Good luck with that one. I hope there is a way to make it happen.

What is even more farcical is the ritual of question time sessions where prepared rhetorical answers are given, mostly consisting of waffle that avoids directly answering the pre-submitted questions. This is supposed to be the "serious" business of managing the nation, but really, it is just some theatre for the supposed benefit of the public. The real business of trying to control the country is handled behind closed doors of the ruling political party.

It is in these cloistered chambers that the legislation bills are dreamt up, to add to the never-ending controls that seem to be a permanent addiction of all Governments.

It is a sad reflection on the political party system that, so much legislation is written in a way that it is beyond the understanding of most of the politicians, and certainly, most of the public; neither of whom have the benefit of legal training. Even with legal training, it seems most legislation is open to different interpretation, as is attested by the innumerable arguments that end up in Courts. As the Senate is ultimately responsible for all the laws that are generated, why hasn't the Senate demanded a complete reform of the way laws are written? All law bills should be self-contained, which would mean eliminating amendments and extracting anything that is relevant to the issue from an earlier law, or laws. This would serve to bring the law up to date for everyone to understand. There is no reason this can't be done.

At the same time, it would be possible to repeal an earlier law that is now updated.

This concept has been included in the new Constitution.

Now, that's something I've had experience with.

What? In trying to understand a law that has been amended?

Yes, precisely. I came across one that had been last updated in nineteen ninety-four when they repealed connections going back to nineteen twenty-three.

That sounds ridiculous. You mean that laws going back to nineteen twenty-three still applied in nineteen ninety-four?

Apparently so, but what was even more ridiculous was some of the provisions that the amendments didn't address.

Like what, for example?

That the Governor General in Council may, at any time, end the appointment of a director for any reason, or none.

Surely that's against any unfair dismissal laws; to sack somebody without a reason?

That's the wording that was left in the Act.

Who's responsible for that sort of thing happening?

Ultimately, it has to come back to the politicians who voted to pass the amendments.

And that, I suppose, is the result of party politics.

Well, it was a thirty-six page Act so, how many politicians do you think would ever bother to read that many pages?

The other major change advocated, and provided for, is the elimination of career politicians. This is achieved in the case of the House of Representatives, by limiting the term in office to three consecutive periods for a total of nine years. It will also apply to the Senate, but their limit will be just the two six-year terms.

This is going to ruffle a few feathers, but why shouldn't politics be a career?

Well, to start with, change is about the only constant in today's world; not that it hasn't always been a factor in the past.

But that's no reason why politics can't be a career.

It certainly is because human nature is such that people who stay in the one job for too long become settled in their ways and find it hard to embrace change.

I suppose that's right. I do know people like that, but politics is different.

Why is it different?

The politicians have to go to the people every three years if they want to keep their job.

That's true, but why are there so many electorates around the nation defined as "safe" electorates for a particular party?

Obviously, because the majority of people in those electorates will vote for that party's candidate.

So, what you are saying is that people just vote for a political party irrespective of whether it is effective or not?

Not always, there will always be some swing voters who vote differently.

But, if there are enough swing voters in an electorate it can't be a "safe" seat?

Hey, you're getting off the subject here. We're talking about long-term politics.

We're not really off the subject because it is party endorsement that contributes to career politics rather than the person.

The responsibilities of the Speaker of the House of Representatives are set out, and one of the major ones is to ensure the creation of an up to date operations manual for the House. The same responsibility applies to the President of the Senate. Essentially, these manuals will eliminate all the unwritten conventions that currently apply to the separate Houses. The manuals will be publicly available so that everyone can know the rules and procedures that apply to the elected representatives and how the

Houses of Parliament are allowed to function. Any unwritten convention that is overlooked, and is later deemed necessary for the functioning of the House, can be added to the manual. The manuals will require the approval of the respective Houses, as will any change or addition, before being officially adopted. There is a time frame set for the compilation of the manuals to ensure they are completed and made publicly available.

Do you really think it is possible to bring all these unwritten conventions out into the open?

Why wouldn't it be? It is something that should have been done years ago, but it suited the politicians to keep them all hidden.

Aren't those conventions all mixed up with tradition and historical customs?

Yes; most of them probably are, but that's no excuse for hiding them.

Surely, we want to keep this sort of traditional heritage as part of our culture?

Why? It's not a part of the modern Australian culture, it is the British culture, and when you look at the pomp and ceremony associated, it comes across as rather superfluous for this day and age.

Yeah, I guess you could be right. As a newly independent nation, it is only logical we should adopt our own procedures.

Too right. Here's the chance for Parliament to bring our system up to date and make it plain and effective for all to see.

Page reference to Chapter 2 Part 2 The House of Representatives 234

CHAPTER 11

Discussing the Role of the Senate

The initial concept of the Senate being a State's House was really a deliberate fraud, as all the "founding fathers" were told, and were well aware of the reality of political parties. Those "founding fathers" chose to ignore the existence of that reality, knowing full well that the Senate would become a political party House and destroy the concept of a State's House.

That's a pretty rude statement, isn't it?

What, that the "founding fathers" were party to a fraud?

Yes. I can't believe that could be true.

Well, it's on record. John Macrossan told the convention in eighteen ninety-one that political parties would control the Senate, but he was ignored.

So, everybody knew about political parties way back then?

That's right; political parties were an established feature of the political scene.

But, the political party system has an enormous influence on how a Government functions.

Precisely. And none of the "founding fathers" could have been unaware of that influence.

So, why do you think political parties were ignored?

I suspect it was because the majority, if not all the fifty delegates to the eighteen ninety-seven convention were basically in favour of federalism.

In other words, you are saying the delegates wanted the federal system to override the colonies?

Not necessarily so, but there was a strong opposition to federalism, certainly in the NSW Parliament, and none of the opposition were elected, or appointed, to the convention.

The concept was that if each Colony/State had equal representation in the Senate, this would be seen as giving each Colony/State the recognition of their equal standing, irrespective of their population. The influence of political parties completely nullified this concept, and it remains a mystery why the "founding fathers" could not see this. On the other hand, if they could see what would happen, and it was very clearly pointed out to them by Mr Macrossan, what benefit did they see in purposely ignoring the threat? Were the "founding fathers" so convinced of the righteousness of their political party system, and genuinely believed the colonies should not have an effective voice in the Federal system, that the subterfuge was justified? But justified in whose eyes?

While only five of the colonies participated in the final set of conventions; Queensland declined to send any representatives; reading the records in the archives, it would appear that the majority of convention representatives were firmly committed to creating a centralised form of government. Was the omission of political party influence a deliberate act for the benefit of the representatives, who had to report to their respective colonial Parliaments?

That sounds awfully dishonest and unethical if the reason for ignoring the power and influence of political parties was just a subterfuge to mislead the colonial Parliaments.

Well, bear in mind, most of the colonial politicians were not privy to what went on at the conventions. They had to rely on the reports of their delegates.

You are talking conspiracy here. I can't believe that would be right.

Clearly, if you read the Chapter on the Senate, it implies that the Senators are elected to represent their respective States, or colonies, as they then were.

Yes, that's true, there is certainly no indication otherwise.

But surely the colonial politicians could realise how the political parties would gain control?

Maybe, maybe not. Just remember, this is the eighteen-nineties we are talking about, and federalism didn't exist at that point in time.

And nor did the communication capabilities either.

That's right. To a large extent, each colony was pretty much a closed community, and interstate communication was more or less restricted to trade practices.

So, maybe you are right. The ultimate impact of federalism may not have been fully appreciated back in the nineteenth century.

It was agreed that each colony would legislate to hold a referendum of the relatively few eligible male voters; hence, it must have been necessary to convince each colonial Parliament that they would be treated as equal partners in the proposed federation scheme. Thus, the subterfuge of the Senate being a State's House would have been necessary to gain that approval.

As with the House of Representatives, the President of the Senate is vested with the constitutional authority to create, publish and maintain a comprehensive Operating Manual for the Senate. The Manual shall set out the rules for the conduct of proceedings and the disciplinary action to be applied to any breach of the rules. In effect, this will require codifying all the currently unwritten conventions, but retain those of practical use and scrap out of date and unnecessary functions based on outmoded tradition. The Manual will be available to the public, and unwritten conventions will cease to exist. The reason for setting out the rules via a Manual is to do away with the unwritten conventions and make the rules and penalties publicly available for all to see. By handing the responsibility to the leader of the Senate to organise the creation of the Manual, it provides a degree of flexibility in making it easier to keep the rules up to date. If the Manual were created through the legislative process, this would unnecessarily involve both Houses of Parliament. Each House can have their own stand-alone rules Manual without needing the approval of the other House. There is no loss of authority by avoiding the legislative process, as the rules Manual is a specific constitutional requirement. Each of the Manuals are to be made publically available, which will tend to ensure the rules and procedures contained therein conform to acceptable rational and ethical standards of the society. Any unwritten convention that is overlooked, and is later deemed necessary for the functioning of the Senate, can be added to the Manual. The Manual will require the approval of the Senate, as will any change or addition, before being officially adopted. There is a time frame set for the compilation of the Manual to ensure it is completed and made publicly available. Should the elected representatives try and manipulate the rules and/or disciplinary actions, there will be ample opportunity for the public to voice their concern and disapproval.

That sounds like a pretty good idea to me. From what I've seen and heard the Senate is almost like some sort of secret society thing that only the initiated members are allowed to know.

Yeah, I guess it could give some people that impression because of the outmoded rituals involved.

I definitely believe the public has a right to know what the rules are, and what discipline is involved when they are broken.

That's only natural. After all, it is the public who own the Parliament, and it is the public who elect the members; they have every right to know the rules and approve the way Parliament operates.

I don't think too many politicians see it that way.

I reckon you are right there. It's been a closed shop ever since it was set up and the pollies have always run it the way they wanted.

Well, it's about time that changed.

The responsibilities of the President of the Senate are set out in a way to ensure impartiality and with the denial of a casting vote. The other major change advocated and provided for, is the elimination of career politicians. This is achieved by limiting the term in office to the Senate to two six-year terms.

What's the reason for preventing politics being a career?

The fundamental reason why a person should choose to go into politics is to serve the public. Today, that reasoning runs a poor second to serving a political party.

But, aren't they the same thing?

When was the last time any political party ever got fifty percent of the primary vote?

I don't know. Has it ever happened?

Not as far as I know. Maybe, in the distant past, but today every party gets into power on the basis of preference votes.

So, what are you saying?

That no political party can ever represent the whole of Australia. The best they can do is represent their party's ideology.

OK, but what's that got to do with career politics?

Well, you must know about all the privileged perks the pollies have been allowed to give themselves over the years?

Yes; some of them are pretty exorbitant, but isn't that justified for sacrificing their lives in the public interest?

Since when did a party politician ever sacrifice anything?

That's being pretty derogative. There's been some bloody good politicians over the years.

Maybe so; it depends on one's perspective, but nine years in one job is enough. If they haven't achieved what they wanted in that time, they should get out.

The original concept of splitting the Senate into two groups is retained in the new Constitution. It will ensure there is a continuity in the representation from one election to the next. This Constitution also specifies the way the Senators will be divided, which is by splitting the representation of each State and Territory in half at the first sitting after the adoption of this Constitution. The split will be done on a random basis by selecting names from a "hat", thus mitigating against political party preference. The option for the dismissal of the whole of the Senate at any time is denied for the reason that continuity of representation is the only justifiable reason for splitting the Senate.

I never did understand why the Senate was split into two classes.
    It seems it is also a mystery to a lot of other people too.
    Why do you say that?
    Well, what other logic is there except to provide a continuity between elections?
    I don't know. Isn't there an explanation in the British Act?
    The British Act is a heap of contradictions.
    What do you mean?
    In one instance it says the Senators will be elected for a period of six years, then it says half of them will only serve three years.
    But, wasn't that just for the very first sitting of Parliament?
    One would have thought so if the logic was to apply.
    So, why didn't it?
    Because, later on in the British Act they wrote in a thing called a double dissolution.
    Which is what? Both Houses get sent up for election?
    Sort of, but it was never explained in the Act whether it meant the whole of the Senate or just the half that would have been due at the next election.
    So, what happened? Was it another of those unwritten conventions that allowed the politicians to assume it meant the whole of the Senate?

That's right, but not so much the Senators, as the PM and the political party in power at the time.

If it's not spelt out in the Constitution, does the PM have the authority to make that sort of decision?

Actually, it is quite unclear how a lot of the conventions originated, but once a convention has been accepted, it seems almost impossible to disregard it.

So, the logical reason for the original split was never part of the consideration?

That seems to be the case. A double dissolution is purely a political tool which a party tries to use to its advantage.

This new Constitution prohibits the concept of a double dissolution by stipulating that all elections are fixed terms. Thus, the party in power cannot vary the term to seek some perceived political advantage. The use of fixed terms is also reinforced by the requirement of the two-thirds majority vote for any proposal to pass through the Parliament. Obviously, if the majority party cannot obtain the required two-thirds approval, there must be something anomalous regarding the proposed legislation. If the main political parties aren't prepared to compromise in the national interest, it will give the public a clear message regarding the calibre of their elected representatives. The Government has the choice to govern in the interests of the nation, or in the interest of their party. Theoretically, there would be no cause for a no-confidence vote in the Government, unless the leadership was so bloody-minded that it refused to compromise. In that case, both the party and the public would be in a position to demand a change in the leadership. Alternatively, a new coalition of parties could come up with a majority to provide a better Government. The fixed term of office, and elimination of double dissolutions rules out the option of calling a snap election, thus placing pressure on the politicians to put the interests of their nation ahead of their party's interests.

A double dissolution sounds like a pretty drastic and expensive decision, just because a Government doesn't get its way?

It is also quite a pointless decision when the British Act clearly provides an alternative way to solve a political hang-up.

What do you mean? Where's it say that in the Constitution?

It's all spelt out in Section 57. If the double dissolution doesn't work, the Governor General can call a joint sitting of Parliament and resolve the problem.

Why have a double dissolution then, if there is an easier way to sort things out?

A damn good question, but it's just another of the perverse ways the "founding fathers" chose to write their document.

Surely, it is more logical to call a joint sitting of Parliament before seeking a double dissolution?

That should have been the obvious sequence, but commonsense seems to be in short supply when one becomes a politician.

In actual fact, if the joint sitting is held and the problem resolved with a majority decision, there would be no need for a double dissolution at all.

How do you work that out?

It would be fairly unusual if the Government couldn't raise a majority vote at a joint sitting of Parliament.

Yeah, I see what you mean. It would have to be a pretty poor Government if it lost the vote under those circumstances.

Page reference to Chapter 2 Part 3 The Senate 239

CHAPTER 12

Discussing the Powers and Authority of the Federal Government

This Chapter deals with the Federal Government, how it is created, what it consists of, how it is administered and the overall chain of command that authorises its legitimacy. At the head of the chain of command is the non-executive Australian Council, which incorporates the Head of the Nation. The actual functioning of the Government comes under the Prime Minister who nominates various Members of Parliament to be appointed as the Ministers of the Government Departments. Once appointed, those Ministers then form the Executive Council, under the chairmanship of the Prime Minister, and become responsible for the policies and planning of the nation's future direction. While the Executive Council is the principle body for formulating and deciding the future direction of the nation, the ultimate executive authority lies with the Parliament where a two-thirds majority is required in each House to pass any motion.

What are you implying here, that a Prime Minister could appoint any Member of Parliament to the Executive Council irrespective of the Party affiliations?

Well, I don't see why that couldn't happen if a Member is well qualified for a particular Ministry, but I doubt any party in power would accept that.

Maybe, maybe not. If the Government needs a two-thirds majority vote in each House of Parliament to get their bills passed, it could make sense to pick Ministers on merit.

That sure would be a radical departure from the existing practice.

But it does make sense, particularly if the domination of political parties is diluted by the two-thirds vote?

You have a point there. If the parties are forced to think nationally rather than from the narrow perspective of their own party, maybe the best person could be selected.

That's going to require a Prime Minister to show real leadership and a lot of guts.

Well, after all, this Constitution is a whole new ballgame in many ways.

There is provision for the creation of a Cabinet consisting of what is considered to be "senior" Ministers, but any Cabinet decisions have to be ratified by the full Executive Council.

Where does this Cabinet thing come from? There's nothing in the British Act that says anything about a Cabinet.

That's true; it's just another of those unwritten conventions that are part and parcel of the Westminster system.

Why is it necessary? What is the function of the Cabinet and what authority does it have?

From a Constitutional point of view, the Cabinet, as such, has no legal authority, but by convention, it is simply a gathering of the so-called "senior" Ministers of the Government.

What does the British Act say about Ministers?

The original British Act provided for a maximum of seven Ministers of State who then become the Executive Council to advise the Governor General on the administration of the Commonwealth.

So, how many Ministries do we have today, and who decides what is a 'senior' ministry and a 'junior' ministry?

Apparently, there are some thirty-nine ministries today of which 27 are classed as 'senior' ministries and twelve in the 'outer' ministries.

So, over the past century, the ministries have grown from the original seven to today's thirty-nine?

That's correct, courtesy of the lovely little Constitutional loophole, "Until Parliament otherwise provides."

But it is logical that there would be more Government Departments required as the Government and the nation grew?

Yes, that's logical and understandable, although it does represent a major alteration to the Constitution, which should have required the approval of the people.

This Chapter also lays down some of the powers and responsibilities of the Prime Minister, who is defined as a Constitutional position in the new Constitution. Whilst the Prime Minister is recognised as the leader of the Government, and is the Chairman of the Executive Council; the position does not have the sweeping authority allocated to it via the unwritten conventions of the Westminster system. While the existence of political parties is seen as a fundamental flaw in the way politics are currently practised, it is considered impractical to abolish them at this point in time. Hence, the method of choosing and appointing a Prime Minister is left in the hands of the political party, or coalition of parties, who command a majority in the House of Representatives.

Why do you say political parties are a flaw in the political system?

Under the Westminster system of Government, a party in power has virtually total authority to do whatever they want, particularly if they control both Houses of Parliament.

But that applies to other systems as well, like the earlier one-party systems of Germany, Russia and China, for example.

True, and in that sense the leader of a party in power can be classed as a dictator, although, in reality, there is no such thing as a "dictator", as no one person can act alone without the support of others.

So, what does this Constitution do that is different?

The requirement of a two-thirds majority vote in both Houses of Parliament nullifies the power of one party to dominate.

But the party in power can still promote the policies it wants?

Up to a point, it can do so, but those policies must be tempered to the needs of the nation rather than the interests of the party.

So, what you are saying, the position of the Prime Minister has to become more nationally oriented rather than party oriented if they want to follow an agenda?

That's correct.

Unlike the current Westminster system, the Executive Council does not have the overriding authority of an unwritten convention to tell the Head of State what to do, or what is more the practice, allowing the Prime Minister to dictate to the Head of State. The Head of State becomes, in reality, the Australian Council, so that the ultimate authority is not in the hands of any one person. While the Australian Council does not have any executive authority to make policy or set an agenda for the nation, it does have the authority to ensure any legislation coming out of Parliament complies with the Constitution.

There seems to be a belief that the Prime Minister should be elected by the people rather than the political party in power. Is that practical?

Under the Westminster system, it is neither possible nor practical. Just think of the ramifications of the idea, particularly if a person were elected who wasn't a member of the party in power.

But, couldn't the candidates come from that party?

Yes, they could, but what's the point of an election if the power of the Prime Minister is curtailed under this new Constitution?

Yes, that's a point. Under the Westminster system the Prime Minister has virtually dictatorial powers, over and above the Head of State, and in that sense, it is an issue of national importance.

Whatever the case, the person who becomes Prime Minister has to be first elected to Parliament, so it really is in the hands of the people from the outset.

So, what you are saying is, that anyone who is elected should have Prime Ministerial potential?

Definitely not, imagine the ambitious backstabbing that would go on if that were to happen?

The Chapter deals in some detail with Australia's involvement in foreign wars and/or conflict zones, either as combatants or non-combatants. The responsibility for any combatant involvement in a foreign war is placed with the Australian Parliament. The one exception being if Australia comes under direct military attack by a foreign nation. The Head of State, as the Commander in Chief of the Armed Forces, is authorised to declare a state of war and initiate immediate action.

That's a very significant issue, the deployment of Australia's defence forces in overseas conflicts. At the moment, the people really have no say in it.

That has been the case throughout our history. We've simply done the bidding of the King of England, or in more recent times, the US.

Except in the case of fighting the Japanese. That really was the only time our army was used for the defence of Australia.

That's right, neither of the European wars were any direct threat to Australia. We just got involved for the sake of Britain.

When you think about it, the same goes for Vietnam and the Korean War. Both were really ideological wars for the benefit of the US. They were nothing of a direct threat to Australia, just as is the current case with Afghanistan, Iraq and the Middle East conflict.

But isn't all our involvement with foreign wars the result of the treaties the Government has signed?

Yes, mostly that is the case. And that's why this new Constitution requires the approval of the people before any treaty can be ratified, especially if it impacts on the people of Australia.

Don't all treaties do that?

Not necessarily, but the issue of treaties does need to come under scrutiny so that we are not compelled to do the bidding of foreigners without the consent of the people.

Wouldn't it be logical to have a "sunset" clause in any treaty so that its effectiveness is automatically reviewed after a given time?

That should always be a compulsory requirement for any international agreement or treaty.

Page reference to Chapter 2 Part 4 The Federal Government 245

CHAPTER 13

Defining the Purpose and Responsibilities of the Federal Government

This Chapter is among the most important in the Constitution because it defines the things we want the Government to do on our behalf.

Let's face it, the sole purpose of creating a Government in the first place is to have a cooperative body that can work towards improving the wellbeing of the overall society. In other words, the primary function of a Government is to serve the public purpose in achieving that goal. But, improving the wellbeing of the overall society is a very generalise aim that can mean different things to different people. So, do we as Australians, have a major overriding national purpose? There is none that I can put my finger on. Is it even feasible to define what we can call a national purpose?

You are getting a bit carried away with your assumptions, aren't you?

Which assumptions are you referring to?

That a Government belongs to us and it is supposed to work for our benefit.

In an ideal world, that should be the case, but our world certainly isn't ideal, and most Governments only pay lip service in working for the people.

Yeah, that's what I've found. All the Governments I know put the Party first and are there to look after themselves.

Our Government seems to spend more time kowtowing to International organisations than doing what is best for Australia.

Well, we are now part of the globalisation process, and there's nothing much we can do about that.

Maybe, we should make it a national purpose to get out of globalisation and put Australia first?

Not much hope of that mate; we are up to our necks in the quicksand, and it's probably too late to get ourselves out.

If we say our major purpose is to be a "democratic" nation, again we are talking in abstracts, as "democracy" is a term with many connotations. But what defines a democracy? It seems there is no one, single, acceptable, definitive answer to that question, although most of the definitions do contain elements of what people would like to include in a democratic system. Perhaps the single most accurate definition of a democratic system is one that maximises the "freedom" of choice for every member of the society, with the limitation that that "freedom" does not encroach on anyone else's "freedom" to choose. Like the term "democracy," "freedom" is also a relative term, just as is the term "free market" and similar expressions. The implication of this definition accepts the assumption that everyone has certain "rights" that cannot be infringed, and the upholding of those "rights" would be a responsibility of a democratic Government.

Now, you're getting into a murky subject. The subject of "rights" is a minefield that can explode anytime.

What do you mean? Most people understand what "rights" they want to have.

Yes, and isn't that the problem? Everyone seems to have different ideas about what is a "right" and what isn't.

Well, there are certainly some fundamental "rights" that everyone should have.

Like what, for example?

Well, like the "right" to life for a start.

So, do you mean we should ban all wars and nobody should be killed?

Well …. Yeah. Wouldn't that be a good idea?

It sure would, if anyone could ever make it happen. So; who would take responsibility for making sure everyone has the "right" to their life?

Yeah; a bit of a problem there.

That is one of the problems with "rights"; they all come with responsibilities to make sure they apply to everyone.

Do they have to apply to everyone?

If they don't, who is going to make the decisions about how to discriminate?

Is that what it would amount to; discrimination within the society?

If you go down that path, you are talking about a dictatorship.

Hey, come on; there has to be a middle road there, somewhere.

When you find it, let me know.

But no form of "democracy" can exist in today's world unless the people are equipped with the economic where-with-all to survive. If we want to associate the concept of "freedom" with "democracy" then the manner in which the economic where-with-all is achieved presents a whole new rethink about the pseudo "science" of Economics. A life of perpetual debt cannot be condoned if we are to talk about "democratic freedom", and by the same token, a society that accepts a level of poverty for some of its members, cannot claim to practice "democracy". Maybe, our primary national purpose should be the elimination of poverty in our nation?

That's a hell of an idea, eliminate poverty in a society?

Well, it is certainly true that if you are destitute and homeless, and suffer from poverty, you have lost a lot of the opportunity to make choices.

But, how can any society do anything about it? I can't see that anyone would be able to eliminate poverty altogether.

Under the present economic system, you are probably right. We only mess around with it at the fringes by relying on charity to help out where it can.

Charity is all very good, but a lot of people resent having to accept charity.

If it is a matter of survival, they may not have any choice. But that's where the economic system comes into play.

What do you mean? How can anyone change the economic system?

Not easily, that's for sure. But, if a nation were to make the elimination of poverty its national purpose, then a lot of changes would have to be made.

Obviously, that purpose of eliminating poverty can be tackled in many different ways, and in the fullness of time, the way to achieve that purpose will change as the nation evolves. First up, we need to set the benchmark for what we can define as the level of poverty. Once that goal is set it provides a focus for managing the situation. On the national level, our "managers" are the Government, and it becomes an integral part of a Government's public purpose to achieve this goal. However, there are other responsibilities we require our Government to address if we are to achieve a standard of living and wellbeing compatible with our modern times. These are the "powers" we choose to give our Government.

That would be a wonderful idea if "we, the people" did have the authority to tell the Government what we wanted them to do.

That's precisely where a Constitution comes into force. It really has to be a document that the people write and control, not the politicians and not the lawyers.

But how in the hell are the people supposed to write a Constitution? Hardly anybody knows anything about Constitutions.

That's true, but there are enough people who do know what sorts of rules a society needs to make the politicians do what the people want.

What do the people want? How do you know what they want?

Well, if a group of ordinary people can get together, and write down all the commonsense things they believe are necessary for a society to function properly, it can be a foundation to build on.

That's all very well, but who is going to listen to a bunch of unknowns who aren't even in Government?

Why do people have to be in Government to know what's needed?

But, Governments and lawyers always tell the people what they can or cannot do.

And isn't that the reason Australia is in the mess it is? Why do you think we have such a stuffed up economy; such a huge debt hanging over our heads, and never-ending squabbling in Parliament?

Yeah, well; I suppose it does come down to the sort of Government we get.

Ain't that right? And why do you think we get that sort of Government shoved down our throats?

I don't know. That's just the way it is.

Bullshit. It's that way because the people let it be that way. They vote for it to be that way. And it really doesn't matter which party gets to run the Government; the end result is always the same.

So, how in the hell are we ever going to change that?

About the only way is to put a draft for a people's Constitution on the table and let the people decide what they want in that draft.

That's never going to work. The Government will never let the people get involved. And besides, most of the people wouldn't know how to decide on a Constitution.

Maybe so, but there are enough people out there who do know what they want, and what they don't want. It's really just a matter of getting the opportunity to have a say.

Good luck mate. I hope I live to see it happen.

In this day and age, everyone's survival revolves around "money". That applies to every individual, as well as the nation itself, and that is a fact whether we like it or not. Thus, when we come to defining the functions we want to give the Government as its primary responsibility, the creation of the nation's money supply must be at the top of the list. It is axiomatic that, in today's society, if we are to achieve the "freedom", and elimination of poverty, as perceived to apply to a "democratic system," that system must be accompanied by a system of "economic democracy".

Poverty and economic insecurity are two factors that exert the greatest strain on human nature. Economic warfare is a contributing cause of these factors and the only difference between economic warfare and military warfare is in method and not in principle. The cure for poverty and the cure for war can be found in the rectification of the money system.

Come on; get real. How in the hell is anyone going to change the money system?

Believe it or not, all the Australian Government has to do is apply the two best parts of the British Act we call our Constitution. Those two parts have always been available to all the Governments since nineteen hundred and one.

That's crazy. How could this old nineteenth century Act change the money system?

It's easy. All the Government has to do, is do what the Act says they can.

That's crap. Where does the Act say the Government can change the money system?

Well, Section 51(xii) of Part 9 of the British Act says the Government has the authority to create all the coins, currency and legal tender the Commonwealth of Australia needs. How's that for starters?

But the Government already does that. How's that going to change anything?

True, the Government is the only organisation that can create all the physical money in circulation in Australia. But, do you know what the percentage of physical money is, compared to all the money circulating in Australia?

I don't know; isn't it a hundred percent?

Unfortunately, no it's not a hundred percent; it's more like three and a half percent.

Don't give me that. There must be billions of dollars floating around out there.

There sure are, but about ninety-seven percent of Australia's money is "digital money", money created by a computer, and not physical notes and coins.

What do you mean, "digital money"?

Money that is in bank accounts that the Banks lend out as a debt, which you have to pay back with interest.

Yeah, so what? That's the way banks work.

So, where do you think all this "digital money" comes from?

From the deposits, people put into their bank accounts, of course. Where else is it going to come from?

Boy oh boy; are you stuffed up.

What do you mean?

Have you, or do you know anyone, who has had their bank account reduced because their deposit has been lent out to someone else?

No, but that's not how it works.

You're dead right. That's not how it works because; the banks just create new money every time they make a loan.

But they can't just create money out of thin air, surely?

Sorry mate, that's exactly how it works.

The fact is that in these modern times the kind of lives we get have already been decided for us by the circumstances of our access to money. This relates to the kind of economics that impacts on our lives. And that, in turn, has been decided, supposedly, by the kind of politics which scored most votes at the last election. "Supposedly", because all but the most deluded of us realised long ago that we do not have the slightest choice in any of this. Unfortunately, while we can vote for any of the brands of politics we are offered, the economics we get is almost always exactly the same, irrespective of who runs the country. The only time it was different was back in nineteen eleven when the Fisher Labor Government created the original Commonwealth Bank of Australia.

When we look at "economics" objectively, we have little choice but to consider the "science of economics" as a "science" steeped in failure. It is a discipline up to its neck, worldwide, in a raging flood of practical problems for which it seems quite unable to suggest any really effective answers. But the great over-riding failure is a universal refusal of its practitioners to question honestly, the very basics of their own "science".

What is economics all about if it is not about money?

It is "economics" itself which stands in the way of possible solutions; it is "economics" itself which stifles our future hopes for better societies, for better ways of living, for a better and a more rational world. "Economics" has indeed become the unacknowledged, central religion of our times; it has become that anointed authority without whose assent nothing in our modern world can be allowed to happen.

This is going to go down like a lead balloon. You can't just dismiss economics as some sort of crackpot theory. For Christ's sake, it's a major academic discipline.

Which one?

What do you mean, which one?

Well, from my last count there are dozens of different economic theories floating around, and none of them have achieved their purported aim of universal prosperity for all.

Who ever said that was the purpose of economics?

What other purpose should it have?

Well, economics is all about the most efficient use of money, isn't it?

Ok, but to what purpose?

Well, doing things efficiently and not wasting money.

What things are you talking about, and how do you define wasting money?

You're starting to get technical now, and it's too big a subject to handle just between us.

That's a piss-weak answer. Economics virtually controls all our lives and is certainly a major issue when it comes to the way a Government operates.

Maybe so, but it's not a subject we can really talk about unless we are properly trained.

Bullshit. You don't have to be trained to understand that in today's environment, money is virtually essential for survival.

There is a real world out there that still exists. In that real world, when people wanted something done they asked: "Can we do this?" Meaning, did they have enough stuff and people with which to do the things they wanted done. Unfortunately, that real world has been overlaid by our later world; our money world. Now, in that money world, when we want something done we ask: "Can we afford this thing?" Meaning, can we find enough money to do it. To the amazement of this later world, wonders were created in the real world, and they can continue to be created if we are prepared to have a rethink about this pseudo-science of "economics."

That will require us to have the courage to ask the unquestionable and unalterable, and most fundamental consideration of the entire discipline of "economics": "How is money created, how is money owned, and how is money issued?" We must also ask, "Is there another way of creating and issuing money which might lead to less human misery and to more human happiness?" Hence it is that the exclusive creation and management of Australia's money supply in every form of legal tender, whether coins, notes or digital "money," is placed at the very top of the "powers" we are prepared to give our representatives in our Parliament. That "power" automatically goes with the authority to control all forms of banking and banking practices in the Australian nation.

You're never going to get away with that; the banks are too powerful. The Government tried to nationalise the banks back in nineteen forty-seven, and the High Court knocked them back.

That was a messy one actually, and the reason the Court used to deny nationalisation has subsequently overturned by a later High Court ruling.

What was their reason for knocking it back in forty-seven?

That's where it got messy because, the Court just ignored Section 51(xiii) that gave the Government control of all banking in Australia, except State Banks, and the Court went for Section 92.

What does Section 92 say?

More or less, that all interstate trade shall be "absolutely free".

Free of what? That's a funny expression; nothing is "absolutely free" apart from maybe the air we breathe.

Exactly. It's a bloody stupid thing to put in a Constitution without defining what they mean.

So, nationalisation could be done now if the Government were to try?

Possibly, but nationalisation isn't really the way to go, as it is unnecessary given the power already granted to the Parliament

You mean under the Australian Constitution?

No, under the British Act. Sorry mate, Australia doesn't have their own Australian Constitution; all they have is the British Act.

But we're not talking about that here; we are talking about banking.

That's true, and under the new Constitution, it is made very clear that the Parliament is in charge of all Banks and banking in Australia.

Yeah, but even so the private Banks could challenge that, just like they did before.

Nope, they couldn't. It's a different situation. The Government isn't trying to take over the banks; what it is doing is overseeing their practices and the way the banks operate.

But the banks could still challenge the Constitution? What makes you so sure they couldn't?

It's simple. If the draft Constitution is accepted by the people at the referendum, then that becomes the Primary Law of Australia, and the Courts have to abide by it.

You are going to be pushing to get that past the people.

I don't see why it would be a problem. The people are well aware of the crisis of two thousand and eight, and they are fed up to the back teeth with the debts the Government keeps racking up. Why wouldn't they take the opportunity to take control of the way their money is created and distributed?

But there is another crucial aspect to our way of life in a "democracy" and that is our choice to live by "the rule of law". As we are often told, "Ignorance of the law is no excuse", but when it comes to one of the most important laws that govern all our lives, the Crimes Act, we find it was first written in nineteen hundred and fourteen. As of today, comprises nine hundred and eleven pages in two separate volumes. It is totally beyond belief that anyone, judge, barrister or lawyer, let alone an ordinary person, can claim to "know" that law. They may know bits of it, but nobody could possibly understand the intricacies and implications of the hundreds of amendments and additions that have been added over the past century.

This is but one "law" on the books, and there are literary thousands of others that were first written in another time and another age, and very likely, for another intended purpose. It is this traditional practice of the legal fraternity to keep trying to update existing laws by way of amendments. That practice produces a goldmine of technicalities for an astute lawyer to plunder in an effort to avoid conviction of their client. While reform has been an ongoing pastime of the legal fraternity for many years, it seems to have achieved little of any consequence to the layman. This Constitution draft seeks to emphasise the need for proper and effective reform by forbidding the common Parliamentary practice of adding amendments to existing legislation. If the existing legislation is inadequate for the purpose, it can only be changed by re-writing the Act and presenting it as a separate stand-alone Bill. If the new Bill is approved by the Parliament and subsequently consented to as law, the earlier legislation is then automatically repealed. As this new Constitution prohibits the application of retrospectivity, any proceedings related to the earlier, and subsequently repealed legislation, shall stand and not be open to challenge. There is a further provision in this draft Constitution that allows public participation in commenting on the proposed Bill by way of submissions, but within a time frame depending on the size of the Bill.

You're a braver man than me Gunga Din if you are game enough to take on both the Banks and the legal fraternity.

Oh, it's no me doing it, it's the hundreds of Australians from back in nineteen ninety-eight and ninety-nine who are fed up with the way the system operates. I'm just a spokesman stoking the fires they ignited back then.

Yeah, well, this latest foray into their world is going to get their shackles up.

I don't doubt that for a minute, but if the people vote for it at a referendum, all it will be doing is re-arranging the priorities in the proper order.

What do you mean, "Proper order"?

All there organisations, such as the Banks and the Courts, and the legal system, are just systems created by man. They are supposed to be there to serve for the benefit of mankind; mankind isn't there to serve for the benefit of the systems.

That would be great if you could ever change it around and make it happen.

Well, it's just like everything else in this world, if we don't get the fundamentals right; if we don't have a solid foundation to build on, there is no way we'll ever get the changes we want.

What are you talking about; the Constitution?

That's it. That's the foundation that underpins everything else the people want to create for their society.

Page reference to Chapter 2 Part 5 Powers of the Federal Government 250

CHAPTER 14

Discussing the Judicial and Legal System

The Australian legal system is based on the English Common Law system, which itself, is based on the various historical Charters going back to the Magna Carta of twelve hundred and ninety-seven, and even further back than that. This system has been adopted by the Australian legal fraternity and modified over time into what is referred to as Australia's Common Law system. It is an adversarial system that relies on the presentation of selected and approved evidence to arrive at a decision. It is a system that is supposed to be unbiased in seeking the truth. Unfortunately, it is swamped in legal technicalities that depend largely on the skill and competence of the lawyers, and/or the bias of the judge. Lawyers, with the time and resources to research the stupendous multitude of previous laws, can use their skill and experience in finding loopholes to exonerate their clients.

That's a pretty rude statement that decisions depend on the bias of a judge. I always thought judges were supposed to be impartial?

In theory, they are, but in practice, no individual, judge or otherwise, can shrug off their upbringing and beliefs that are indoctrinated in them throughout their lives.

But if we have a jury system, how can a judge influence that?

Unfortunately, the judge can do that by deciding what evidence can be presented and what arguments the jury is allowed to hear.

But surely, evidence is evidence, and no one has the right to decide if it is relevant or not?

Well, under our legal system it can depend on how the evidence was obtained, and if there is a question as to the reliability of the evidence.

OK, I can accept that false, or fabricated evidence should not be allowed, but is a judge equipped to determine that?

Mostly, the evidence can be challenged on a legal technicality, and the authenticity of an issue comes down to one person's word against another.

Isn't there a better way to carry out an independent investigation before a case comes to Court?

Officially, that's what the police are supposed to do, but they are in the best position to muddle things up if they so choose.

But in the movies, it always seems to come down to the prosecution and defence lawyers to try and sort out the truth. Is that the way it works?

Mostly that is fiction, but there does seem to be room for some form of independent review before it gets to court

Possibly, but it is never going to get off the ground with the established legal system in Australia.

Can't the new Constitution do something about that?

Not really, apart from allowing Parliament to initiate avenues for reform.

Such as?

Well, for one example, eliminating the amending of existing laws and making the changes self-contained in a new law that incorporates any applicable parts from the earlier laws.

That would be a hell of a reform if it can be done.

I don't see why it can't be, and it would be done if the new Constitution is adopted.

So, in effect, any new laws that come out of Parliament must be self-contained and not subject to precedent.

That would be the ultimate aim, but it would take a while to achieve that.

Thus it is, in many cases the application of legal process depends on how much money a litigant has for employing the best advice. By and large, there is one legal process for the rich and another for the poor. Supposedly, "justice" is served through an appeals process to a higher Court. An aggrieved person can mount an appeal if they believe they have been unjustly served in a lower Court. Depending on the circumstances, and very much on the amount of money a person has to pursue the appeals process, it can go as far as the High Court of Australia, which is Australia's supreme legal body. However, the appeals process is not an automatic option for seeking justice, as the path is strewn with numerous legal obstacles apart from the factor of money.

The Australian legal system is also part of the Australian political system, despite the hypocritical assumption that, like religion, politics and the law are supposed to be separate and independent. In the draft Constitution, Section 143(ix) under the powers of Parliament, does give the Parliament the authority to initiate other types of legal processes as long as they are independent of the Government. This provision allows the Parliament to establish various types of Commissions or bodies of inquiry that can be seen to be independent of politics.

It seems to be a common assumption that most of the Government inquiries are set up to obtain a pre-determined outcome.

Yes, that can be the case if the Government is allowed to set the terms and conditions for an inquiry.

But that's wrong. It shouldn't be allowed to happen that way.

If it is up to a political party, then some of these inquiries are more like a public relations exercise. No political party is willing to set up an inquiry if it is likely to reflect badly on the party.

Well, that's logical so, how can you stop that from happening?

I'm not sure we can unless public sentiment is strong enough to demand an independent inquiry.

The Constitution requires a two-thirds majority vote in both Houses of Parliament for any decisions to be ratified. Hence, if there is a public or Parliamentary demand for an inquiry, it is most unlikely any one political party is going to control the terms and conditions that will apply.

But it could also make it much harder to get an inquiry off the ground.

That's a point which needs addressing, although the political risk in being seen to try and rig an inquiry would give pause for consideration.

As long as the judges of the Australian Federal Courts can be appointed by the Government of the day, there will always be an element of bias in their selection and appointment. This Constitution tries to minimise that bias by delegating the selection and recommendation of Federal judges to a Select Committee made up of members of the House of Representatives and the Senate. It also delegates the recommendation of remuneration for all levels of the judiciary to this bipartisan Committee, who must then submit their recommendations to Parliament.

So, fundamentally, all judges and Court officials come under the category of Public Servants?

Yes, that is correct. If they are paid by the Government, they are employed to serve the public.

And what does that mean; that no judge, or any other public servant, can be paid more than the Prime Minister?

Yes, that's right. Obviously, the Prime Minister has to be the most senior public servant in the governmental system, and it doesn't make sense that any public servant should receive a higher pay than the Prime Minister.

Does that apply to the President too?

No, not so because, the President is the titular head of the nation, and as a member of the Australian Council, like all the other members, their basic remuneration is set by the separate State Governments. The Constitution provides for the additional loading on the salaries and conditions in relation to their role as Australian Council members.

As the issue of a trial by jury has become a contentious issue for both State and Federal Constitutions, this Constitution defines the conditions that shall apply to the trial by jury process. Namely, any conviction that carries a penalty of imprisonment of a year, or more, or a fine of five thousand dollars, or more, shall allow the accused the option of trial by jury, by a single judge, or a panel of judges, if so chosen.

That's a good approach to set this out clearly and define the conditions that will apply to a trial by jury.

By virtue of the provision that State law must conform to Federal law, it also makes it clear as a national standard.

To date, there seems to be a lot of confusion regarding the right to trial by jury.

That's right. Some of the States have different provisions for a jury trial, and it isn't a universal practice throughout Australia.

I guess there is a valid argument that the expense and time factor of a jury trial is hardly justified for relatively minor offences.

That's the basis for the State and Federal Government's argument, despite the fact some people consider trial by jury is a fundamental legal right.

As far as this Constitution is concerned, this is a starting point. All the provisions in the Constitution are open for amendment through the Periodic Constitutional Review process. So, if the people want to change the provisions in the future, it can be done via a referendum.

Page reference to Chapter 3 Part 1 The Judiciary 259

CHAPTER 15

Discussing the Role of the High Court of Australia

By virtue of the Preamble, this Constitution is clearly defined as the property of the people, both because it has originally been drawn up by ordinary people, and subsequently adopted by them at a nationwide referendum. It emphatically denies it is the property of seven unelected judges sitting in their rarefied positions on the High Court of Australia. Under this Constitution, the High Court is not granted any executive authority to make law or to alter the purpose and intent of any law made by the Parliament. When the High Court is required to interpret the wording of a law the Court must now take into consideration, as a guideline, the principles set out in the Preamble of this Constitution. This consideration shall apply to existing laws, even though those laws would have been created in a different time frame and under different conditions. It is not within the Court's prerogative to ignore the guiding principles of the Preamble should a conflict arise. Despite the established practice of the past of recognising precedent, when such precedent is based on different parameters, and in conflict with the principles laid down in this Constitution, the precedent shall not apply.

Thus, it is entirely appropriate that a unanimous decision should be reached whenever a Federal law is challenged. If unanimity can't be reached that is verifiable proof that there is something wrong with the law. As the High Court does not have executive powers, the Court shall report back to

Parliament, explaining their perceived problem, with or without recommendations for remedying the impasse.

Ahh, but isn't that the perennial problem, understanding the intent and purpose of the laws from the way they are written?

It certainly is, especially when a law is subject to ongoing amendments over a long period of time.

Why do they have to keep making amendments? If there is something wrong with the original law, why don't they just re-write a new one?

There's probably a couple of reasons for that.

Yeah, and what are they?

Well, firstly, it is probably a traditional thing. All the bills that go to Parliament are routinely written by trained legal people. They are never written by the politicians who, as a whole, are mostly untrained in the legal field.

Yeah, well that's fair enough, isn't it?

From the point of view of the legal fraternity, it certainly is because it leaves the door wide open for arguing technicalities.

How come? What do you mean?

Well, when you add amendments to amendments to earlier amendments, in relation to a law that was originally written in another time, and under different circumstances, and possibly, for a different purpose, it presents a Pandora's Box of opportunity to raise questionable technicalities.

But, why do the politicians allow that to happen?

And that's probably the second reason. Most politicians can't understand the legalities, and also the fact, most of the back bench simply vote the way they are told to vote.

You're talking party politics again?

Yeah, I'm afraid so.

The quaint and traditional concept of "judicial review", as developed over the decades for the express benefit of the legal fraternity, is specifically denied in this new Constitution. Similarly, the acceptance of split decisions from the bench of the High Court is henceforth forbidden. The unelected members of the High Court are not endowed with infallibility, certainly not with this new draft Constitution. It is an obvious fact that if the seven, supposedly, top legal brains in the nation cannot come to a unanimous decision, then the decision has to be based on something else other than legalese. Justice Gleeson is on record, as published in The Australian newspaper on the seventh of July two thousand, *"Judges are accorded a measure of respect, and weight is given to what they have to say, upon the faith of an understanding by the community that to be judicial is to be impartial. But to deploy judicial authority in support of a cause, risks undermining the foundation upon which such authority rests. The expertise which the members of the (High) Court are required to bring to bear on that function is their expertise as lawyers. The Australian community would be properly concerned if they decided to base their decisions upon the exercise of other supposed talents. What those talents might be, when and how they were acquired, and by whom they might be assessed, are questions that would need examination if legalism were to cease to be the base of decision-making. The quality which sustains judicial legitimacy is not bravery, or creativity, but fidelity to the Constitution"*.

While Justice Gleeson is probably quite correct in saying the community may well be concerned about decisions being based on "other talents," as distinct from legalese, there is virtually nothing the public can do about their concern. Under the present system, any High Court decision, split or otherwise, is considered sacrosanct, and there is no higher avenue of appeal. In other words, the High Court is granted infallibility, even when there can be cogent and logical argument against a decision, especially if it is a split decision. The new Constitution does provide an avenue of last resort, but with split decisions being barred, and the problem handed back to Parliament, the influence of those "other talents" would be significantly suppressed.

That's a quaint expression, "fidelity to the Constitution". What does it mean?

That is a question which defies a logical answer, especially regarding the currently used nineteenth century, British Act.

Don't give me that. The expression must mean something if a High Court judge uses it?

Well, seeing it is the High Court itself that is called upon to interpret much of the Constitution, how is anyone to know what the Constitution really stands for?

Fidelity means faith, doesn't it? How can anyone have faith in something that is, more or less, in a constant state of flux?

That's the problem, isn't it? But possibly, the more important aspect of the judge's statement is the reference to "other supposed talents."

Yeah, and I was also wondering what those "talents" might be.

When it comes to expressing an opinion, then that opinion has to represent the personal makeup of the person involved.

What do you mean?

Well, basically, it is the sum of one's character. Every one of us forms our opinions based on our life experiences, which includes our upbringing, our education, our prejudices, our politics, and all the inherent biases we accumulate, consciously or unconsciously.

Are you saying a judge can't ignore those sorts of "talents" and be impartial?

They can try, but when it comes to expressing an opinion, it is virtually impossible for anyone to go against what they inherently believe to be valid.

I agree, and those "talents" must come into play every time a split decision is made?

Let's face it, every judge on the High Court is ultimately appointed by the Prime Minister of the day, and no Prime Minister in his right mind is ever going to appoint a judge who is not compatible with his political beliefs.

Doesn't that system of appointment taint the impartiality of the High Court?

Of course, it must, especially when legalese is tossed out the window, and the judges have to resort to their "other talents".

Obviously, any split decision by the High Court must involve a difference of opinion regarding the issue at hand. As such, there is no justification for assuming a majority opinion is any more correct than a minority opinion. Legalese is not a matter of personal opinions, assumptions, or inferences. If the law is unclear in the way it is written, and the seven judges cannot reach a unanimous decision, it is not within the authority of a few of the judges to interpret what is intended. When unanimity can't be reached the duty of the High Court is to return the issue to the Parliament, pointing out the inconsistencies and problems with the law. The Court must leave it up to Parliament to clarify their intentions by addressing the law involved. The Court can make recommendations to Parliament if it so chooses, but only Parliament has the executive authority to change the law or define its intent.

But, hasn't interpreting the Constitution, and the law, been one of the primary functions of the High Court?

It has been in the past, but it is a function assumed to be germane to the High Court, even though it is not provided for in the British Act.

So, where did it come from? Who gave the High Court that sort of authority?

I guess it is one of the many traditional myths that have been fostered over time by the legal system.

Yeah, and what other myths are there?

Well, there's the myth that politics must not interfere with the legal process, but that furphy is blown right out of the water from the start.

How come? The Government can't interfere with a judge's decision?

Maybe not directly, but it certainly can indirectly, through the appointment of the judges.

Yeah, I can see the problem there. No Government is going to nominate a judge who is not compatible to their policies.

And there is also the Attorney General's Department, which can have a direct influence on the way the legal system is conducted.

Well, of course. It is the Government that makes all the laws that really controls the way the system works.

So, there is no way the legal system can truly operate independently of the politics and the Government?

Under the current arrangement that's pretty much the fact, but a certain amount of change is possible if the appointment of judges is divorced from the Government.

However, when the High Court comes to dealing with Australia's Primary Law, the British Act we use as Australia's Constitution, they appear to be entirely out of their depth. The nineteen ninety-nine Sue v Hill split-decision is a prime example of the ludicrous reasoning applied to a case that really wasn't even within their constitutional jurisdiction to hear. They took the astounding decision to classify the UK as a "foreign country" when they knew full well that the British Act is the only authority that justifies their creation and existence. The High Court is created under Part 9 of that Act, and the Court can only legally rule on issues related to that Part 9. The preceding eight parts of the Act are wholly and solely, the responsibility of the British Parliament to deal with in any way they so choose. The High Court of Australia has absolutely no authority to tamper with any of those eight preceding parts. Hence, there is absolutely no rational way Britain can legally be construed as a foreign country, as long as we continue to use their law as our Constitution, a foundation law that has never been repealed.

This is getting a bit tricky. What actually is the Australian Constitution?

I guess the correct answer to that is, Australia doesn't have one.

That can't be right? They are always talking about the Australian Constitution.

Yes, that's true, different people do talk about an Australian Constitution, but they seldom say whether they are talking about Part 9 of the British Act or the whole of the British Act itself.

OK, they are two different things, but didn't the Australians spend all that time back in the nineteen hundreds drawing up an Australian Constitution?

Well, to start with, they are not two different things. Part 9 is just one part of the British Act so; it is really just a part of the same thing.

But what about all those conventions and referendums Australia had in the nineteen hundred's?

Well, forty-nine Australian politicians and lawyers, and one banker did get together to draft up a document for Part 9 of the British Act, but only that Part and not the preceding eight Parts.

But isn't that Part 9 called the Constitution?

Yes, it is, but that Part 9 is different to what the Australian politicians presented to the British Government.

How come?

The British Government insisted on changes before they would allow the original draft to go to the British Parliament and be included as Part 9.

How many changes did the Government want?

That seems to be unclear, but I have read that up to seventy changes were demanded although this hasn't been verified.

That's a lot so, I can understand why you say Australia doesn't really have their own Constitution.

The British Act is really the British concept of a Constitution for their enlarged Australian colony.

What was just as damning on the part of the High Court was the assumption that Australia was an independent nation, but no one on the Court could define how and when this transition from a Dominion of the UK to an independent nation was supposed to have occurred. And in a display of appalling arrogance, Justice Callinan made the statement, "The truth is that the defining event in practice will, and can only be a decision of this Court ....." The real truth is that Australia's independence can only be achieved in two ways, the first and easiest way is to have the UK Parliament repeal their Act. The second way is for the Australian people to take unilateral action and declare Australia an independent nation. At no time will that decision be in the hands of seven unelected people sitting in the High Court of Australia, let alone the politicians sitting in Parliament. Australia's independence from the UK can only be ratified by a referendum in Australia of all eligible voters.

Page reference to Chapter 3 Part 2 The High Court 263

CHAPTER 16

Discussing the Financing of
Australia and its Economy

The pseudo "science" of economics has gained an almost unchallengeable control of everyone's life in today's world. It's now at the point where virtually every nation's survival depends on how its "economy" is managed. Ultimately, the economy of any nation is all about money. The issue and control of a nation's money supply are of the utmost importance in striving for a harmonious, productive and equitable society. Unfortunately, there is a huge, no, colossal misunderstanding, throughout history and around the world, as to the origin and purpose of having a money system.

That's bullshit. We have a great money system in Australia that's worked fine for the past hundred years or more.

Geez, what rock have you been hiding under? We are just like the rest of the world and have a totally screwed up money system.

What's screwed up about it? I can go to almost any bank and borrow money.

Yeah, that's pretty much true, but the bank will only lend you the money if you sign a contract to pay it back with interest.

So, what's wrong with that?

Well, to start with, they don't lend you the money to pay the interest; do they? And they probably don't actually lend you the money itself; they just write some figures in an account with your name on it.

Yeah, so what? Once I have an account I can draw on the money anytime I want it.

That's the neat little trick the banks use. They write some figures in an account, and at some stage, you can transfer all or part of those figures into physical cash, if you want to.

Yeah, that's right, that's how it works.

That's true, but what do you do with the money when you get it?

I spend it of course, or maybe I save it.

Why in the hell would you want to save money that you have to pay interest on?

Yeah, well, probably, I just spend it.

OK, now tell me, where are you going to get the extra money to pay the interest on what you've borrowed?

Well, I don't know. I suppose I'm going to earn it somehow, either from working or making things to sell.

And what if all that extra money you need has to come from somebody else who has had to borrow their money from a bank?

But that's crazy, a lot of people have their own money and don't need to borrow it.

Are you telling me people can make their own money just like that, whenever they need it?

No, of course not. Nobody is allowed to counterfeit money.

So, where did they get it from?

I don't know, maybe their parents, maybe the Government, or maybe they won lottery.

Well, the Government gets most of their money from taxes, or from borrowing, and that's why they are up to their eyeballs in debt. And all the lottery money comes from the millions of people who gamble, and like taxes, most of that money comes from a bank to start with.

But a lot of parents have money set aside, from superannuation, or maybe the sale of a property, or maybe the parents are just rich.

Well, if you really want to know the truth; around 95% of the money in circulation in Australia today, is created by the private banks and lent out as interest-bearing loans. The Government only creates about 5% in notes and coins.

That's got to be crap. Everyone has notes and coins, that's what money is.

That's back to where we started. Hardly anyone knows how the money system actually works.

There really is only one single purpose for having a money system, and that is to provide a convenient medium for the exchange of goods and services. The fundamental alternative is the cumbersome system of barter trade. Money itself has no intrinsic value and is useless unless it can be exchanged for something that is needed or wanted. Of course, the more you have, the better your choices, but the accumulation of money achieves nothing unless it is put to some use. Some people say that only gold or silver, or some other rare and valuable metal, should be used for the money system, but that's ridiculous. Those metals are commodities, and there is only a finite supply of them in the world. Some nations have those metals, other nations don't, and it is completely ridiculous to say a nation that doesn't have those metals cannot have a money system. A practical and workable money system must have two fundamental properties. Firstly, the tokens used for the system must be universally accepted within the given society. Second, the tokens must come with some form of guarantee they are not false tokens.

What about Bitcoins; where do they fit into the money system?

Technically, they don't. Bitcoins are the same as casino chips, except, as a form of digital currency, they are imaginary.

That's crazy. I just read the other day where a young chap became a millionaire from investing in Bitcoins.

Investing or gambling? They are the same thing when you talk about Bitcoins, and shares too for that matter.

But many companies now take Bitcoins as payment for their sales.

Maybe so, but they do that entirely at their own risk. Bitcoins are not recognised as legal tender and only exist as a form of digital keystrokes in cyberspace.

So, why are they so valuable?

Valuable in what sense? Fundamentally, they are worthless unless they can be exchanged for something else.

But isn't that what happens when they are used to buy something?

Yes, it is, but where is the guarantee that they exist in the first place?

Well, what's the difference between digital Bitcoins and the digital "money" that the banks create when they make a loan?

Virtually none, except that the banks are registered organisations under Government legislation and are supposed to operate within specific parameters.

Are you saying the Bitcoin isn't like that?

That's correct. The Bitcoin comes under the category of buyer beware. There are no guarantees, and your holdings could disappear tomorrow.

Are you saying the Bitcoin is a Ponzi scheme that depends on enticing customers to buy something that doesn't really exist?

Exactly. Show me the proof that a Bitcoin exists.

But, why is a bank account different? Where are the guarantees for them?

Bank accounts are only guaranteed up to certain limits. No bank can sustain a run on the bank if all the customers want to withdraw their money at the same time.

Only too true, I've read the stories about banks having to close their doors, and even going bankrupt.

An appropriate name isn't it? But having a run on a bank is a risk the government, and the banks, are willing to take.

Under most circumstances, the only authority that is in a position to guarantee both the properties of universal acceptance and authenticity of the money supply is the nation's Government. As the Government is an instrument of the people, it means that the people of a nation are the rightful owners of the money system that is created to serve the needs and wants of the people. Creating and providing the money system is one of the major public purposes for having a Government in the first place. This draft Constitution addresses that responsibility by creating the publicly owned Bank of Australia with the independent mandate to manage and arrange the nation's supply of money according to agreed parameters. Under this new Constitution, in the same way, it was provided for in the British Act, the Parliament is responsible for legislating to cover all banking in Australia, whether publicly owned, privately owned or foreign-owned.

Hey, hang on there. Isn't that the greatest risk for any society; to allow the Government to control the money supply?

It can be a risk if there are no constitutional controls on how the Government must manage their creation of the money supply.

Yeah, well I bet there were constitutional controls in Germany and Zimbabwe, but that didn't stop the hyperinflation.

Ahh, the pet argument of the private banks. Never let the Government control the money supply because it will lead to hyperinflation.

But isn't that true? History proves it.

Sure, it has happened, but what about all the boom and bust cycles that have occurred throughout history when the money supply has been controlled by the private bankers and money lenders?

That's different. Everybody doesn't lose their money like they do with hyperinflation.

Yes, it is different. There are a lot of losers, but there are also a lot of winners, and mostly the winners are the bankers and the people with lots of money to start with.

Don't give me that. What about all those stories of rich people committing suicide when a depression occurs?

Yeah, I read those stories about people jumping out of windows because they have lost all their money, but that's because they gambled with more than they could afford to lose.

Yeah, that could be the case, but I know there are a lot of ordinary people who suffer when there's a depression or even a recession.

Depression and recession are really just terms used by economists for the physical conditions that occur when the banks and the Governments withhold the issuing of credit and manipulate the money supply.

Why would they do that?

It comes under the umbrella of "fighting inflation".

But why is inflation such a horrible thing that it has to be fought to the extent of bringing on a depression?

That's a long story, but really, inflation only occurs when there is more money available than there are goods and services.

So, it's a supply and demand problem?

Precisely; if the productive capacity of a nation is related to the consumption capacity, then inflation cannot become a serious problem.

If it is that easy, why isn't it done?

A good question that really can only be answered by looking at the history of economics and the way money is created.

That's a bit rude, and too simplistic an answer. Do you have any proof of that?

Most economists are still using Adam Smith's really stupid 18th-century idea that an invisible hand controls the economy.

Well, considering all the booms and busts we've had over the last couple of centuries, the invisible hand doesn't seem to have had much control.

Hence it is, with this Chapter on Finance, the draft Constitution is setting out the conditions and controls that need to be in place if the Government is going to be the sole supplier of the nation's money supply. The primary control is the establishment of what can and must be seen, as an independent body authorised to assess the level of money needed for a growing nation and the related population levels. This independent control is created through the establishment of a Monetary Authority. The Authority consists of ten representatives from the various peak bodies covering the Australian community. It will be chaired by the Governor of the newly established Bank of Australia.

How do you expect this Monetary Authority to be seen as independent?

As it is going to consist of eleven people, only one of them will be appointed by the Government.

Surely the Governor of the Bank will be a Government appointee?

No, he or she will be a Parliamentary appointee. Each of the other representatives will be appointed by their peak body, independently of the Government.

That sounds fair enough. But what about the Banks; shouldn't they be represented?

The banking and finance industry will appoint their representative.

They're not going to like that, just one voice in eleven.

In the real world the Banks are really nothing more than service organisations; set up to facilitate the distribution of the money supply.

I bet the Banks will never agree to that sort of definition?

It won't be up to them. If the people of Australia choose to adopt this Constitution, then the Government will be the sole issuer of the nation's money supply.

What in the hell do we need the Banks for if that's the way it's going to work?

The retail banking sector will do what it is supposed to do; distribute the money to the private sector on a proper due diligent basis.

But if the Government is going to control the issue of money how will the Banks get it?

As legitimately registered businesses they will be allowed to apply to the Government for access to a quantity of "credit" depending on the capital of the business, its location and its customer base.

That sounds complicated.

Not at all. It is standard business practice. That's why we have urban banks catering primarily to urban housing and/or commercial activities, and rural banks catering to the rural industries.

So, if they buy a quantity of "credit" from the Government they can pass it on at a higher price than it cost them; is that the idea?

Exactly. Healthy competition would control how much extra they could charge their customers, but the Government is in a position to relate the productivity to the consumption and thus avoid inflationary pressures.

What about investment banks; where do they fit in?

They will be completely separate and totally denied any access to Government support.

Where is their money going to come from?

From investors in the private sector who are prepared to risk their money knowing there will be no backup, or support, from the Government if the investment goes bad.

The investors aren't going to like that at all.

Who gives a shit? All they are doing is gambling in the hope of making a profit. Why should the people support gamblers if they make a bad bet?

Naturally, as the population grows more homes are required, more infrastructure to cater for those homes, and more goods and services will be in demand. This is where the relationship between the nation's productive capacity and its consumption capacity must be related.

There is absolutely no point in producing anything if it is not going to be consumed. That represents a waste of time, of effort, of resources and of money. Consumption, however, has to be calculated on both domestic consumption and external consumption, which means our export of goods and services. Both production and consumption require access to various levels of capital, and to date, the provision of capital for productive purposes, generally speaking, has not been a significant problem. Unfortunately, the supply of productive capital has been mostly at the mercy of the private banks, who have the Government authorised power to manipulate the supply of credit in a way that best suits the banks. The major problem throughout history has been the mechanism for supplying "capital" to the consumption sector of a nation. Ultimately, this sector comes down to the people. Virtually, every single individual in a society, whether domestic or overseas, represents the consumption sector. For example, there is no point in building a bridge, or any other type of infrastructure, unless it is going to be used by people. To date, the only universally accepted way for the vast majority of people to earn the "capital" they need for consumption, is by being employed and working at a job, either for themselves or someone else.

The problem with this system is that the wages a person is paid will always represent less than half of the cost of any product produced. The other half, or more, of the cost, is taken up with the raw materials, overheads, taxes, advertising, marketing, interest payment on borrowed money, and lastly, the profit margin. Consequently, the wage earner is always short of the money they really need to maintain the modern standard of living now regarded as "acceptable". The only way the workers can achieve the standard is by borrowing money for their house, their car, their TV, the schooling of the kids, and all the thousands of other items that are needed in today's world. Of course, the banks love this situation and are only too willing to help place the debt noose around the necks of anyone and everyone, prepared to sign a contract.

Surely that's not right? Wages can't be that small a percentage of the cost of things?

Unfortunately, it is. All the other costs are relatively fixed, in the sense they can't be changed to any significant degree by the producer, except for the profit margins.

But the profit is the last thing the producer wants to change; isn't that right?

That's right if they can't make a profit they won't stay in business.

So, that leaves wages as the main area to focus on?

Yes, exactly. Hence the push for automation. Reduce the workforce, or reduce the wages you have to pay, and you reduce the costs.

But that doesn't make sense? If the people are the primary consumers, the more people you throw out of work, the less purchasing power is available to the nation.

That's right, but when you look at the industrial history of the past 200 years, the whole thrust of progress has been to produce more with less labour.

But all the Governments are still mouthing the mantra of full employment, while at the same time promoting mergers, amalgamations and increased productivity?

Yes, it's all an illogical contradiction. Just look at the rural sector; the cry for the past decades has been to get big or get out. As a result, the rural workforce is a fraction of what it was 50 years ago.

It's much the same in the cities, even with all the new industries that have been created.

Unfortunately, the unemployment figures are all manipulated these days by mixing up part-time, and even casual work of a few hours, with full-time employment.

Yes, it's true, you can create the statistics to read any way you want.

An additional function of the Monetary Authority is to set up a Remuneration Committee to recommend to Parliament the appropriate remuneration packages for all grades of politicians and senior public servants, with the provision that no public servant shall be paid more than the Prime Minister. The Committee is authorised to review these packages on an annual basis.

Page reference to Chapter 4 Part 1 Finance 267

CHAPTER 17

Discussing Domestic and International Trade and Foreign Debt

The Chapter 4 Part 2 deals with both the domestic and international trade and commerce and provides for the establishment of an IMPEX system, explicitly designed to manage all the trade in foreign currencies. The ultimate aim of the IMPEX system is to achieve a balance between Australia's import requirements and its export capacity. All foreign currency transactions are handled through a single gateway called the IMPEX facility, which is operated and managed by the Government-owned Bank of Australia. The concept of an IMPEX system is a truly "free" market system. The exporter is paid in IMPEX dollars, and the only way an importer can acquire the necessary foreign currency is by purchasing IMPEX dollars via the IMPEX market. The IMPEX system has another indirect, but quite practical purpose in encouraging local industry, both to increase export production and develop local manufacture of products that would otherwise be imported. The system can do this through the creation of IMPEX dollars. On receiving payment in a foreign currency, the IMPEX facility creates the equivalent in Australian IMPEX dollars at the going exchange rate. The exporter receives IMPEX dollars, which they can then sell on the Impex market to importers. When there is a demand for IMPEX dollars, the dollars can be sold at a premium. This provides the extra incentive to produce for export while discouraging imports. It also provides a potential to set up and produce previously imported goods directly within Australia. The process encourages downstream processing of raw materials to provide for both the domestic and export markets. The beauty of the system is that it offers virtually no incentive for speculation. The IMPEX dollars are only issued to exporters and can only be acquired through the single Australian IMPEX facility, and to that extent, it is a self-contained, closed and monitored market.

In terms of economics, a nation's wealth is measured by all the assets it owns plus all the assets it imports, less everything it exports.

That doesn't sound right. I thought we become richer when we export stuff?

Richer, or wealthier, in what way?

Well obviously, we get paid a lot of money for the stuff we sell overseas.

Yes, but that's not entirely true. If the Government allows a foreign-owned exporter to exploit our resources, the foreigners reap the benefit.

But Australia collects royalties, and whatever tax it can get that isn't avoided. And of course, the foreign company does create employment in Australia.

Well, that's a pretty good reason for foreign investment, isn't it?

Not really. Australia is a monetary sovereign nation, so, there is no reason why any Government needs to rely on foreign investment to develop any of our resources.

But we don't have the knowhow or the machinery, to compete with those big foreign companies.

I'm not too sure about the knowhow. Australia is well endowed in a great many fields, and what we don't have we would be able to hire from overseas.

What about the machinery?

That could be bought from overseas, at least to start, but there is no reason we couldn't build the machinery in Australia.

So, are you really saying we don't need foreign investment at all?

That's the truth of it. The Australian Government can create all the money it needs to fund any project it wishes to undertake, and without going into debt.

Why in the hell don't they do it then?

Because they sold our sovereignty to the Bretton Woods deal back in 1945 and became enmeshed in the web of globalisation.

An issue that needs to be addressed is whether any nation wants to be an independent nation, or alternatively, what degree of independence they are willing to accept? Most of the European nations have sacrificed their sovereignty and a considerable degree of their independence by joining the European common market. This is especially so in accepting the common currency of the Euro, which each nation has to borrow from the European Central Bank. While the amalgamation has been good for some nations, it has been bad for others, certainly, monetarily wise.

So, the question is, is independence a worthwhile goal for any nation?

However, another name for independence is self-sufficiency. Although it seems inevitable that foreign trade is an essential feature of modern life, this should not mean a nation has to become dependent on foreign trade for the nation's survival. In this modern world, for a country to maintain at least an element of independence it needs to earn enough "foreign exchange" from the goods and services it exports to roughly balance its level of imports. Australia, as an island continent, and blessed with abundant resources, is in an ideal position to resist this global domination if the people were ever to demand their leaders take up the challenge.

That's a pretty tricky question these days; what does independence really mean?

Yes, I suppose it is; seeing that nearly every country is dependent on imports from foreign countries.

So; can any country really be independent?

We probably should also ask if any country can be self-sufficient these days, or for that matter, whether they would want to be?

Well, if a country were self-sufficient it wouldn't have to rely on any other country for what it needs, or wants.

That's true, but could they only do that by being isolationists and unwilling to share anything with the rest of the world?

Not at all. All it would mean is that the country balances the trade between what it exports with what it imports.

So, it would still have to import stuff that it can't produce itself?

Yes, to that extent it would be dependent on other countries and couldn't be classed as independent?

Well, I guess you are right, but that's not the same as becoming dependent on foreign markets to survive as a nation.

One of the significant problems of almost every country in the world is the difficulty in achieving a balance in their foreign trade. The clamour for globalisation has not helped the situation, if anything, it has made it worse. Similarly, the drive for a one world Government and the suicidal aim of eliminating national borders will destroy cultures and ultimately prove self-defeating. The ulterior aim of globalisation is, in reality, to destroy the independence of nations around the world.

In nineteen forty-three, the United States of America belatedly entered the war against "the Axis", after watching their "allies" exhaust their economies and their resources in total war. Back in the Great War of nineteen fourteen to nineteen eighteen, the USA did the same thing, not that the war in Europe had anything to do with the US. While the other nations did most of the fighting, the US then took the lead role in the ultimately damaging peace negotiations that sowed the seeds for World War Two. In nineteen forty-four the United States of America took the first steps to formalise, what would later be called globalisation. Forty-four nations met at the USA resort of Bretton Woods to plan the post-war world. The USA then openly began to act as a power without rivals by dominating Bretton Woods as the planet's most powerful nation.

Though everyone thought Bretton Woods was to be about the post-war reconstruction of Europe, in truth, it turned out to be all about the USA's three main post-war objectives:

1. World free trade with no discrimination against the USA.
2. Freedom for the USA to invest in foreign economies.
3. Unimpeded access by the USA to foreign materials and resources.

Out of Bretton Woods came a "General Agreement on Trade and Tariffs", (GATT), a "World Bank", and an "International Monetary Fund" (IMF) all, over time, to be dominated and controlled by the USA. The prime objective of the GATT (later the World Trade Organisation), was the reduction of barriers against imports across the world. Strangely, the United States of America managed, in practice, to exempt itself, unapologetically, from this reduction. It is still trying to do this, but less effectively with the rise of China. The globalisation gospel was earlier inspired by the Chicago School of Economics from nineteen twenty-six onwards, but it was significantly boosted by Robert S. McNamara, the "architect" of the Vietnam War, during his presidency of the World Bank between nineteen sixty-eight and nineteen eighty-one. McNamara upgraded the rules of globalisation by officially redrafting them as "Structural Readjustment".

Those rules are divided into two groups:

The first group is aimed at destroying national independence by trade disruption through:

1. Removal of tariffs, export subsidies, and import restrictions.
2. Removal of foreign-exchange controls.
3. Downgrading of import-replacing local production.
4. Adjustment of price structures to the world market.

As of two thousand and seventeen, this has proven to be a very successful program that now impacts on virtually every nation in the world.

The second group was meant to subject the world's nations to the unelected, US-dominated, globalisation elite by using the following practices:

5. Currency devaluation.
6. Over-riding priority to be given to the payment of foreign interest.
7. Reduction of government social spending so that interest could be paid without reducing the outstanding deficits.
8. Government assets and undertakings to be privatised (sold off) preferably to foreign investors.
9. Promotion of exports, and the foreign sale of national assets to boost foreign-exchange earnings.
10. Corporate and Financial Deregulation.

The point to be noted here is, that once a nation had lost its financial independence under the Group 1 policies, it would be unable to resist the application of the Group 2 policies; so the Group 1 actions were always the first line of attack, always under the banner of "Free Trade." Once the first attack succeeded, the Group 2 policies could be applied to complete the destruction of the victim nation's independence.

A nation, which is made so dependent upon imports that it cannot earn enough foreign currency from its exports to pay for them, has no option but to make up the shortfall by borrowing from foreign lenders. Alternatively, they are forced to sell off assets (land, buildings, companies, other local possessions) to foreign buyers. Few people seem to realise that, in this, there is no other choice.

And isn't that Australia's position today?

Is there a way to untangle us from this nation destroying web of globalisation? Probably not. The UN and the WTO have the power to impose sanctions on any nation that tries to buck the system.

Is that what frightens everyone; being hit with sanctions?

It certainly makes life more difficult for the people of any nation that gets hit with sanctions.

But, isn't it the Government that's responsible for the problem? Why should the people have to suffer?

Most Governments now do what they are told. Foreign organisations, multinational corporations and international finance pretty much control everything.

That's a bit rich. Are you one of those conspiracy nuts?

Why is it a problem not wanting to be dictated to by foreign organisations and multinationals?

It's a problem because it is out of step with globalisation and the idea of a one world Government.

So, are you saying that because we are all part of the human race and we all live on this one small planet, we should sacrifice our independence?

That's what it comes down to, but we are also all individuals, and none of us are really the same.

There is a relatively straight forward and practical system available that can allow any nation to control its foreign trade dealings, and ultimately, achieve a balance, as well as reducing any accumulate foreign exchange deficit. That system is called an IMPEX system, and it is a system that aims to reward foreign earnings and discourage, or otherwise control, the flow of imports and other foreign spending. This can lead to the balancing of the nation's foreign-exchange transactions. This Constitution provides for the implementation of an IMPEX system. Ultimately this system can put an end to the nation's foreign deficit, and eventually start clawing back its accrued foreign debt.

But, isn't such a system in direct opposition to the aims of globalisation, the World Bank and the World Trade Organisation?

It certainly is, but if any nation considers it has a moral responsibility to preserve its identity, and the self-respect of its people, then it has no choice but to fight back against the destruction reeked by globalisation.

But won't international sanctions cripple any country that tries to buck the system?

Sanctions could undoubtedly make life more difficult, but they could also provide an impetus to reclaim a lot of the industries that have been destroyed.

But we couldn't just rebuild an industry without getting foreign investment.

That's absolute crap. Australia is a monetary sovereign nation, and we don't need foreign investment to start up any industry we need.

But nobody is going to invest in any enterprise if they can't be guaranteed a profit.

Are you saying nothing can be done unless there is a profit to be made?

Of course. That's the whole basis of the capitalist system. If you can't make a profit, you go bankrupt.

But if they are things that everybody needs, why should they only be available if someone can make a profit out of supplying them?

That's capitalism.

Surely, the point of having a Government, is to serve a public purpose in planning and providing the essential services the nation needs?

Ahh, now you are getting into the hypothetical.

Page reference to Chapter 4 Part 2 Trade and Commerce 273

CHAPTER 18

Discussing the Issue of States and Territories and new States

Although it appears to be a contentious issue with some people, the existence of the States is a fact of life. Concerning the history of the Commonwealth, it was carefully selected politicians from the six colonial Parliaments who promoted the concept of a unified nation. Theoretically, and probably in practice too, the colonies saw the idea of a Federal Government as a beneficial way to better coordinate the arrangements in trade and commerce, in defence, and in standardising issues between the colonies. Those issues included such necessary things as weights and measures, a uniform monetary system, and uniformity in law and business practices.

As the colonial politicians were the purveyors of the Federal concept, it is a matter of conjecture as to which side was perceived to be the more politically powerful, the colonies or the Federal Government. The fact that the colonies were prepared to accept the authority of Federal law over State law could be more related to seeking uniformity in lawmaking rather than a reflection of political dominance. In fact, what has happened is an ongoing competition between the State Governments and the Federal Government. The Federal Government has been able to establish its perceived superiority with the help of its appointed High Court, and the monopoly for proposing amendments to Part 9 of the British Act. The States have never been given the authority to propose amendments. Hence, the majority of the proposals coming out of the Federal Parliament have been aimed at increasing the power of the Federal system over the States.

What are you saying; that the States are more important than the Federal Parliament?

No, that's not what I'm saying. I'm just pointing out that it was the colonial politicians who initiated the move to create a central Government.

OK; so, the colonies came first, and there is no way we can get rid of them?

Getting rid of the States is what some people would like to do because they claim Australia is over-governed.

Well, we are when you add the third tier of Local Government.

So; what do you want to do, hand Australia over to a Central Government, sitting in Canberra and virtually isolated from the people?

Well, it would certainly cut down a lot of duplication, and get rid of the antagonism between the States and the Federal Government.

Maybe, to a degree, but do you honestly believe Canberra is capable saying which street in your neighbourhood needs resurfacing, or what priority should be given to the guttering and kerbing on your street?

That's getting a bit mundane, isn't it?

Not at all. It's just one of the hundreds of things Local Government does because Local Government is the closest to the people and is better able to understand the community needs and wants.

Yeah, maybe you're right, but that doesn't explain why we need State Governments.

At this point in our history State Governments are a physical reality, which is impossible to ignore. It would be a hell of a transition to phase them out, and in any case, that would have to be a decision of the people; certainly not the politicians.

The colonial politicians were very conscious of the disparity between the colonies, particularly in respect to population, the wealth of resources and political authority. Hence, they came up with a concept to neutralise this disparity. They dreamt up the illusion of the Senate where each colony would always have equal representation. The founding fathers maintained this illusion despite officially being told the truth that political parties would negate the concept. The "founding fathers" of Part 9 of the British Act chose to ignore the existence of political parties, and consequently, the Senate has never worked as a State's House, right from its very inception.

That sounds like a pretty low trick on the part of the founding fathers. Why would they do that?

That's an interesting question. When I think about it, I've never seen it raised before.

All those guys were pretty well educated, weren't they?

One has to assume so, as they were all past or present members of their colonial Parliaments, plus the banker, of course.

And it's not as though political parties were something new to them, after all, it was a well-established system in Britain for more than a century.

That's true, so why would they ignore the existence of political parties, especially after they had been told what it would do to the Senate?

Could there have been an ulterior motive for ignoring political parties?

Well, just think about it a bit. Here were fifty politicians and lawyers, all in favour of federation. No opposition voice was allowed to be part of that last series of conventions.

But there was pretty strong opposition, particularly in NSW, wasn't there?

Yes, the anti-Billites, as they were called. They were strong enough to force a quota for the Yes vote in the NSW Parliament.

A quota that wasn't reached in the first referendum.

That's right. But remember, each colony, except Queensland, had sent its ten representatives to that last series of conventions

*and they each had to go back to their Parliament and convince
them to call a referendum for federation.*

*Now, that's a thing, isn't it? If each of the colonial Parliaments
thought they were going to have equal representation in the Senate,
it would be easier to get the Parliaments to agree to the referendum.*

Surely, the old bastards weren't that sneaky?

Well, they were politicians and lawyers, weren't they?

In the fullness of time, the boundaries of the colonies and Territories
became settled, to the extent that, as of today, there are no
contentious issues about the State borders. However, there are some
proposals being aired to change the established status. For example,
to convert the Territories to States and to divide Queensland into
two States. There are also potential issues related to native title that
might affect State boundaries at some time in the future. Any such
change will have a direct effect on the Parliamentary arrangement
as it currently stands. With that in mind, any changes to the current
State and/or Territory borders is seen as a national issue and would
have to be dealt with via a national referendum.

*That becomes pretty involved when you start to think about
changing State boundaries.*

*It sure does, as it has a direct bearing on population figures
and then on the State or Territory representation in the Federal
Parliament.*

*It would make a huge difference if the Territories were to
become States.*

That would be a major change.

What about Native title? How could that affect things?

Ahh, that one is a real unknown.

*Do you think it might be possible for the Kooris to create their
own State within Australia?*

*I have no idea, but the last thing I think anyone would want to
happen is to set up some sort of apartheid situation in Australia.*

What about Queensland; do you think they will ever split into two States?

Anything is possible, but I think they are going to need a lot bigger population in Nth Queensland before that can happen.

One of the major changes that will have to occur with the adoption of a new Constitution for an independent Australia is the amendment to all the State Constitutions. Each State Constitution is a product of letters patents handed down by various legitimate monarchs of the UK. Hence, all reference to their origin will need to be deleted and each Constitution updated to recognise the new standing. As this could be a drawn-out exercise, there is provision for existing terminology to be interpreted as applying to the new Constitution.

Do you think the States will be prepared to go along with that?

I don't see they will have any choice if the people of Australia choose to adopt this Constitution at a referendum.

What if one of the States don't approve?

Well, we all know the rules for the referendum; a majority vote and a majority of the States. Any State that doesn't get a majority will still have to abide by the rules.

That's going to be big job converting all the State Constitutions.

There's no doubt about that, but it might also be an opportunity to properly update those State Constitutions.

Update them, but in what way?

Most of the State Constitutions are a combination of different Acts rather than being presented as a single understandable document.

And I suppose, very few people in the States know very much about their State Constitution?

Apart from some of the lawyers, that is probably dead right.

Queensland tried to update their Constitution a few years back, and I know from personal experience, they stuffed up the job.

How do you mean they stuffed it up?

It is still covered in several Acts, and it still uses legal jargon that only lawyers can understand.

So, the attempted reform didn't achieve much at all?

Precisely. It was kept in the hands of the legal fraternity, and the fob off of public participation was just a smokescreen.

Page reference to Chapter 5 Part 1 States and Territories 276
Page Reference to Chapter 5 Part 2 New States 280

CHAPTER 19

Discussing the Election Processes
Applicable in Australia

As the election process is deemed a fundamental function of a democratic system, it is considered essential that election procedures should be dealt with in the Constitution.

Another of the principles of a democratic system is trying to maximise the choices available to people, but of course, there have to be some restraints in place, as nobody can have total freedom to do whatever they want. Thus, it is with the election process in Australia, which combines a degree of freedom and a degree of restraint. The two major factors taken into account for Australia's electoral system are the relatively small voting population and the fact there are, typically, multiple candidates for each electorate. According to the latest Census figures, of the approximate twenty-four million population around nineteen million of them are of voting age. Despite the fact very few other countries have compulsory voting, and the further fact there is a general sense of apathy regarding politics in Australia, compulsory voting is the only option likely to provide the most accurate gauge of the political will.

So, you believe compulsory voting is OK, and people should be made to vote whether they want to or not?

I believe everyone should be guaranteed the opportunity to vote and making voting compulsory does provide that guarantee.

But what if there is no one you want to vote for?

You just do an informal vote.

You mean I have to go all the way to a polling station just to register an informal vote?

Is that really a problem, just having to go to a polling station about once every three years?

But most Australians don't give a damn about politics and couldn't care less who gets elected.

A lot of people tend to say that, but I'm not too sure how true that really is.

That's why people keep talking about the donkey vote.

That's a furphy they keep throwing around, but as far as I know, there are no statistics on just how many votes are supposedly donkey votes.

Well, I shouldn't have to vote if I don't want to.

Not voting, or even voting informally, both have an effect on what happens.

How can it if the vote doesn't count?

It's a cop-out because; all you're doing is handing over your responsibility to someone else for the Government that gets to run your life.

That's bullshit. I don't vote because I don't like politics.

Well, whether you like it or not, politics runs your life, and if you don't care, then you don't have any cause to complain.

Non-compulsory voting opens up many avenues for manipulation of the voting public, not the least in "buying" the vote and rigging the attendance. As politics affects everybody in the society, everybody has a responsibility for the representatives who are elected, whether the individual chooses to vote, or not. The argument for the system of first past the post only holds up if there is a maximum of two candidates standing. As soon as there are more than two candidates, and no candidate can get at least the fifty percent plus one of the votes, the system falls apart. The result then shows that more voters oppose the "winning" candidate than approve of him or her. If the first past the post were coupled with non-compulsory voting, as is the case in the UK, the result is a gross distortion of a so-called 'democratic' electoral system.

Why do you reckon first past the post isn't a democratic system; it seems logical enough to me?

When only two candidates are standing, it is OK, but if there is more than two, then it becomes harder for anyone to get fifty percent of the vote.

Even so, whoever gets the most votes should be elected.

Why? If no one gets fifty percent, then that means there are more people against the so-called winning candidate than there is for him, or her.

Is that why the preferential system is used? Your second preference gets counted until someone gets the fifty percent?

That's correct. That's the idea behind preferential voting, but even then, if voting is not compulsory, fifty percent can still be a minority of the voters in an electorate.

Well, that's their fault if they don't vote.

Precisely, they deserve all they get.

Regarding the second factor mentioned above, that of multiple candidates, Australia has long used the preferential system where the voter numbers each candidate in order of their preference. The objection to this system is that the vote can finish up being counted for a candidate whom the voter opposes. The obvious solution that is now being applied is optional preferential voting. Under this system, the voter only numbers the candidates they prefer and can ignore the others.

First past the post and preferential voting are the systems that can apply to the House of Representatives, but the Senate comes under a different system. The illusion of the Senate being a State's House is still being dishonestly perpetuated by using the ruse that each State has an equal number of Senators, irrespective of the State's population. In fact, the Senate was taken over by the political parties from its very inception and has never been a State's House. Either it is a handmaiden to the Government in power, or it is an obstacle to that Government.

But isn't the Senate supposed to be the House of review?

Technically that's what it was created for; to be part of the check and balance over the House of Reps to make sure the interests of the States weren't ignored.

So, why doesn't it work that way?

Because of the political party system, and especially when there are only two major parties.

So, if the party in Government also has the most votes in the Senate, then there are no checks or balance on what they do?

That's right, they get to do anything they want, and there is no opposition.

But if they don't have control of the Senate, then they can't do much at all?

They can if they are prepared to compromise and consider the other side of the argument.

That shouldn't be too hard to do, should it?

No, it shouldn't, but the ingrained adversarial Westminster system seems to create ideological blockages for the two parties to work together.

Because each State is treated as a single electorate, and only twelve candidates can be chosen to, theoretically, represent the State, a voting system, known as proportional representation, was chosen in nineteen forty-eight. Compulsory voting still applies, but in nineteen eighty-four the system was changed again as a result of the nefarious referendum of nineteen seventy-seven. That referendum introduced political parties into the Constitution. The voters were given a choice to vote for a minimum number of political parties, or a minimum number of candidates in order of their preference. Although the change aimed to maintain the dominance of the two major parties, the proportional representation system provides an avenue for the minor parties, and some independents, to get elected.

From all accounts, it is a bit of a strange system, when an independent, or a minor party can get elected with a very small percentage of the vote.

Yes, it can appear strange, but at least a wider range of views can get representation.

But is that a good thing to upset the stability of the two-party system?

That's a false analogy because; while there are two major parties only one of them gets to govern.

But all these other parties and the independents are making it harder for the Government to govern appropriately.

What do you mean, to govern properly? If the Government governs for the benefit of the nation rather than their narrow party benefit, it would be no problem in getting legislation passed.

That's a good theory, but it doesn't work like that in practice.

Well, this Constitution is going to make it work like that because the Government will have to get a two-thirds majority if they want to get any bills accepted.

If you do that, then nothing is going to get done.

Which might not be such a bad thing, considering all the crap they keep coming up with.

But, I suppose, with a bit of luck, it might kill off this stupid adversarial system that is now used.

Yeah, you could be right. After all, the Federal politicians should really be there for the benefit of the nation, not just to score points for their party.

Page reference to Chapter 6 Part 1 Elections 281

CHAPTER 20

Discussing the need to Control Political Parties

While political parties are recognised in this Constitution, a definition is provided as to precisely what conditions shall apply to any such entity. The definition is uniform for any political party related to State and Federal elections. Although political parties can represent one of the most dangerous aspects of any political system, it is an accepted fact that people of like mind will always congregate together. It is also an accepted, although unfortunate fact that the mostly unknown executive body of a political party can have a strong influence over the members who get elected to Parliament. This influence is exerted in relation to party endorsement at the next election, but also through policy decisions.

That's kinda harsh to say political parties are the most dangerous aspect of the political system.

Well, they certainly can be if they get total control of the Parliament.

Yeah, but that doesn't happen too often in Australia, and besides, Australians don't elect radical politicians.

That's relatively true, as we seem to be stuck with the two major parties.

So, what's wrong with that? Doesn't that make for a more stable government system?

Yes, I suppose you could say that, especially as the difference between the parties is almost negligible.

Don't give me that. The Libs are all fired up conservatives, and the Labor is the opposite.

Bullshit. They are both middle of the road, and there is very little change whichever party gets to form a Government.

Well, Whitlam tried to change things, and so did Howard.

Yeah, and look what happened to both of them. The public tossed them out when they got off the middle of the road.

That's democracy for you. The Australian public won't tolerate any political party that tries to go down the wrong road.

A nice theory, but the buggers can still do a lot of damage in the three years between elections.

The fundamental flaw with political parties is that the elected members must give their loyalty to the party ahead of the constituents in their electorate. While electorates tend to be classified according to the dominant party vote, most spending allocated to electorates tends to focus on boosting the support for the particular political party that happens to be in power at any given time.

The other major flaw in the political party system stems from the stupidity of the adversarial tradition endorsed by the Westminster system of government. In a country like Australia, with its relatively small population and relatively small number of Federal politicians, it is pathetic that these people cannot be allowed to put the interests of the nation ahead of the interests and policies of their party.

Don't you think the Westminster system is too ingrained to be changed?

I hope not because, after all, it is just a system created by people and anything created by people can be changed.

I must admit, some of the sessions of Parliament I've watched on TV were more like school kids carrying on in the playground.

That's the unfortunate part of the system; it sets up two sides to fight each other rather than encouraging people to work together.

That certainly seems the case. If one side says something, the other side has to oppose it.

Let's face it; here we have just a couple of hundred people sitting in Parliament to represent the twenty plus million people in Australia; don't you think they should be able to work together for the benefit of the nation?

Seems not, when everything revolves around which party they represent.

To me, that sounds like a pretty good reason to try and change things.

This new Constitution attempts to address this glaring fault by forcing a two-thirds majority vote in each House for any bills to succeed. That provision will achieve two major things. First, it will force the major political parties to agree on a compromise that will result in more equitable legislation in the interests of the nation as a whole. Secondly, it will demand a much closer scrutiny of every bill presented to Parliament to ensure its purpose has a better chance of being achieved.

The common parliamentary practice for most ruling political parties is to instruct the party members to vote according to the dictates of the party's Executive, usually, without serious debate on the bill. Then, of course, there is the occasional nefarious practice of the "midnight" vote with almost no debate at all. These expediencies are often adopted because of the legal way the bills are drafted and the general lack of legal training by the majority of the backbenchers. A two-thirds majority vote will serve to counter this practice and force all the politicians to take a closer look at the bills.

I don't like the idea of compromising. How do you achieve a compromise between something good and something bad?

Yes, I've heard that argument before. How do you compromise by mixing water with poison?

That's right; you always finish up with poison in the glass.

I guess it comes down to a matter of degree. One would hope that no party wants to deliberately push bad policies so, any compromise should lead to a better outcome.

The two-thirds majority would undoubtedly eliminate one party pushing their barrow and ignoring any alternative proposals.

That has to be a good thing, surely?

I've had a look at some of these bills that come out of Parliament and become laws, especially where amendments are involved.

But what's wrong with amending a law to bring it up to date?

Nothing is wrong with trying to do that; it is the way they go about it.

Why, what's wrong with the way they do it?

Mostly, the bill just lists the changes to various Sections of an existing law and states the alterations or additional words to be used.

So, what's the problem?

The problem is that the amendments can't be understood unless you have the whole law in front of you and can understand the impact.

So, you are saying the bill to make amendments doesn't include the whole of the law?

That's right. Often the original law was written decades ago, and some of them cover hundreds of pages so, unless you know the whole law, it is hard to know just how the amendments will apply.

Yeah, I can see that could be a bit of a problem.

Unfortunately, it is the bread and butter stuff of the legal fraternity, and the reason so many Court cases hinge on technicalities.

Why is that; is it because the amendments create complications?

Quite often that is the case, but more often it is the convoluted way the law is written and the legal jargon that is used.

This Constitution has an additional provision to enhance the better evaluation and understanding of bills being promoted in Parliament. The provision requires that each bill must be a stand-alone bill, as amendments to existing bills are no longer allowed. The past practice of adding amendments to existing laws, many such laws dating back decades and often subject to many earlier amendments, can make these laws virtually incomprehensible to most people, including the legal fraternity. By making each bill a stand-alone bill, all the outdated and irrelevant sections of the earlier law can be deleted, but the pertinent sections can be re-drafted in a way that all the politicians can read and understand the need and purpose for the bill.

That sounds like a great idea. Make all the new laws stand alone and complete. It would really help to clean up a lot of the obsolete laws on the books and make the new laws understandable.

That's the idea. From all accounts, law reform has been an ongoing occupation for some people, but it doesn't seem to have made the legal system any easier to understand.

Maybe, the legal people like it that way?

I bet they do.

That's why it is bloody stupid to say that ignorance of the law is no excuse.

The ways the laws are written, it is probably the most valid excuse anyone can have.

Page reference to Chapter 6 Part 2 Political Parties 284

CHAPTER 21

Discussing the Concept of Citizen's Recall

The citizen's recall provision in this Constitution is part of the system to put more control in the hands of the people and to make the people's representatives more accountable for their actions. To date, about the only practical opportunity the people have to make their representative's accountable is the vote every three years, or so. While there are some reasonably justifiable conditions related to any recall action, the fact that the provision is written into the Constitution may give some of the politicians, and bureaucrats, pause to reconsider their actions. If a citizen's petition is considered justifiable, then various avenues are available to address the issue, right up to the ultimate level of impeachment.

Why is this idea of Citizen's recall preferred to the more conventional Citizen's Initiated Referendum?

There are a couple of reasons, but probably the main one is that it places a spotlight on the individual to discourage dishonest and corrupt practices.

Why should elected representatives be singled out for that?

It's not only elected people, but it can also apply to appointed public servants.

Why are you focussing on them as well?

I guess it comes back to that well known saying, "Power corrupts, and absolute power corrupt absolutely."

But you can't tar and feather everyone just because they are elected or appointed?

Definitely not, the recall provision doesn't do that at all. All these people are in positions of authority over others, and thus, they are in positions to show favours.

And you reckon some of them are going to succumb to temptation?

Unfortunately, that happens to be part and parcel of human nature.

So, a recall provision puts them on notice that people are watching them?

That's right. It provides an avenue for people to take some appropriate action if they have proof of any wrongdoing.

That makes it quite a bit different from a Citizen's Initiated Referendum.

It is, but the CIR system isn't aimed at the individual the way the Citizen's recall system is.

But the CIR could be the result of unacceptable practices by individuals?

Yes, that's true, but it would be a much longer and less direct system for addressing individual malpractice, or corruption.

By giving the people the authority to determine the powers, privileges and immunities being granted to their elected representatives, this Constitution reinforces the importance of the recall and impeachment processes. Those powers, privileges and immunities are the very crux of what must be in the hands of the people to determine. It should never have been handed over to the people's representatives to determine these for their own benefit without any input from the people.

Are you saying the old Constitution gave the politicians the authority to determine whatever powers, privileges and immunities that wanted?

Yes, unfortunately, that is what it did, and it is one of the glaring weaknesses of the document.

I'll say. That is like giving the inmates the keys to the asylum.

Well, not exactly a good analogy, but reasonably accurate.

Surely the people would object to handing that sort of authority over to the politicians?

The people of the nineteenth century didn't have any say in it, and the people you refer to would have been the few eligible men who were allowed to vote at the referendums.

But surely, even if there were only a few men involved, they must have been intelligent enough to understand what they were voting for?

Yes, they would have been intelligent enough to know whether they were voting for "unity of the colonies, or disunity,"

But they voted for the Constitution too, didn't they?

No, that's one of the historical lies that have been perpetuated over the years. They were never asked to vote for the Constitution, only for "unity or disunity of the colonies".

So, the fifty appointed and elected guys at those early conventions got to say whatever they wanted?

That's it. The people were never a part of those conventions, and certainly, no opposition voices were allowed to participate.

The other issue that impacts on the people's control of their representatives is the elimination of career politicians. The fact that this Constitution limits every politician to a limited number of consecutive terms in office will prevent the rorting of the system through exorbitant superannuation and other payouts when they lose office. The so-called justification of serving the public is largely a furphy, and most candidates go into politics for the power and perks it offers. There is really no reason politics should be considered any different from any other occupational career. Hence, the conditions imposed on the people through legislation must apply equally to any elected representative.

They're not going to like that; putting a limit on the time they can spend in politics?

Why not? It's the politicians who have insisted on contracts for senior public servants so, why should politicians be treated any different?

But isn't going into politics a way to serve the people and the nation?

It'd be wonderful if that were true, but most of the politicians today are there to serve the party.

So, how is limiting their term in Parliament going to make any difference?

To start with it will eliminate the practice of paying ongoing benefits to the politicians when they get kicked out, or retire.

That would be a good thing considering the ripoffs they've given themselves over the years.

Limiting the time in office will also create the opportunity for fresh ideas.

Maybe, but won't the political parties still control the policies?

Possibly, but to a lesser extent. The system will force changes, especially if some sitting members get kicked out before reaching their limit.

Page reference to Chapter 7 Part 1 Citizen's Recall 286

CHAPTER 22

Discussing the Impeachment Process in this New Constitution

An impeachment process should be a compulsory necessity for any genuine democracy. Unfortunately, it is only included in a relatively few Constitutions of the many nations around the world. Impeachment is the most powerful deterrent that can apply to any person who chooses to "serve the people", irrespective whether it is an elected or an appointed position.

By placing an impeachment process in a Constitution, it covers every person in Government employment, right to the very top of the political and bureaucratic chain of command.

Aren't there already enough provisions in the Crimes Act and other legislation to deter people from doing the wrong thing?

That is probably true for ordinary people, but politicians and bureaucrats are in a different category from ordinary people.

How come? Why do you say they are different?

Politicians and bureaucrats are employed by the people to serve the people, that is a responsibility an obligation that makes them different.

That's a bit rich. Most of them think they are there to tell the people what to do.

That's the essence of power, and it is also why there is a difference.

So, what are you saying? That because of their position, they have the power of authority over other people?

Exactly. And that puts them in a different category to ordinary people.

But they can still be charged and prosecuted under criminal legislation, can't they?

In most cases, they probably can, but their positions are directly created by the Constitution so, the Constitution has an obligation to deal with any misconduct.

Under most normal situations, actual impeachment is a relatively rare event and even rarer in the most senior ranks of the political arena. The very existence of an impeachment process has a sobering effect on people who are in a position to affect the lives of others. Of course, impeachment is only as effective as the legal system a nation chooses to adopt, but as long as the principle of innocent until proven guilty is upheld, then the rules of valid evidence will apply.

So, impeachment is just like a trial in a court?

In some respects, it is, but other aspects make the impeachment process different.

What aspects?

Politicians and bureaucrats are under oath to serve the people so; we can be dealing with ethical and integrity issues, as distinct from criminal conduct.

But there still has to be evidence presented, doesn't there?

Under normal circumstances that would be the case. Nobody could get impeached on the basis of heresy, or rumours.

So, there is a pretty tight system involved before an impeachment action would take place?

Definitely. Impeachment is the last resort really.

Impeachment is a very serious step, and the process is carefully structured to ensure anyone likely to come under its umbrella is given the proper opportunity to defend their actions. Perceptions can sometimes cause as much damage to the integrity of a senior position as a case of proven misconduct. Hence, there is an option available to allow a conditional resignation under certain circumstances.

Page reference to Chapter 7 Part 2 Impeachment 289

CHAPTER 23

Discussing the Need and Purpose
of a Periodic Review Process

Although Citizen's Initiated Referendum (CIR) has been around for many years, and the concept seems quite popular, there has been relatively little success in having it implemented. The intended purpose of CIR proposals is to place greater authority in the hands of the people. However, the CIR system tends to be more an ad-hoc approach that looks at the Constitution in a piecemeal way.

A Nation's Constitution is also its Primary Law and its value, and integrity depends on it being recognised as an integrated document that has to be addressed in its entirety. It is also a document that needs to be assessed over a period rather than being subject to the expediency of the moment, or for the benefit of some perceived popular or political gain. Hence, there is a provision written in the Constitution for a periodic Constitutional review process to take place every few years. This will allow individual and interested people, or groups, to propose constitutional changes. The periodic concept will also allow a better assessment of the constitutional provisions concerning how they are applied in practice, and whether they are achieving their intended purpose.

But Citizen's Initiated Referendum represents a direct way for the people to express their views.

Up to a point because most CIR systems depend on a group of people getting a required number of signatures on a petition.

So, what's wrong with that?

If the issue is clearly a national one, and we are talking about a certain percentage of signatures needed for a petition, then that percentage should cover the nation.

OK. That's not a big problem in today's world of the internet. There's already a lot of groups setting up petitions for all sorts of things.

That's true, although most of those petitions have been pretty specific in their aim.

But there's no reason the system couldn't be used for a constitutional issue?

That's also true, but CIR does tend to be more of a random single issue process, rather than a planned and comprehensive overview process.

Probably, the most crucial factor in dealing with a Constitution is in acknowledging its ownership. Once ownership is established, then it is axiomatic that only the owners have the authority to propose changes, and only the owners have to authority to say which changes should be made. In a genuinely democratic system, it should be obvious that the people are the rightful owners of their nation's Constitution. It is the people who must agree to how much authority they are prepared to allow their representatives, and it is the people who determine what sort of governmental and bureaucratic structure they will allow to govern their lives. However, by accepting the proposition that the people are the rightful owners of their Constitution, it does present a challenge. After all, a Constitution is really all about people and how their society should function so, by any logical reasoning, it is up to the people to say what should, or shouldn't be in their Constitution.

The challenge arises because of the historical tradition, which has fostered the claim that a Constitution is a legal and political document, and not something untrained and ordinary people should meddle with. This traditional belief goes back centuries, and even to the time of the Magna Carta. That document was really just a contract to share "power", meaning control over the people, between the aristocratic Barons and the King, but with the Catholic Church, very much, thrown into the mix. In fact, that mentality has persisted right through to today's world. Without a doubt, the politicians and the legal fraternity have jealously maintained their claim to ownership of the Constitution. They have done this by ensuring the people are never allowed to propose changes. The people are only allowed to have a say in whatever proposals the existing Government chooses to initiate. Our history over the past century has shown that the Government mostly makes proposals that will inevitably increase their power over the people, or the States. Fortunately, the people are imbued with an inordinate amount of common sense, and rather than being "conservative", as is often claimed, they can see through the grab for more power. Hence, only eight of the forty-four proposals put up by the Government in the seventeen referendums we have had since nineteen hundred and six, have been accepted.

So, you are saying the population isn't conservative at all, but are showing a lot of common sense?

I reckon that is pretty obvious when you look at all the proposals put to them by the two main political parties.

Why do you single out the two main political parties?

It's another one of those unwritten conventions. Any proposal has to have the agreement of both Houses of Parliament, but as most proposals aim at benefiting the Government, only the two main political parties are ever in a position of forming the Government.

So, both parties have an interest in increasing the Government's powers?

Exactly. That's why thirty-six of the forty-four proposals put to referendum since nineteen hundred and six have failed.

Failed for the Government, you mean, but have been successfully defeated by the people?

That's right, and isn't that a display of common sense rather than being conservative?

I don't know. Maybe the people just don't like change?

If they don't like change, why did they approve of the eight proposals?

Yeah, I see your point. Those changes didn't seem to give the Government more power.

And the referendum of nineteen sixty-seven is a prime example, when it removed that racist Section 127 from the British Act, and thereby recognise the Aborigine race in the Constitution.

But that is not to say that any Constitution can ever be set in concrete and should never be subject to change. Change is the only constant we really have in this world, and all our customs, traditions and practices do need to accept the inevitability of change. However, when it comes to a nation's Constitution, it should always be looked at in a systematic and coordinated way. Changes need to be considered regarding their impact on other parts of the Constitution and also in respect to the fundamental philosophy underpinning the Constitution. For these reasons, an independent periodic Constitutional Review Process is proposed to allow any interested person, or organisation, to be involved in submitting proposals. The Process is designed to be conducted on an Australia-wide basis and entirely independently of the Government, but all Governments and the legal fraternity can participate.

Do you think it is possible to set up such a review system that is independent of the Government?

Probably not under the present system. No Government would ever willingly relinquish their control over the Constitution.

So, how do you reckon it is ever likely to happen?

It can only happen if the people want it to happen.

And how are we going to know if the people want it to happen?

That's easy. It is written into this new Constitution, and if the people accept the new Constitution at a referendum, then it will become part of the Primary Law.

But even so, how can you design a system that is going to be independent of the Government?

That is the challenge because whatever system is set up it will need money to function.

And the money will have to come from the Government; correct?

Yes, that's correct. But as it has to be a nationwide system, and all forms of Government, Federal, State and Local can make submissions, as well as any groups or individuals, the cost could be shared between the Federal Government and the States.

So, what's the initial concept?

The initial idea is to establish separate State commissions to solicit proposals, and have the proposals coordinated for presentation to an eventual National Convention.

And what happens with the outcome of the National Convention.

The new Constitution makes it compulsory for the Government to have a referendum on whatever proposals are agreed by the National Convention.

Sounds complicated, but it might work.

Well, it definitely places the ownership of the Constitution in the hands of the people, and it does set up a better-coordinated approach to look at the Constitution as a whole.

Page reference to Chapter 8 Part 1 Constitutional Review Process 294

CHAPTER 24

Discussing the Amendment of the Constitution by Referendums

Over the years there has been considerable discussion about the difficulty in changing the Constitution through the referendum process. This is a quite deliberate distortion of the position. There really isn't any problem getting the Constitution changed if the change is seen to benefit the people and not the Government. However, there are thirty or more loopholes in Clause 9 of the British Act that allows Parliament to change the meaning and intent of the Constitution without going to referendum. This is accomplished through the wording "Until Parliament otherwise provides...," or similar. Parliament can do this through legislation without changing a word in Clause 9 of the British Act. Over the century, Parliament has done this hundreds of times. A classic example is using the nineteen seventy-five Common Informers (Parliamentary Disqualifications) Act. It completely nullifies Section 46 of the Constitution. That Section specifies the penalties to be paid for every day a member sits in Parliament when unqualified. Sub Section 4 of that Common Informers Act reads, *"On and after the date of commencement of this Act, a person is not liable to pay any sum under Section 46 of the Constitution, and no suit shall be instituted, continued, heard or determined in pursuance of that Section."*

That is absolutely incredible. I thought they could only change the Constitution by referendum.

You, and along with almost everyone else.

Are you saying there are all these other ways the Parliament can make changes without getting the people's OK?

Yes, it's a fact, but the Parliament can't use those provisions to change any of the wording; all they can do is change the intent and meaning of the Sections.

That's bad enough, isn't it? But, why did the "founding fathers" need to make those provisions in their draft?

A couple of reasons, I suppose. One reason could have been to provide some flexibility, and the other, to keep the Constitution up to date.

Have they done that?

Well, they've certainly used the flexibility to change things, but not so much to keep it up to date; it's been much more to benefit the political party system.

Like that example in shutting down Section 46?

Exactly. There must have been some sitting politicians in nineteen seventy-five who should have been disqualified under Section 44.

And they would have had to pay the penalty for every day they sat if proven unqualified?

Correct; and that original penalty was one hundred pounds a day.

So, this nineteen seventy-five Act effectively stopped any disqualified member from paying any penalty at all.

Yes, that's right, and it was a pretty low trick just to make sure their mates in Parliament were looked after.

The nineteen sixty-seven referendum is another glaring example. When the people were made aware of the racist attitudes of the "founding fathers" they were appalled. The people voted overwhelmingly to remove the obnoxious Section 127 that excluded Aborigines from being counted in the census.

The government, however, used what was expected to be a "successful" referendum to throw in another question related to the aborigine people. While removing Section 127 was a morally and ethically correct decision, the removal of the words. "other than the aborigine race in any State" was quite another issue.

To do that the Government relied on the appalling ignorance of the general public regarding, what should be, the people's Constitution. By removing the above words from Section 51(xxvi) it effectively gave the Federal Government total control of the Aborigine population in Australia. Before the "successful" results of this referendum, the welfare and administration of Aborigine affairs was the responsibility of the States. Whether that is a good or a bad thing isn't really the issue. The issue was transference of power to the Federal Government; something that was not made abundantly clear at the time. That nineteen sixty-seven referendum allowed the creation of a substantial new federal bureaucratic Department. Although that didn't happen till nineteen seventy-two, it did lead to the setting up of a Federal Department in opposition to, and competition with, the existing Aborigine Affairs Department in each of the States.

But, that nineteen sixty-seven referendum is said to be the most successful referendum ever held in Australia?

In terms of the percentage of approval, it certainly was.

Why was that one so easy to get passed?

Mainly because so few people know anything at all about the Constitution and were appalled to find out how racist it was in the way it treated the Aborigines.

You mean not counting them in the Census?

Exactly. If people are excluded because of their race that is just plain racism, and it makes all the Aborigines second class people.

So, why was that put in the Constitution in the first place? After all, the Aborigines were here first, and it was their country to start with.

I guess the only way to answer that is to go back to the eighteen hundreds. Here were all these Pommies arriving with a bunch of convicts, to a land where there were no recognised towns and no apparent Government, just some primitive natives who threw spears at the new arrivals.

Yeah, well I'd probably be doing the same if I got invaded.

To the Poms, it wasn't an invasion. It was just part of the European tradition of colonisation; a system that had been in practice for a few centuries.

So, colonising a country is different from invading it?

Yep, colonising was an accepted and legal thing back in the seventeenth and eighteenth centuries.

But that doesn't make it right, does it?

Right, by whose standards, and in what period of history?

Yeah, as they say, might is right, and a spear is no match for a gun.

We've had seventeen referendums since the first one in nineteen hundred and six, and only eight of the forty-four questions asked have been "successful." The reason for their "success" is, because, they weren't seen as a grab to increase the already extensive power of the Federal Government. The conventional excuse of blaming the conservative nature of the Australian people for the "failure" of most referendums is, in fact, a deliberate misrepresentation. The Government and their acolytes refuse to acknowledge the very high level of common sense displayed by the people, in denying the Government more power.

However, according to Section 128, and a proper legal standpoint, it is questionable about the constitutional legality in the way these referendums have been conducted. Section 128 states clearly, and explicitly, that "the proposed law" must be presented to the people at a referendum. It says this eight separate times in that Section; hence, there should be no doubt about what is intended. There is nothing in the Section that allows a simplified question to be used. Neither is there a provision in this Section that includes the words, "Until Parliament otherwise provides…" There is also an anomaly with respect to Section 51 and the thirty-nine powers allocated to the Federal Government. There is no specific provision for the Commonwealth Government to make laws dealing with electoral matters, although subsection 51(xxxvii) is probably manipulated to cover this oversight.

Apparently, the Electoral Act of nineteen hundred and six, and subsequent amendments tries to cover the stipulation of "the proposed law" being presented at a referendum. It requires the said "proposed law" to be published in two newspapers in each State. The glaring anomaly of this practice is illustrated in the nineteen twenty-eight referendum. A simple question was asked to allow the Federal Government to take over State debts, but it wasn't until some months later that Section 105A was added to Clause 9 of the British Act. Had the people been fully aware of what was to be included in Section 105A, it is almost certain the referendum would have failed.

Sub Section 5 of that Section reads, *"Every such agreement and any such variation thereof shall be binding upon the Commonwealth and the States parties thereto notwithstanding anything contained in this Constitution or the Constitution of the several States or in any law of the Parliament of the Commonwealth or of any State".*

Nobody is above the law, and to write this provision into the Constitution is bordering on criminality. The people of Australia are ultimately responsible for any debts incurred by either the State Governments or the Commonwealth Government, but any contract has to come under the rule of law. This is even more alarming when it is realised that the debts are mainly between the Governments and the private bankers and investors, and this provision gives those "lenders" total freedom from any Australian law whatsoever. Stanley Bruce was looking after his English banker mates to ensure they got every penny owed to them. The other appalling thing about this subsection is that it has been allowed to fester in the British Act since nineteen twenty-nine and there hasn't been one single move to have it repealed.

That really is incredible that somebody had the audacity to write such a provision into the nation's Primary Law.

And what does it say about the politicians and the legal fraternity who seem to have accepted such a despicable arrangement?

And don't forget the Press.

It is unbelievable that something like this could have been subject to any sort of rational debate.

Is there one single lawyer, or Judge, in this country who could honestly agree that any contract is above the law of the nation?

For the life of me, I cannot think of any logical justification for accepting that subsection 5.

And as you say, what is possibly even worse, is the fact that the subsection has been allowed to remain there without challenge all these years.

I guess that provides a sort of confirmation of how little is known about the Constitution.

Anything to do with changing the wording of the Constitution must automatically impact on the States, and therefore, as per the existing arrangement, a referendum would require a majority vote and a majority of the States approving any proposal. Under the new Constitution, this type of referendum is called a Class 1 Referendum. However, the new Constitution introduces a second type of referendum, one that depends on a majority vote independently of how the States vote. This is a Class 2 Referendum and is used for issues of national importance, as distinct from being State or constitutional related issues. Questions such as euthanasia, for example, or possibly, what represents a legitimate religion. In every case, whenever a referendum is called for, whether Class 1 or Class 2, the complete details of the proposed legislation, or changes to the Constitution, must be made available at the time. When the proposed changes are presented to support the referendum, they cannot be subject to any subsequent alteration.

That makes a lot of sense, having two types of referendums.

There's obviously a lot of issues of national importance that don't directly relate to the States.

I've often heard complaints about requiring a majority of States having to agree to a referendum for its acceptance.

I've heard those complaints too, but it is a logical requirement for issues dealing with changing the Constitution.

Why do you say it is OK for that?

Well, the Constitution involves all the States, big and small, and if it is just left to the overall majority vote, then the population of New South Wales and Victoria would probably control most of the referendums.

Yeah, I suppose you could be right. But what sort of national issues are you talking about?

Issues like signing a treaty that will impact on our Australian laws and way of life.

And like the same-sex marriage issue?

Yes, that's right. It really doesn't have anything to do with the States directly; it's very much a national issue.

And what about getting involved in foreign wars?

That's certainly a national issue. It really isn't even a Government decision, unless Australia were to come under direct attack by foreign military.

Yeah, that's right. Our military is supposed to be for defence, not for fighting other people's wars.

Page reference to Chapter 9 Part 1 Amending the Constitution 297

CHAPTER 25

Conclusion

Of course, this is nowhere near the end of our journey, just as it isn't the end of this book. We have a long way to go in changing the perceptions that have been built up over the years. It is but a first step in trying to show people that they are responsible for their society and the type of politics they are prepared to accept in running their lives.

It is absolutely true that politics do control all of our lives, but it is up to us to say what sort of politics we want. Although the concept of self-government is sometimes perceived as an ideal situation, human nature makes it difficult to see how such a concept could be translated into a practical system. Until a wiser generation evolves, it would seem we are stuck with a form of representative Government. Possibly, the words written in the dedication offers a clue to what sort of Government we should aspire to – *"a more honest system; a system less corruptible by money, and one that can give us better control over our elected and appointed representatives."*

This draft Constitution does attempt to provide a roadmap to lead us in that direction.

One of the major problems of the present political system is the way political parties operate. Despite the fact that the Westminster system of Government is not the system defined in the nineteenth century British Act, it is the system used in our

Parliament. It is a traditional British adversarial system, based on the outmoded concept that the dominance of two major political parties provides the essence for stable Government. That system has many flaws, not the least that the elected politicians must always represent their political party ahead of their constituents and their electorate. Fundamentally, all political parties have one primary objective – to get enough candidates elected to form the Government. Unfortunately, in our modern society, the only way that objective can be achieved is through money.

As history has shown over the past few centuries, political parties have been responsible for an incredible amount of carnage, destruction, bloodshed and misery, to millions of people around the world. Unfortunately, the damage political parties have done to the world far outweighs the good they have achieved. Sure, there has been an amazing degree of progress in the course of our history, but if we look at it objectively, invariably, it is more often the result of individual ideas and initiative, whether supported by the Government or not.

Is there a better way?

At this point in time, it is difficult to believe political parties can be eliminated, because, human nature is such that people of like mind will always congregate together. The other aspect of human nature is the fact that people tend to come in two fundamental categories – leaders and followers. However, while we may choose to accept the existence of political parties that is not to say a Constitution should not attempt to control the way they operate. In truth, controlling political parties has to be a primary responsibility of a good Constitution.

This Constitution attempts to do that in several ways. First by forcing our Federal politicians to think nationally rather than from the narrow perspective of their party's ideology. The draft Constitution does that by requiring all bills to achieve a two-thirds majority vote for acceptance, in both Houses of Parliament. The bill then goes to the Australian Council for ratification that it complies with the Constitution. If the Council agrees, the Head of State is then authorised to give consent to the bill.

Another thing is the elimination of career politics. All politicians of the House of Representative are limited to a maximum of three fixed terms of office. The Senators are limited to a maximum of two fixed terms. Double dissolutions are eliminated to ensure there is always half the Senate in place to provide continuity after every election.

The Constitution also provides for a Citizen's Recall process and an Impeachment procedure, which dramatically improves the ability of the people to hold their elected and appointed representatives accountable. These measures are reinforced by requiring every elected representative, and all senior bureaucrats, to swear allegiance to the people of Australia and our Constitution. The Constitution also addresses the electoral process, lobbying and accountability for the money involved in elections.

These steps are coupled to a more independent High Court, by mitigating political bias from allowing a Prime Minister to make the appointments. Each State shall appoint a Judge, and one from the Territories, to make up the full bench of the High Court. The Constitution also demands that all High Court decisions must be unanimous; otherwise, the Court must hand the issue back to Parliament to sort out. It is clearly undemocratic to allow seven unelected people to make laws or to create an interpretation that is not endorsed by Parliament. Under this Constitution, Parliament is the only body with executive authority, apart from the specific and limited authority granted to the Head of State as Commander in Chief of the Armed Forces.

Possibly, the single most crucial function provided for in this draft of a new Constitution is in clearly and definitively, declaring Australia a monetary sovereign nation. That declaration places the total responsibility on the Government to issue and manage the nation's money supply on behalf of the people. The

Government shall have the sole authority in designating the specific form of tokens to be recognised as legal tender, for use as the nation's medium of exchange. Virtually, every aspect of our modern way of life revolves around money. It is, therefore, essential that the issuing and controlling of the nation's money supply, is a fundamental public purpose, and responsibility, for having a Government. The establishment of the official Monetary Authority, and the controlling factors of population levels, balanced productive and consumption capacities, are designated in the draft Constitution. The private banking system shall continue to fulfil their primary function of distributing the money supply to the nation, but at their own risk and according to the parameters laid down by the Monetary Authority.

These are but a few of the innovative ideas incorporated in the draft Constitution.

This draft Constitution is designed as a roadmap for the future. It is not something that is set in concrete, but merely a series of ideas for placing on the table. It is designed as a starting point, in the hope of generating an open and constructive discussion that will lead to an improved version. A version suitable for national acceptance, and its eventual adoption by the people of a genuinely independent Australia.

Graham L Paterson

PART 2

A DRAFT
for a
CONSTITUTION OF AN INDEPENDENT AUSTRALIAN NATION

(As updated December 2017)

CONTENTS

PREAMBLE

We, the people of the Commonwealth of Australia, a Federation which was constituted under the Act of the British Parliament (63 and 64 Victoria, Chapter 12) dated the ninth day of July 1900, have agreed to adopt this new Australian Constitution governing the Federal Commonwealth Parliament, the Government, and all the Federal Courts of our Nation, in accordance with our beliefs, as set out in this Preamble.

As this Constitution also represents the Constitution of our independent Australian nation, any Federal law shall take precedence over State law should conflict arise.

In setting out these fundamental beliefs and principles governing the application of this Constitution, this Preamble must always be treated as an integral part of the Constitution in the formulation of Laws and judicial decisions.

WE hold to the belief that all Australians, including the descendants of the original Aborigine inhabitants, are created equal under the rule of Law, that we are endowed with certain inalienable rights; these include the right to life, liberty within the law, responsible free speech, ownership of property, self-defence, and the pursuit of happiness. It is the responsibility of every elected member of the Parliament to guarantee, under oath, that these Rights are universally sustained within the nation.

All Rights are ordained as the possession of the people, but in the interest of our society and the Commonwealth of Australia, those rights come with the responsibility not to unlawfully encroach on the rights of anyone else.

WE further hold to the belief in the Rule of Law as the only viable option for a Democratic Society. This belief is based upon the universal values contained in our historical Common Law heritage. This heritage is derived from the Great Charters of England, handed down to us through the centuries as part of the development of British Common Law and subsequently incorporated into Australian Common Law. While it is recognised that laws do impact on the unrestrained rights of the people, this Constitution defines good Government as subordinating all laws to maximising the concept of individual freedom for the people legitimately living in this nation.

WE hold these values to be inviolate and that no Parliament, or Court of the Commonwealth of Australia, shall have the right to deny, or rescind, the inherited rights, freedoms and obligations of any Australian citizen as provided by our Common Law heritage.

WE, the people of Australia, hereby declare that we are a sovereign independent Nation made up of Australian States and Territories.

WE, the people of Australia, further declare that our Parliamentary system shall comprise of an Australian Council, a House of Representatives and a House of Senators, each of which shall be formed and function in the manner set down in this Constitution.

WE also declare that the Government of Australia shall be vested and maintained in the four principal, non-political areas covered by the Public Service Departments, the Police Service, all sections of the Judiciary and the Defence Forces of Australia.

All Members of the Australian Council, as well as every Member of the Australian Parliamentary system, and of each of the Government Services designated above, shall at all times, be responsible to the People of Australia and shall, as provided for in this Constitution, swear to such allegiance by the Oath of Office contained herein. Any infringement of this sworn obligation shall be open to challenge through all legitimate means, including the Citizen's Recall procedures as set out in the Constitution, and possible impeachment procedures, if applicable.

WE, the people of Australia, declare that the responsibility for the Government of the Commonwealth of Australia shall be vested in the Members of the House of Representatives whom shall appoint, or elect, from their membership, a Prime Minister, with the powers and authority as specified in this Constitution.

The Prime Minister shall then select Members from either House of Parliament to act as Ministers in charge of the various Government Departments; with the duties and responsibilities, as provided for in this Constitution. No one person shall be a Minister of more than two such Government Departments at any one time.

The Ministers selected by the Prime Minister shall form an Executive Cabinet with the duties and responsibilities as set out in this Constitution.

The High Court of Australia shall be as provided for in this Constitution and any judicial decisions relating to this Constitution must be with the unanimous agreement of all the Judges hearing the case.

In the light of the changes that are taking place in our modern society, an independent periodic Constitution Review process involving public participation is included in the Constitution to ensure it is kept relevant and up to date,

Every part of the Constitution, as listed in the Contents, shall only be amended by a nationwide Referendum, unless there is specific provision for either, or both Houses of Parliament, to make changes. The purpose of any such provision is limited to keeping the Constitution up to date and retaining a relevance to the changing society. Every such provision is specific in its application, and cannot be subverted to a wider application unless approved at a Referendum.

The power to set aside this Constitution, or its respective provisions, is not granted under any circumstances, but changes may be made via either a Class 1 or a Class 2 Referendum, except for any Sections designated as permanent.

DEFINITIONS

To properly understand the intent and purpose of this Constitution, it is essential that the meaning of the various terms and titles used must be defined, and uniformly applied. These words, titles and expressions are listed in relation to their perceived importance.

This list is subject to amendment and additions, as new words come into effect, or the meaning of older words are modified, but any changes can only be made with the approval of both Houses of Parliament. While these definitions are an integral part of this Constitution, amendments, additions and changes can be made without need of a Referendum.

The Australian Constitution

The Australian Constitution represents the Primary Law of the **Commonwealth of Australia**, and is a document that has been presented to the people of Australia in its entirety, and approved by them at a Referendum for adoption as a sovereign and independent nation. This Constitution can only be amended and changed by a nationwide referendum, except for the special provisions allowing either or both **Houses of Parliament** to make certain specific changes. As stated in the **Preamble**, the purpose of any such provision is limited to keeping the Constitution up to date and retaining relevance to the changing society.

The Preamble

This is a brief but comprehensive statement setting out the principles and philosophy by which the Government, and the legal system, must comply with the making and interpreting all laws. **The Preamble** is, at all times, an integral part of the Constitution and shall never be treated separately.

The Australian Council

An independent body set up by this Constitution to provide an overriding authority for the integrity and functioning of the Constitution in relation to the political, governmental and legal system adopted by this Constitution. Any reference to the **Council** in this Constitution shall mean the **Australian Council** unless otherwise defined. The powers and limitations are set out in the Constitution. The **Council** has no executive powers.

The Commonwealth of Australia

The Commonwealth of Australia is the nation of Australia, which was created by combining the separate **Colonies** of the 19th century under a federated arrangement, and includes any Territories under Australian Government jurisdiction. This term can be shortened to **the Commonwealth**, all of which have the identical meaning as the **Federation of Australia** or the **Australian Federation**. The full geographical definition of the Commonwealth is contained in **Schedule 3**

The Federal Parliament or the Commonwealth Parliament

In terms of this Constitution, the above titles will include both the **House of Representatives** and the **House of Senators**. Unlike the definition in the original British Act, this title does not include the

Australian Council which is a concept to replace specific functions of the Monarchy. **The Federal Parliament** is also referred to as **the Commonwealth Parliament**, or the shorter version of, **the Parliament**, all of which are identical in meaning.

Any reference to **Parliament** in this Constitution includes both Houses in relation to the issue concerned.

The State Parliaments

In terms of the States, the **State Parliament** means the existing Parliamentary arrangements in the respective States, whether that **Parliament** consists of one House or two Houses.

The House of Representatives

Commonly referred to as the **Lower House,** is the larger House of the Commonwealth Parliament, as set up in this Constitution.

The House of Senators

This House was originally conceived as a States' House, with each State having an equal number of elected Senators. The House is commonly referred to as the **Senate,** and in other respects, as the **Upper House.** It too is set up in the manner defined in this Constitution, covering its purpose and functions. The concept of a **Double Dissolution** of Parliament is denied in this Primary Law, and at no time shall the whole of the Senate membership be dissolved simultaneously with the House of Representatives. Only that half of the Senate due to stand at the next election shall be affected at any time.

Referendums

A Referendum is a nationwide process, as set out in this Constitution that allows every eligible voter to pass judgement on any proposal to alter, amend, or add to the existing wording of the Constitution, which is not otherwise covered by specific provisions in the Constitution. Two types of Referendum are contained in this Primary Law. Any question relating to changes to this Constitution will require majority approval by the voters, as well as the approval by the majority of the States. The second type of Referendum will deal with questions of national importance and only require agreement from the majority of the eligible voters.

Political Parties

A Political Party is an organisation set up for the principle purpose of getting members elected to the Australian Parliament. The organisation must be registered in conformity with the relevant legislation, both existing and any subsequent legislation, and comply with the conditions set out therein, as well as the provisions of this Constitution. The Political Party system is the weakest link in any aspirations for "good governance", especially when one party gets control of both Houses of Parliament. That is when the party members rule the nation in the interests of the Party, and invariably, at the expense of the nation as a whole. Thus, a Political Party with total control can represent the greatest danger for any nation. This Constitution aims to counter this potential threat by requiring a larger Parliamentary majority approval for identified national issues and by interposing the higher authority of the **Australian Council** in the process of assenting to laws.

Direct or indirect pecuniary interests

The definition of the above terms is to be read in the widest interpretation and shall include any form of remuneration or benefits received from any entity associated with any government-funded project, program or related entity. Indirect pecuniary interests will also include the elected politician's family or other forms of trust funds, and interests in any foreign organisation with related Australian government association, State or Federal.

Retrospectivity

The principle of applying laws in retrospect is expressly prohibited in this Constitution. Any legitimate actions or decisions based on the laws as they applied at that time, shall remain legitimate and shall not incur any penalty that may apply to a subsequent law or amendment of the previous law. This does not prevent an earlier action, or decision, from being modified to comply with the later provisions, if such is required, but no retrospective penalty or imposition will apply.

Citizenship

Citizenship of Australia applies to any person born in Australia to Australian parents or born to one parent who is an Australian citizen, irrespective of whether both parents agree or not. Citizenship also applies to people born outside of Australia to Australia parents, or as in the case above, to one parent who is an Australian citizen. Citizenship also applies to any person who complies with the requirements for naturalisation and completes the naturalisation process. Citizenship of Australia is exclusive to the Commonwealth of Australia and no citizen wishing to stand as a candidate for any Commonwealth, or State Parliament shall hold allegiance to any other nation by way of dual citizenship or any other obligatory condition. This does not prevent a naturalised citizen from receiving any pension entitlements from a foreign country, provided that entitlement is declared.

Australia's Population

As the population figure for Australia, and the respective States, is used in the formula for calculating each State's allocation of

Members for the House of Representatives, it is necessary to define what is meant by "population." Although the Parliament has a responsibility for every person living in the Commonwealth of Australia, for the purpose of the formula, only the recognised legitimate citizens of the nation, whether in Australia, incarcerated, or overseas, shall be included in the term "population." This term shall not be modified to apply only to eligible voters, as Parliament has a wider responsibility to include all the newly born and youths not yet of voting age. This population figure will be determined by the Bureau of Statistics as at the most recent Census.

Commonwealth Assets

The people of Australia are the rightful owners of all Commonwealth facilities, property and assets of any type, and the elected Government is always the caretaker of these assets and responsible for their proper maintenance and upkeep.

As caretakers, the Government also has a responsibility to assess the economic viability of the maintenance of these assets. Any proposals involving the leasing or selling of any Commonwealth asset shall require the approval of the rightful owners via a referendum before the proposed action can be implemented. The Government is obligated to publicly recommend whatever action can be taken that will be beneficial to the owners of Commonwealth facilities, property and assets.

Australia's money supply

The nation's "money" supply consists of all the physical "money" used in Australia, meaning the notes and coins produced by the Government as legal tender, as well as all digital "money" created as interest-bearing debt by the private banks licensed to operate in Australia.

Australia's status as a monetary sovereign nation is retained in this new Constitution by virtue of Section 144(i) and (ii). This means that the Australian Parliament has the sole authority for the creation of Australia's total "money" supply, and that includes the way the private banking sector operates.

Foreign Exchange

All financial transactions involving foreign currencies will be handled through the IMPEX system as set out in this Constitution.

A Periodic Constitutional Review Process

The Periodic Review shall be a process independent of the Government and the legal profession, but open to any interested person, group, or organisation, as well as the Local, State and Federal Governments, to submit proposals for amending the Constitution. The aim is to create the opportunity for every interested Australian Citizen to become involved in formulating changes to *their* Constitution.

This concept embraces a fundamental philosophy that must apply in our Democracy – that the Constitution of Australia is the exclusive property of the Citizens of Australia - it is *never* the property of the Government. *It is therefore rejected that the Commonwealth Government has the sole right to propose amendments to 'our' Constitution.* The right to alter the Constitutional intent rests solely with **the People** and not with the Government and certainly not with the High Court.

What is important is that the final outcome of the Process will be translated into definite action through a mandatory referendum of the publicly approved amendment proposals.

Commonly understood words

For the purpose of understanding the meaning of words in this Constitution, their commonly understood meaning shall always be used. For example, the word "may" indicates an indefinite state, where optional actions can apply, compared to the word "shall," which represents a clear and definite instruction without any options suggested, or implied.

A Parliamentary Session

A Parliamentary Session shall mean the continuous period from the official opening of Parliament to the official closing of Parliament at the end of the three-year term for elections. All elected members are required to be available for every sitting, as per the program agreed between the Houses of Parliament. There shall be no restrictions on how many sittings may be held during a calendar year, beyond the constitutional minimum of ten sittings, nor how long any sitting might last.

A Communications Monopoly

A national communications monopoly shall mean the single ownership more than two forms of national communication outlets in either the print media, the television media, the radio media or any combination of these.

CHAPTER 1

TRANSITION

A. An official referendum will be held for the adoption of this Constitution, which will be conducted under the existing rules of requiring a majority of the eligible voters and a majority of the States to approve its adoption. A simultaneous referendum will also be held to ask the people which title they prefer for the Head of State, Governor General, or President, and automatically, Governor or Vice President for the States. The result of this simultaneous referendum will be decided by the nationwide majority vote without the majority of the States being required. The Constitution shall be amended to use the agreed title without need of a referendum.

B. The acceptance of this Constitution represents a formal declaration of Australia as an independent nation and thus severing all political and monarchical ties with the United Kingdom. This act of severance shall apply to each State and Territory of Australia, irrespective of whether the State voted in favour of the Constitution or not.

C. With the adoption of this new Constitution, there will be a transition period until new elections are completed for all Federal Parliamentary seats and the successful candidates sworn in. During this transition period, the established Commonwealth and State

Parliamentary Governments and bureaucratic instrumentalities will remain in place and function as normal. No changes shall be made to either the State or Commonwealth bureaucratic personnel, or standard operating procedures.

D. The existing Commonwealth Government and bureaucracy shall become an Interim Government and bureaucracy until the transition phase is complete.

E. The State Governments and bureaucracies shall continue to function as normal, but as the new Constitution affects the regal appointment of the State Governors, as well as the Governor General, this will require changes to each of the State Constitutions. The States shall be given three months to appoint a Vice President/Governor by the two-thirds majority vote of their respective State Parliaments, as provided for in Section 17 of this Constitution. The States shall then proceed to implement the appropriate changes relating to the monarchy, as applicable to their respective Constitutions and their legislation. As that change over will be a long and complex procedure, the States can provide blanket legislation to cover the reinterpretation of regal terminology as an interim measure.

F. As part of the transition period, the existing State Governors shall participate as interim Australian Council members.

G. The Interim Commonwealth Government is not authorised to initiate any new legislative bills after the adoption of this Constitution but may continue with business in progress. Such business would then come under the auspice of the newly formed Australian Council at the expiration of the transition period.

H. On the adoption of this new Constitution, the Governor General, shall become the Acting Head of State, and within 30 days following the finalisation of the Referendum results, he/she shall convene a meeting of the six existing State Governors at the Government House in Canberra. This meeting will represent the inaugural meeting of the interim Australian Council under the conditions as defined in Chapter 2 Part 3 of this Primary Law. The interim Council shall declare a date for new Federal elections at an agreed time within six months from the adoption of the Constitution. All existing Parliamentary seats shall be declared vacant, as of the agreed date for elections. A period of one month shall be allowed for election campaigning. The elections will be held under the currently established procedures, for electorates and voting, but may be qualified according to the provisions specified in this Constitution. Any such qualifications will be set out in the writs provided by the interim Australian Council and signed by the Acting Head of State.

I. Upon convening this inaugural meeting, the existing Governor General will make available suitable facilities and staff of the office for the temporary use of the interim Council members.

J. The Governor General, as the Acting Head of State for the independent Australian nation, shall chair this inaugural meeting, as per the provisions as set out in Section 26 of this Constitution. All existing staff and facilities of the Government House will remain in place until the official Head of State takes up residence, and after that, at his/her discretion.

K. The existing Governor General, and each State Governor, whose appointments are dependent on the authority of the Queen (or King as the case may be) shall formally submit their resignation to that authority when the States select and appoint their replacement Vice President/Governor, as per Section E above. The Governor General will submit his formal resignation after chairing the inaugural official Australian Council meeting and the selection of the official Head of State from their membership, as per Section 22 of this Constitution. Mutually agreed arrangements will be made between the Governor General and the official Australian Council regarding vacating Government House and including approved remuneration for any truncated term of office. Similar arrangements shall be required in each of the States for the handing over of the Governor's office.

L. In the interim period between the Referendum and the completion of the above Federal election and the installation of the new Parliament, the Reserve Bank of Australia shall guarantee continued funding according to the approved budgetary expenditure from the previous or interim Government. This will apply to the functioning of all existing Federal Government services and facilities.

M. The Transition period shall expire when the following functions are complete,

(a) The official Australian Council is established and sworn into office as per the Oaths of Office listed in Schedule 1 of this Commonwealth Constitution.

(b) The Head of State is chosen and appointed from the Council's membership, and sworn into office by the Chief Justice of the High Court of Australia, as per Schedule 1.

(c) After each newly elected member of the Federal Parliament is duly sworn into office, as per Schedule 1, the official opening of Parliament shall be proclaimed by writ and conducted by the Head of State at a time and date specified by the Australian Council, but no later than fourteen days after all members have been sworn in.

From that point, the Transition period shall be declared expired.

N. At no time will the independent nation of Australia be without an Official or Acting Head of State, nor without the normal functioning of the established State and Commonwealth bureaucracies.

O. This part of Chapter 1 will become redundant, as from the opening of the newly elected Federal Parliament. If deemed appropriate, Parliament can then remove it from any subsequent publications of this Constitution without the unnecessary requirement of a referendum, but it will remain on record in Hansard.

CHAPTER 1

PART 1

THE FOUNDATION OF
THE AUSTRALIAN COMMONWEALTH

1. This new and relevant Constitution for an independent Australia adapts some of the concepts from the original Constitution of the Commonwealth of Australia as established by an Act of the British Parliament on the 9th July 1900. This new Constitution defines certain of those concepts as the foundation for establishing the primary law of the Australian Commonwealth. A significant difference between the original Constitution and this new Constitution is the philosophical declaration outlined in the Preamble. It represents the underlying philosophy of the society, which the people of the sovereign and independent Australia, choose to live by.

2. The legal principles of this new Australian Constitution are based on Australia's inherited Common Law practices, but shall be as modified and/or defined in this Constitution. Australia's Common Law is derived from the British Common Law, as contained in the established and accepted Charters from past centuries of British history.

3. The sovereign and independent nation of Australia shall be known by its full title as the Commonwealth

of Australia. For the purposes of this Constitution, and other appropriate use, the short title of the Commonwealth can be used.

4. The ultimate authority of the Commonwealth shall be vested in the Australian Council as defined in Chapter 1 Part 2 of this Constitution. The Federal Parliament of the Commonwealth shall be as described in the Preamble and consist of a House of Representatives and a House of Senators, whose duties and functioning are detailed in Chapter 2, Parts 1, 2, 3 and 4.

5. The Parliaments of the Commonwealth, both State and Federal, and the entire Australian Governmental system, which includes the office of the Nation's Head of State, the Australian Council, and all Australian Courts, shall be bound by the principles contained in the heritage of British Common Law, which subsequently forms the basis of Australian Common Law.

6. While these principles are derived from the British Common Law Charters and enactments, of which some of the main ones are as listed:

> Edward I. (Magna Carta) c. XXIX 1297:
> Charles I. c. I (Habeas Corpus) 1640:
> Charles II. c. 1 (Habeas Corpus) 1679:
> Bill of Rights 1688 Will and Mary
> English Bill of Rights 1689
> George III (Habeas Corpus Act) 1816:

The Charters themselves shall not be used as applicable laws within the context of Australia's Common Law and Australian Courts, but the principles contained therein shall not be denied.

None of these Charters and/or enactments shall limit the subsequent development of Australian law and practice concerning the principles of democracy, egalitarianism, and a sense of fair play that is an inherent part of the Australian character.

7. Australia shall be governed as one independent Nation, and no Federal Parliament shall legislate to divide the Nation. This does not prevent the formation of new States within the nation if the will of the people should consent to such action through a referendum.

8. The Federal Parliament shall not delegate the making of, or variation of laws, or the setting of regulations subject to laws made by this Parliament, other than under the principles provided for in Sections 5, 6 and 12 of this Constitution.

9. The Australian system of a three-tier elected, Local, State and Territory, and Federal Government, under the office of the Australian Council, through the Nation's Head of State, shall continue in accordance with, and subject to, this Constitution. Local Government shall remain under control to the respective State Governments unless approved otherwise with a Class 1 referendum.

10. Australia is declared a monetary sovereign Nation and the administration of its money supply is hereby placed and shall remain, under the total control of the Nation's Parliament through a Monetary Authority as set up in Chapter 4 Part 1. The supply of the Nation's money in whatever form it takes shall be regulated in accordance with the production and consumption capacity of the relevant population figures and the dynamics of the economy. A fundamental purpose of the Commonwealth Monetary Authority shall be in optimising the employment opportunities for any citizen willing and able to work. The Australian

money supply shall be issued under laws made by Federal Parliament, subject to the provisions set out in Chapter 4 Part 1 of this Constitution.

11. The Australian flag shall be adopted in accordance with the will of the people, as determined through a nationwide plebiscite. The Australian flag shall be flown each operating day at all schools and all State and Federal Government offices.

12. The reference to good government in this Constitution shall mean, but not be limited to, the framework and maintenance of a society that fosters, and practices, the right of independent personal and economic freedom that does not unlawfully encroach on the similar right of other people. Good government also means that the citizens of Australia shall be free from government, or other unwarranted interference, or prying. This shall include the freedom to use, within the law, all public places and facilities without fear from any sector, and the freedom to have and enjoy one's property and privacy without unwarranted and unlawful intrusion by any person whatsoever. While this Constitution recognises that all Government laws do impact on the unrestrained freedom of the people, those laws can also serve to protect their freedom. Thus good government requires that all laws be subordinated to maximising the concept of individual freedom for the people legitimately living in the Australian nation and its Territories.

13. This Constitution is clearly defined as the property of the people of Australia; therefore, it shall only be amended or altered by way of the provisions contained herein, and specifically in Chapter 9 Part 1, but with the exception of any sections prohibiting alteration, e.g. Section 103 and Section 270.

CHAPTER 1

PART 2

THE AUSTRALIAN COUNCIL

14. The institution of the Australian Council is hereby established as the supreme, non-political authority for the Australian nation, on the basis that Australian is a federation of the six States, New South Wales, Victoria, Queensland, Tasmania, South Australia and Western Australia. Provision is provided for the Territories of Canberra and Northern Territory to be included in the Council subject to the conditions contained in this Constitution.

15. The Australian Council shall, in principle, replace the Monarchy and the British Crown in all aspects whatsoever of Australian life and property.

16. Depending on the choice of title for the nation's Head of State, the Australian Council shall consist of the State Governors, or Vice Presidents, of the six Australian States, each of whom shall be chosen and appointed according to this Constitution.

17. As the current State Governors are appointed by the Queen, they shall be replaced in accordance with the process set out in this Constitution. Each State legislature, whether consisting of one or two Houses of Parliament, shall hold joint sittings, as applicable; to select and nominate a suitable replacement by a vote

of at least two-thirds of the total elected members. No business of any State Parliament shall proceed until a replacement Governor/Vice President is selected.

18. The chosen candidate shall then be sworn into office by the Acting Head of State during the transition period, or after the transition, by the official Head of State as chosen by the Council according to Chapter 1 Part 3, Section 38.

19. Whenever the population of Australian citizens exceeds one million for either of Australia's Territories, or when either Territory should become a State, as provided for in Chapter 5 Part 2, those Territories/States shall be entitled to select, appoint and remunerate, with the approval of two thirds of their elected Parliamentary members, a Representative to join the Australian Council.

20. In the event of a Territory or a newly created state, being in the position to appoint a member to the Council, that member shall have all the rights and authority applicable to each State member, including being nominated as Head of the Nation.

21. All existing Australian Acts of all the Parliaments of the Commonwealth and the States and Territories are to be progressively amended to replace the words 'Monarch', 'Sovereign', 'Queen', 'Crown' or any other words to the same effect, with the words 'the Australian Council'. Until such amendments are complete, the relevant words shall be interpreted as meaning "the Australian Council".

22. With the inaugural meeting of the official Australian Council, the State Governors/Vice Presidents shall elect one of their members to assume the position of Australia's Head of State. The election shall be by unanimous agreement, or secret ballot until one

member is selected by a clear majority. Subsequently, within thirty days before the expiration of the Head of State's appointment, the Australian Council shall convene a special meeting at the Government House in Canberra, to elect one of their members to replace the retiring Head of State, as per the conditions stipulated above in this Section.

23. The designated title for the Head of State shall be determined by a majority vote at a referendum of the Australian people to be held in conjunction with the referendum for the adoption of this Constitution, as provided for in Chapter 1 Part A.

24. Upon the election of a State Governor/Vice President, or a Territory Representative, to become the Head of the Australian nation, that person will resign their current position and the State or Territory will appoint a replacement, who would then become a member of the Australian Council.

25. The conditions, duties and responsibilities associated with Australia's Head of State are contained in Chapter 1 Part 3

26. The newly elected Head of State will take up the position as Chairperson of the Australian Council, but will not have a casting vote in the event of any evenly split decisions, under which circumstances; the decision will be decided in the negative. The Chairperson is denied a casting vote to prevent decisions being based on the views of a single person. It will also negate any potential influence relating to the prestige and status as Head of the Nation. This condition will still apply if a Territory appoints a member, which results in a Council of seven members, plus the Chairperson.

27. In the event the Chairperson is not available to attend, or participate in a scheduled Council meeting,

the members shall select a temporary replacement Chairperson for the duration of the meeting, along with that member's voting rights. Modern communications can allow the official Chairperson to participate without being physically present at the meeting.

28. The salaries and special conditions relating to the State Governors/Vice Presidents will remain in place, but in line with their dual responsibilities associated with membership of the Australian Council, the Commonwealth Government will recompense each Council member with a twenty-five percent loading on their existing remuneration from the State or Territory, as well as covering all cost and expenses relating to their Council responsibilities.

29. The members of the Australian Council shall be prohibited from receiving any other remuneration, or inducements, during their service on the Council, but neither shall their salary and conditions be reduced during their term on the Council.

30. It is recognised that there can be variations in the timing and duration of State Governor/Vice President appointments, and a possible Territorian appointment, but on the expiration of an appointment, the Council member will automatically be replaced by the newly appointed State Governor/Vice President, or Territory representative.

31. The Australian Council shall meet at least once a month, and a permanent schedule will be agreed by mutual consent, to establish the time, date and place of future meetings. The meetings shall be by rotation in the relevant State or Territory Government Houses if so agreed, but the Council may hold other meetings, as required by circumstances and events.

32. The Australian Council has the authority to resolve any controversial or political crisis, ideally by negotiation, but with the provision that the Council has the ultimate authority in the case of an unresolved crisis, to send the issue back to the people to vote at a new election.

33. The Australian Council has the responsibility for authorising the Head of State to assent to Parliamentary legislation, but only after it has been confirmed by a majority of the Council as being compatible with this Constitution. The Australian Council does not have the authority to approve any legislation that seeks to deny or revoke the principles inherent in the Common Law Charters and enactments referenced in Section 6 above.

34. The Australian Council shall have a period of not more than 90 days for deciding on the consent of any Commonwealth Parliamentary legislation, but if permission is not given, the legislation shall be returned to Parliament, with a public statement detailing the reservations why assent is not granted. Parliament can either amend the legislation or withdraw it entirely.

35. In the case of an appeal being justifiably accepted, at the discretion of the Australian Council, the Council shall be the ultimate authority in the observance of this Constitution in respect to any appeal related to:

a. All the Courts of the Commonwealth including the States and Territories

b. All Federal Government Departments.

c. All Police Services including Federal, State and Territories.

d. The Government Departments of all State and Territories to the extent they must comply with the provisions of this Constitution.

e. The Australian Council shall act as a body of last resort in relation to any High Court decisions, other than in a case involving impeachment. Within ninety days from any High Court decision, the Council shall have the authority to consider any formal appeal, and if found justifiable by the majority of the Council, it can instruct the High Court to review its decision. The review shall be based on the published reasons why the Council finds a conflict with the Constitution's intent and purpose. Any subsequent unanimous decision by the High Court shall be binding.

f. The Council shall decide on the acceptability and legitimacy of any issues brought before it and shall have the authority to make public their recommendations, which the relevant authorities shall then be obliged to consider. The Council is not granted any executive powers to enforce their recommendations in relation to any acknowledged issue, but no pending action in relation to the issue shall proceed until the recommendations are addressed and the issue resolved between the appropriate authorities and the party or parties concerned.

g. The Council shall be the party of last resort in deciding if the High Court shall address an issue should the Court have previously declined to allow a case being heard. The proponents of the issue shall have the opportunity to justify their reasons for a hearing to the Council, but the Council's decision is final.

36. Should any position on the Australian Council become vacant for any reason, the relevant State or Territory Parliament shall choose a replacement according to the procedures in place for appointing their nominee.

37. A quorum for every Australian Council meeting shall be a minimum of five members, but if a quorum is not available, a new meeting will be convened within seven days of the initially scheduled meeting.

CHAPTER 1

PART 3

THE HEAD OF STATE

38. As contained in Section 18, the inaugural meeting of the official Australian Council will elect one of the State Governors/Vice Presidents to the position of Australia's Head of State. The title of Governor General or President shall be determined by the simultaneous referendum associated with the referendum to adopt this new Australian Constitution.
39. The election and appointment as Governor General/President shall be for five years from the date he/she is sworn in by the Chief Justice of the High Court, with the Oath of Office as provided for in Schedule 1 of this Constitution.
40. The Nation's Head of State shall substitute for the functions of the Monarchy and the British Crown, in a sense, they represent a form of non-political authority. The Head of State is a representative of the Australian people in all symbolic aspects whatsoever of Australian life and property but without any implications of royal prerogative or hereditary succession.
41. The Head of State will take up the position as Chairperson of the Australian Council, as per Section 26.

42. The function and responsibility of the Head of State are to act as the nation's titular leader in performing the ceremonial and representative duties applicable to the position. The Head of State shall not perform any political function other than those related to ceremony, and the issuing of writs for proclaiming the opening of each session of Parliament. The Head of State shall not publicly express any political opinions.

43. At the expiration of the five year period, a new Head of State shall be elected from the Council members, under the conditions as contained in Section 22, with the provision that the retiring Head of State shall not be eligible for re-election.

44. The Head of State under this Constitution shall inherit all the responsibilities, applicable to the position of Governor General under the previous Constitution, but exclude any provisions of individual "reserve powers", or any other applicable written or unwritten convention.

45. The Head of State shall give assent to all Federal legislation on behalf of the Australian Council, but only after its compliance with this Constitution is considered and endorsed by a majority of the Australian Council.

46. All such assent, and other significant official documentation will be provided under the Seal of Australia, which is defined in Chapter 2 Part 4, Section 134, and is for the sole exclusive use by the Head of State.

47. The Head of State shall be the nominal Commander in Chief of the Defence Forces of Australia but shall not have the unilateral authority to command those forces contrary to Australian Council approval, or the

provisions of Chapter 2 Part 4, Section 137, except for the provision in Section 138 of this Constitution.

48. In the event of any temporary incapacity of the Head of State to perform his/her duties, the members of the Australian Council will choose a temporary replacement to act on behalf of the Head of State.

49. In the case of a more severe or permanent incapacity, a new Head of State shall be chosen in accordance with the procedure set out in Section 22.

50. In the event of the Head of State attempting to exceed his/her authority under this Constitution, any member, or members of the Council, shall have the authority to convene a special meeting of the Council for the exclusive purpose of deciding if impeachment of the Head of State is justified and/or warranted. If so decided, impeachment proceedings shall be conducted as per Chapter 7 Part 2.

51. The salary and expenses related to the office of the Head of State will be met by the Commonwealth Government, as provided for in Chapter 2 Part 4. The Head of State shall not be entitled to receive any additional remuneration, other than that specified in this Constitution, during the term of office, and nor shall his/her remuneration be reduced during the time in office.

52. The Governor General/President shall, with a mutually agreeable arrangement pending the transition period, as provided for in Chapter 1 of this Constitution, take up residence at Government House, and at his/her discretion, along with the staff and amenities associated with the position as Head of State.

CHAPTER 2

Part 1

THE COMMONWEALTH PARLIAMENT

53. The Commonwealth Parliament shall consist of the House of Representatives and the House of Senators, and the shorter title, the Parliament, is used in this Constitution when any parliamentary procedure must involve both Houses.

    i. There shall be a minimum of ten sittings of Parliament in any calendar year, but this shall be adjusted pro rata depending on the date of the adoption of this Constitution and after the first sitting defining the end of the Transition period.

    ii. The Head of State shall issue a writ proclaiming the time and date for the first sitting of Parliament at the commencement of the Parliamentary session following each three-year election. The program of sittings shall be agreed between the President of the Senate and the Speaker of the House of Representatives, after the inaugural sitting under this Constitution.

    iii. The Prime Minister, with the agreement of the Executive Council, may request writs to be issued for additional sittings outside of the agreed program, as and when deemed necessary.

54. Each House of Parliament has the Primary Law authority to implement specific rules and procedures independently of the other House. These rules and procedures, as developed and amended from time to time, shall be appropriately recorded in the publicly available Operations Manual applicable to each House. No unwritten conventions shall henceforth apply. These Manuals shall include a general range of disciplinary actions applicable to any breach of the Rules. The creation and maintenance of these manuals shall be the responsibility of the Speaker for the House of Representatives and of the President of the Senate, positions as provided for in Chapter 2 Parts2 and 3.

55. All powers, privileges and immunities applicable to every elected Member of Parliament shall be defined as in Schedule 2 of this Constitution and only amended with the agreement of the Australian Council following a written submission proposing each amendment. If a majority of the Council members agree with the amendments, the approved amendments shall be put to the Australian people via a Class 2 Referendum requiring only a majority of votes for acceptance, without need for a majority of the States agreeing.

56. Any Constitution provisions referring to Parliament shall mean the involvement of both Houses, whether by way of joint sittings or other means, but in accordance with the Constitution specifications for affirmative decisions.

57. Every elected Member of Parliament shall take the Oath of Office contained in Schedule 1 of this Constitution, and promise to serve the people of Australia by upholding the principles and intent of this Constitution, as defined in the Preamble, and in the Constitution itself.

58. Every candidate for election to Parliament must be an Australian citizen, either native born or naturalised, and shall be at least eighteen years of age, and not older than seventy years of age, which is the mandatory retirement age for Judges on the Australian Courts.

59. No person shall be eligible for election to both Houses of Parliament at the same time, but there shall be no restriction, other than the age limits in Section 58, to prohibit any Member who has served in one House and chooses to nominate for the other House.

60. No person shall be eligible to stand for Parliament if they are under any acknowledgement of allegiance, obedience or adherence to a foreign country, or are a citizen of a foreign country and holding rights or privileged relating to a foreign nation.

61. No person shall be eligible to stand for election to Parliament if they are an undischarged bankrupt, or declared insolvent in a Court of law, or if they are serving a criminal sentence, or subject to be sentenced. A person with a past criminal record, and no outstanding or other restrictions for the prior seven year period may stand as a candidate, provided that record is made public.

62. No person with direct or indirect pecuniary interests, as defined in Definitions above, in any Federal or State Government funded activity shall be eligible to nominate, unless all such interests are declared in a public Statutory Declaration, to include an official declaration renouncing all declared interests if elected. Any sitting Member of Parliament who chooses to stand for re-election must provide a similar public Statutory Declaration of their interests, along with the renunciation of those interests if re-elected. Any

direct benefits related to their previous parliamentary service shall be retained and continued if re-elected.

63. Each of the provisions in Sections 57 to 62 shall apply to any past or present member of the Commonwealth Defence forces, Public Service, Police Services and the judiciary should they wish to stand as a candidate for election. The payment of any pensions due shall be suspended during the time a candidate is elected and sits in Parliament.

64. The Parliament shall not make any legislation that alters or otherwise diverts the intent of the above provisions in Sections 57 to 62 but may seek any appropriate changes by a referendum of the people.

65. All the above relevant and applicable information shall be provided to the Electoral Commission by every candidate standing for election, whether a sitting member or a new candidate. Any sitting member in breach of the above provisions in Section 57 through to Section 62 shall be ineligible for re-election.

66. No elected Member of Parliament shall receive any other remuneration or benefit from any source while sitting as a member, other than those provided for in this Constitution, and periodically adjusted, as per the guidelines contained herein.

67. Each House of Parliament shall establish a bipartisan Parliamentary Rules Committee, consisting of at least five Members, but no more than nine. The Committees to include at least one member from each political party in each House, with the member chosen by secret ballot. The responsibility of the Committees is to ensure the rules laid down in the Operation Manual of the House are observed, and

to receive, and investigate, any official allegations or complaints made in writing, from any source, including the Citizen's Recall process, regarding a breach of the rules by a sitting Member. A Member so charged shall have the right to defend themselves in a manner of their choosing.

68. If a Member is found guilty of a breach of the Parliamentary Rules, as distinct from the constitutional rules laid down in Sections 57 to 62 and Section 66, the Committee shall recommend the appropriate disciplinary action to be imposed, as allowed for in the Manual of Rules. Any breach of the constitutional rules shall be directly referred to the Australian Council, with or without a recommendation for appropriate action.

69. If a sitting Member of Parliament is reported to the Parliamentary Rules Committee and alleged to have breached any provision in Sections 57 to 62 and 66, the Committee shall evaluate the report, and if deemed justified, submit a report to the Australian Council. The Council shall authorise the appropriate action, including initiating Impeachment procedures, as per Chapter 7 Part 2. Pending the outcome of the Impeachment process, the Council shall act accordingly, and if applicable, authorise the Head of State to officially expel the Member from Parliament. All entitlements and benefits otherwise due shall be denied, plus the possible refund of all, or part, of any remuneration and benefits, received from the time the breach of the rules occurred. The Member may also be open to civil jurisdiction if such is applicable.

70. Any issue deemed to have national importance, and to affect the whole population of Australia, shall require the approval of a minimum vote of two-thirds

of the total members in both Houses of Parliament. Such issues shall include, but not be limited to, for example:

a. Any declaration of war against any foreign country, other than if Australia is directly invaded by armed aggression, in which case the authority rests with the Commander in Chief to take immediate action, as per Section 47 above.
b. Any involvement of the Australian Defence Forces in any foreign conflict, or as a peace-keeping force
c. The implementation of any Treaty, Pact, or other Agreement that is intended to apply to the people of Australia and impact in any way on commerce and trade, or the public laws of Australia
d. The conditions for the sale or leasing of any publicly owned Commonwealth property, facilities or assets, to any foreign or domestically owned enterprise, but only after getting the people's approval to sell or lease each specific item through a nationwide referendum

CHAPTER 2

Part 2

THE HOUSE OF REPRESENTATIVES

71. The House of Representatives shall be the primary House of Parliament with its membership being based on a formula, which shall be related to the population figures, as determined by the latest Bureau of Statistics official census for the respective States and Territories.

72. For the purpose of this formula, the population figure shall be defined as every Australian citizen living in Australia and its Territories at the time of the most current Bureau of Statistics Census, plus any overseas Australian citizens who participate in that census.

73. The formula mentioned above provides a number, to be called a quota. This quota figure is determined by dividing the total population by twice the total number of Senators allowed for each State, plus the Territories of Canberra and Northern Territory.

74. The arrangement under the previous Constitution, of allowing each State to have twelve Senators and each Territory, two Senators, shall continue under this Constitution. Thus, the total number of Senators in the Australian Parliament, as provided for in Chapter 2 Part 3 Section 99 of this Constitution, is seventy-six (76)

75. Therefore, the quota is determined by dividing the total population figure by 152, being twice the number of Senators.

76. The number of House of Representatives Members allowed for each State is determined by dividing each State's population by the above quota.

    If the remainder in the State's calculation is more than half of the quota figure, then the State shall be entitled to one extra Member for the House of Representatives.

77. Each State population is determined in the same manner as the Commonwealth population figure, namely, from the latest Bureau of Statistics census.

78. The conduct of an election and the qualification of electors shall be as contained in Chapter 6 Part 1 of this Primary Law.

79. Until altered by the people of Australia through a referendum, members of the House of Representatives shall be elected for a fixed three-year term of office, except for the occasion of a vacancy occurring, whereby the replacement member shall only sit for the remaining portion of the three-year term.

80. Three consecutive terms in office shall be the maximum allowed for any member of the House of Representatives, after which they are disqualified from standing as a candidate for the House of Representatives at the next election. This does not prevent a person from standing for a Senate position, and it does not prohibit a person from seeking re-election to the House of Representatives at a later election.

81. The first sitting of the House of Representatives after an election shall be proclaimed by the Australian Council within 30 days of the finalisation of vote

counting and the declaration of the State and Territory members, irrespective of any subsequent or pending electoral disputes.

82. The first order of business after each election for the House of Representatives shall be the election of a Speaker to control the conduct of proceedings.

83. As a guarantee that the Speaker has the full support of the House, and is considered to be an honest, impartial and unbiased leader, the election shall require at least two-thirds of the total House membership approving the appointment.

84. The election shall be by secret ballot until one candidate is elected. No other business of the House shall proceed until a Speaker is elected.

85. The Speaker shall be present at all sittings of the House of Representatives, but if he or she is not available, an Acting Speaker shall be elected in the manner as set down Section 83 above and shall act as required in the Speaker's place for the duration of that sitting.

86. The Speaker, or the Acting Speaker, if applicable, shall not vote on any issue being decided on in the House, nor shall he or she participate in the debate other than in respect to the conduct of the proceedings.

87. Voting in the House of Representative shall only proceed when there is at least ninety percent of the total membership present and accounted for by the Speaker.

88. Any motion before the House shall at all times require an affirmative vote by a minimum of two thirds the members present before that motion can proceed to the House of Senators. Each member shall be entitled to one vote. The unwritten convention known as "pairing" shall no longer apply.

89. All bills relating to the annual budget for the normal functioning of the Government shall originate in the House of Representatives. Such bills shall not originate in the Senate. Apart from budget-related bills, the Senate shall have equal authority to initiate any other bills related to finance and/or financial issues. Any bill relating to finance, other than the budget bill, shall only deal with one specific finance issue, or proposal, and shall not include other unrelated items.

90. A Member may resign his or her place in the House of Representatives by submitting a letter to the Speaker, with copies to the Commonwealth Head of State and the State Governor/Vice President.

91. If a Member is absent from any session of the House of Representatives for four consecutive weeks, without the permission of the Speaker, the position shall be declared vacant. The Speaker shall duly notify the Head of State of the vacancy with a copy to the relevant State Governor/Vice President.

92. If a House of Representatives position becomes vacant for any reason within six months, or less, till the expiration of the three-year term, the position will remain vacant until the next election.

93. The Head of State shall issue a writ for a by-election to fill any declared vacancy, but only if the vacancy is the result of the death of a sitting Member, or the Member's incapacity to serve the term through illness, accident, or compassionate grounds.

94. A vacancy created for any reason other than those defined in Section 93 above, will not be filled, and any member relinquishing their position for whatever reason will be ineligible for a government post for ten years thereafter.

95. It shall be the responsibility of the Speaker to initiate the creation and maintenance of an Operations Manual, as per Chapter 1 Part 2 Section 54, covering the rules of procedures and conduct of business for the House of Representatives and the elected members. A general range of disciplinary actions applicable to any breach of the Rules shall be included in the manual.

96. The Speaker shall establish a bipartisan Committee consisting of one representative from every political party sitting in the House and one representative for whatever number of Independents may be elected. This Committee shall have a period of up to 90 days to compile the Manual. Any unresolved issues will be decided at the discretion of the Speaker.

97. This bipartisan committee shall also be responsible for liaising with the similar committee from the Senate in determining the definitions of any new word, phrases, or entities that may be necessary to add to, or amend, the list of definitions at the forefront of this Constitution. The joint recommendations shall be approved by the Parliament before being adopted and inserted into the Constitution. A Referendum shall not be necessary for this process, but public consultation can be allowed if deemed appropriate by the Joint Committee.

98. Any changes to Chapter 2 Part 2 shall only be allowed through a nationwide referendum.

CHAPTER 2

PART 3

THE SENATE

99. The House of Senators shall always consist of an equal number of members elected from each State, irrespective of the State's population. On the adoption of this Primary Law each State is entitled to elect twelve members, and the Territories of Canberra and Northern Territory, are entitled to two members each. Until altered by a referendum, these entitlements shall be adopted.

100. Senators shall only be elected for a maximum of two continuous fixed terms of six years, except as provided in Section 101 below. This does not prevent a retiring Senator from standing at a later election for either House of Parliament. The Senators shall be elected by the current electoral system of proportional representation as specified in Chapter 6 Part 1 of this Constitution. The qualifications of all candidates for the Commonwealth Parliament are defined in Chapter 2 Part 1.

101. After the first election under this Constitution, each of the newly elected State and Territory contingent of Senators shall be divided into two groups of equal number. The first group shall serve three years in office and the second group shall serve the six years in office.

The method of dividing the Senators into groups shall be by the random selection of numbers from a hat. The first six numbers of the State Senators and the first drawn number of the Territory Senators shall form the first group and the remaining numbers, the second group. After this first election under this Constitution, all Senators shall serve their fixed term of six years.

102. The existing arrangement for half of the State and Territory Senatorial positions becoming vacant at the expiration of three years shall continue with the adoption of this Constitution. The election for half the Senate positions shall be held simultaneously with the expiration of the House of Representatives three year fixed term of office.

103. This Constitution forbids Parliament from making any provision, or law, after the Transition period, for the dissolution of the whole of the Senate at any time, irrespective of any political or other reason.

104. The one exception being for the initial dissolution of the Parliament on the adoption of this new Constitution. Irrespective of the timing for the initiation of the inaugural Parliamentary elections, as per Chapter 1 Transition Section G, the whole of the Senate shall be vacated, and any person shall be eligible to nominate as a candidate, including the Senators vacating the office.

105. The first sitting of the House of Senators after any election shall be proclaimed by the Australian Council within 30 days of the finalisation of vote counting and the declaration of the State and Territory members, irrespective of any subsequent or pending electoral disputes.

106. The first order of business following an election and the resumption of sittings for the House of Senators

shall be the election of a Senate President to control the conduct of proceedings.

107. As a guarantee that the Senate President has the full support of the Senate, and is considered to be an honest, impartial and unbiased leader, the election shall require the vote of at least two-thirds of the total Senate membership approving the appointment.

108. The election shall be by secret ballot until one candidate is elected. No other business of the House shall proceed until a Senate President is elected.

109. The Senate President shall be present at all sittings of the House of Senators, but if he or she is not available, an Acting President shall be elected in the manner as set down Section 107 above and shall act as required in the Senate President's place for the duration of that sitting.

110. The Senate President, or the Acting President if applicable, shall not vote on any issue under deliberation by the Senators, nor shall he or she participate in the debate other than in respect to the conduct of the proceedings.

111. Voting in the Senate shall only proceed when there is at least ninety percent of the total membership present and accounted for by the Senate President or the Acting President.

112. Any motion before the Senate, including those listed in Section 106 and Section 108, shall at all times require an affirmative vote by a minimum of two thirds the members present before that motion can proceed. Each Senator shall be entitled to one vote, and all voting shall be by secret ballot.

113. As per Chapter 2 Part 2 Section 89, the Senate shall not initiate any bills relating to the annual budget but may propose amendments to such bills for consideration by the House of Representatives.

114. If a bill from the House of Representatives is presented to the Senate three times, with or without amendments, and the Senate is unable to agree to the bill, the Head of State, with the agreement of the Australian Council, shall call a joint sitting of Parliament. If a two-thirds majority vote is obtained, the bill will then go to the Australian Council to check its compliance with the Constitution, and eventual assent by the Head of State, if and when cleared.

115. The Senate has full authority to initiate bills in respect to any other issues, including financial or monetary, provided the issues are not directly related to the budget or funding for the normal functioning of the Government. Any bill dealing with such other finance or monetary issues shall deal with one specific item only and no other unrelated items.

116. It shall be the responsibility of the Senate President to initiate the creation and maintenance of an Operations Manual, as per Chapter 1 Part 2 Section 54, covering the rules of procedures and conduct of business for the House of Senators and the elected members. A general range of disciplinary actions applicable to any breach of the Rules shall be included in the manual.

117. The Senate President shall establish a bipartisan Committee consisting of one representative from each political party sitting in the Senate and one representative for whatever number of Independents may be elected. This Committee shall have a period of up to ninety days to compile the Operations Manual. Any unresolved issues will be decided at the discretion of the Senate President.

118. As per Section 97 above, this Senate bipartisan committee shall also be responsible for liaising with the

similar committee from the House of Representatives in determining the definitions of any new word, phrases, or entities that may be necessary to add to, or amend, the list of definitions at the forefront of this Constitution. The joint recommendations shall be approved by the Parliament before being adopted and inserted into the Constitution. A Referendum shall not be necessary for this process, but public consultation can be allowed if deemed appropriate by the Joint Committee.

119. A Senator may resign his or her place in the Senate by a letter to the Senate President, with copies to the Commonwealth Head of State and the State Governor/Vice President.

120. If a Senator is absent from any session of the Senate for four consecutive weeks without the permission of the Senate President, the position shall be declared vacant. The Head of State shall be duly notified of the vacancy by the Senate President with a copy to the relevant State Governor/Vice President

121. The Head of State shall issue a writ for filling the vacancy only if the vacancy is the result of the death of a sitting Member, or the Member's incapacity to serve the term through illness, accident, or compassionate grounds.

122. If a Senate position becomes vacant for the reasons listed in Section 121 above, and before the expiration of the six-year term, or three years as applicable, and that vacancy relates to a political party, the State Governor/Vice President shall invite the next person on the political party's Senate list, as of the last election, to fill the vacancy for the remainder of the term. If he or she declines the offer, the Governor/Vice President shall proceed down the list of candidates

until the offer is accepted, or the list of candidates is exhausted.

123. If no candidate is available from the political party related to the vacancy, the Governor/Vice President shall invite the next person eligible, as defined by the Electoral Office and according to the votes cast. Should that offer be declined, the State Governor/Vice President shall choose a candidate at his or her discretion to fill the vacancy for the remaining term of office.

124. A vacancy created for any reason other than those defined in Section 121 above, will not be filled, and any member relinquishing their position for whatever reason will be ineligible for a government post for ten years thereafter.

125. Any changes to Chapter 2 Part 3 shall only be allowed through a Class 1 nationwide referendum, as per Chapter 9 Part 1 Section 275.

CHAPTER 2

PART 4

THE FEDERAL GOVERNMENT

126. The Australian Council is the supreme Constitutional authority concerning the functioning of the Australian Parliament and all branches of the Australian Federal Government. It is also responsible for the administration of oaths required from all elected Members of the Australian Parliament and all Department heads of the Australian Government services including the Defence Department. The Australian Council, through the Head of State, is responsible for confirming the appointment and dismissal of Government Ministers, High Court and Federal Court Judges, Head of Government Departments and senior Defence personnel, in accordance with the recommendation of the Federal Executive Council, as defined in Section 131.

127. The Australian Council is also responsible for the Constitution compliance of all Parliamentary legislation, and the recommended actions proposed by the Executive Council. If these are deemed acceptable by the Australian Council, assent is granted through the Head of State for implementation.

128. The Australian Council has no executive power to become involved with the normal functioning of

the Australian Parliament, or the Australian Federal Government, other than as expressly provided for in this Constitution.

129.   The political party holding the majority of seats in the House of Representatives, or any coalition of elected members, which can claim a majority, shall have the Constitutional authority to elect one of their members to the position of Prime Minister. That member shall then be sworn into office by the Head of State under the oath contained in Schedule 1.

130.   The Prime Minister shall then have the authority to select and nominate elected members of either the House of Representatives or the Senate, to act as Ministers in charge of the various Government Departments, but so as no one person shall be the Minister of more than two Government Departments at the same time. Each nominated Minister shall swear before the Head of State, the oath as contained in Schedule 1, to serve the Australian people with honesty and integrity.

    i.   A Minister of a Commonwealth Government Department shall be ultimately responsible for the actions of that Department in complying with the legislation and ensuring the Department functions in accordance with its agreed annual budget.

    ii.   The appointed Head of each Bureaucratic Government Department shall also be required to take an Oath to serve the people of Australia, as provided for in Schedule 1 of this Constitution.

    ii.   All public servants employed by the Department shall perform their duties with honesty, fairness and in an unbiased manner in respect to the public, and shall be held accountable by the Minister for any breach of this responsibility.

131. The Prime Minister shall be the Chairperson of the Federal Executive Council which shall consist of all the appointed Federal Government Ministers as nominated and recommended by the Prime Minister and sworn in by the Head of State.

    i. On the adoption of this Constitution, the number of existing Ministries shall be retained as the base for the functioning of the Government and membership of the Executive Council.

    ii. Any increase in the number of Ministries shall require the approval of the people via a Class 2 referendum. However, the total number of Ministries can be reduced by five at the Government's discretion via amalgamation, or other means, without the need of a referendum.

    ii. The membership of the Executive Council shall expire at the discretion of the Prime Minister, or when a Member ceases to be elected.

132. The Federal Executive Council shall meet officially at least once a month, or more often as required, with a quorum of eighty percent of the Ministers present for ratification of decisions, as decided by a majority vote. Minutes shall be kept of all Federal Executive Council meetings.

133. If a Prime Minister chooses to create a group of what is termed "senior" Ministers, commonly referred to as the Cabinet, any decisions from this group must be ratified by the Federal Executive Council before implementation or passing a recommendation to the Australian Council.

134. The Federal Executive Council shall be responsible for the design and creation of the official Commonwealth

of Australia Seal, to be used by the Head of State with the approval of the Australian Council, for ratifying all official documentation relating to the independent Australian nation.

135. The Federal Executive Council shall be responsible for developing Government policy that is subsequently reflected in legislation. This shall include the amalgamation and/or creation of Government Departments, as conditions require. It shall also be responsible for developing and publishing a five year forward plan for Australia as part of the long-term planning of the nation, both of which shall be established in coordination with the elected State Governments.

136. The Federal Executive Council shall have the authority to formulate Australia's foreign policy and to recommend to the Australian Council the acceptance of any negotiated international treaty, which if it impacts on Australian laws, shall be put to referendum before ratification and implementation.

137. The Federal Executive Council is also authorised to recommend to the Australian Council the official non-combatant deployment of any Australia military or Government personnel to overseas assignments related to any conflict zone. The Council may confirm the deployment with or without adding conditions to the recommendation. No deployment shall exceed one calendar year in duration from the date of embarkation.

138. The Head of State, as Commander in Chief of the Armed Forces, shall have the authority to immediately declare Australia in a state of war only if Australia is directly attacked or invaded by hostile military forces. Under no other circumstances shall

the Head of State unilaterally declare war on a foreign country on behalf of the Australian people. Any combat deployment of Australian forces to a foreign country shall only be allowed if a formal declaration of war has been made by a two-thirds majority vote of both houses of the Australian Parliament, on the recommendation of the Federal Executive Council, and ratified by the Australian Council. Australia shall not become involved in a foreign war at the request of another country, except as provided for in this Section and the limited provisions in Section 137.

CHAPTER 2

PART 5

THE POWERS OF PARLIAMENT

139. Any draft legislation related to the responsibilities listed below in Section 143 shall be completely self-contained, and shall not rely on previous legislation for its implementation. Earlier legislation shall be repealed after assent is given to the new legislative bill, which may or may not incorporate relevant parts of any previously applicable legislation. As per this Constitution, retrospectivity is not allowed; hence, any decisions based on prior legislation shall not be open to challenge.

140. Parliament shall register and classify any recognised religious organisation wishing to practice in the Commonwealth, as provided for in Section 143(xl), but shall not make any law prohibiting the free exercise of any registered and recognised religious belief. Parliament shall not make any laws imposing a religious belief, or practice, on anyone in the Commonwealth of Australia. Parliament shall have the power to make laws concerning any religious activity or practice that involves coercion, intimidation, enforcement or violence against any individual in the Commonwealth. No religious test shall be allowed to disqualify any citizen from

employment with any public or private organisation, corporation, club, or group membership, within the Commonwealth.

141. All draft legislation created under Chapter 2 Part 5 of this Constitution, and subsequently agreed by both Houses of Parliament, shall be made available, in full, for general public comment and formal submissions, for a minimum period of four weeks from the date of Parliamentary agreement. Any draft legislation consisting of more than fifty (50) pages, or fifteen thousand words, shall require a minimum period of eight (8) weeks for public comment and submissions.

142. Following the designated period for public comment and submissions, both Houses of Parliament shall establish bipartisan Review Committees to evaluate the submissions and publicly determine if they warrant any revision to the draft legislation. Upon final agreement from both Houses of Parliament, the draft legislation shall be delivered to the Australian Council for assent by the Head of State as per Sections 33 and 34.

143. Subject to the identified provisions set out in this Constitution, and any subsequent amendment through a national referendum, the Federal Parliament shall have the power to draft laws for the effective and economic functioning of the following responsibilities.

   i. The exclusive creation and management of Australia's money supply in every form of legal tender, whether coins, notes or digital "money", but controlled in relation to the population growth, Australia's productive capacity and capability, and Australia's consumption capacity, as provided for in Chapter 4 Part 1.

ii. The legislative control of all forms of banking and banking practices within Australia and its Territories, other than State Government owned banks that operate within State boundaries, provided the State Banks comply with the national and prudential banking practices.

iii. The permanent separation of all commercial retail banking, private and publicly owned, from investment and equity banks, as per Chapter 4 Part 1.

iv. The establishment of an import/export facility to control all Federal, State and private foreign currency transactions, as detailed in Chapter 4 Part 1.

v. The implementation and management of Australia's foreign currency transactions according to the Impex system as set out in Chapter 4 Part 2. This involves the creation of the separate currency to be called Impex dollars. The Impex system shall be the responsibility of the Bank of Australia as provided for in Chapter 4 Part 2.

vi. The implementation and management of a universal debit tax system, without exemptions, on all financial transactions within Australia and its Territories, up to but not exceeding one percent of the value of the transaction. This limiting rate shall only be changed by referendum and not by legislation. Any attempt to avoid paying this tax shall be treated as tax avoidance, and the appropriate legislation will carry substantial penalties, including fines and up to five year's incarceration.

vii. All forms of international and domestic trade and commerce with other countries and between the

States, with the exception of ratifying any trade treaty unless the treaty is approved by a national referendum. The purpose of this provision is to encourage Australian enterprise and initiative but within the parameters of laws laid down by the Parliament.

viii. The defence of the Australian nation and its Territories, and the adequate maintenance of defence forces necessary for that purpose, including national service if deemed appropriate. At no time shall the defence forces be used to quell civil unrest within the Australian nation. Any deployment of Australia's defence forces outside of the Australian nation is provided for in Section 137 and 138 of this Constitution.

ix. The legislative control of Australia's legal system to ensure it is confined to the Parliament and remains as independent of the Government as is possible. Parliament shall have the authority to initiate legal processes it deems appropriate and necessary in the interests of justice and truth.

x. The establishment of a Federal Police service for dealing with federally related criminal activities and police procedures outside of a State's jurisdiction. The Federal police shall provide Police services for the Territories and all Federal Courts when required, but in cooperation with the State Police service, if appropriate.

xi. The continuation of a publicly owned essential communication service, including postal services, telecommunications and any other forms of electronic communication deemed necessary for Australian commerce and national defence.

xii. The establishment of a Foreign Investment Board for the regulation of all foreign corporations, enterprises, subsidiaries or joint ventures, trading and/or operating within the limits of the Commonwealth under any capacity whatsoever. The Board must ensure at least fifty-one percent genuine and legitimate Australian ownership within five years of the commencement of any foreign owned or controlled business.

xiii. All forms of navigational aids for sea and air navigation, regularly upgraded to ensure the best possible safety record for public, private, commercial and defence operations at sea and in the air.

xiv. All forms of commercial shipping in Australian waters whether national or international carriers, but excluding State commercial ships that operate within State waters, except all shipping must conform to the federal safety standards for commercial shipping operations.

xv. Astronomical and meteorological observations:

xvi. A comprehensive quarantine service, to ensure, as far as technology and practical surveillance allows, that the entry of persons, goods, organic material, or livestock coming into Australia, in any form whatsoever, shall not potentially expose the people, property or the environment to danger, or represent a hazard to the nation's wildlife and plant life through disease, or pests, or an introduced species of any type whatsoever.

xvii. The continuation of the five-year Census program and the collection of statistics under strict privacy conditions by the Bureau of Statistics, for public use within six months of the completion of the Census.

xviii. The regulation of all forms of commercial fishing, both national and international, within Australian territorial waters, and any land or sea-based processing of the catch, but in cooperation with the States regarding State fisheries regulations, quotas and licences that do not conflict with the national regulations.

xix. The regulation of all national and foreign insurance business related to Australian interests, to ensure prudential viability and policies compatible with Australian law. State insurance business and policies applicable within the limits of the State concerned is exempt, provided any such business complies with federal prudential and policy standards.

xx. The overseeing of national metric weight and measure standards throughout Australia, and in respect to the import and export of any goods or products whatsoever.

xxi. Bankruptcy and insolvency within the context of Australia Law.

xxii. Copyrights, patents of inventions and designs, and trademarks.

xxiii. The regulation of immigration quotas in relation to Australia's employment requirements, refugee obligations, willingness to accept and adapt to the Australian cultural standards and way of life, but subject to verifiable security checks to minimise the entry of criminals or other unsuitable immigrants into Australia.

xxiv. The naturalisation of aliens after a minimum of three years continuous residence within the Commonwealth, who can demonstrate their ability to speak, read and write English to a reasonable standard of Primary School level. All candidates for naturalisation must renounce any allegiance to a foreign power and be prepared to swear allegiance to Australia. Dual citizenship shall be permitted and acknowledged on application to the Minister of Immigration specifying the reason and/or purpose why dual citizenship is necessary.

xxv. Regulations regarding marriage, divorce and matrimonial issues to be uniform throughout the Commonwealth, including same-sex relationships, and applicable to Australian citizens wherever domicile. These regulations shall apply to parental rights and the custody and guardianship of infants. Australian law applies to all parents domicile in Australia, irrespective of nationality. Outside of Australia, the law only applies to Australian citizens.

xxvi. Earnings and asset-based means-tested age pensions for every Australian citizen of sixty-five years of age and over that shall not fall below 30% of the national average weekly wage, and similarly for invalid pensions, which shall be paid to all Australian citizens entitled, by a Doctor's certification, for the disability.

xxvii. The provision of earnings and asset-based means tested maternity allowances, widows' pensions, child endowment, unemployment benefits, pharmaceutical, sickness and hospital benefits, medical and dental services benefits, family allowances, and educational allowances.

xxviii. The service and execution throughout the Commonwealth of the civil and criminal process as they relate to Commonwealth matters.

xxix. External affairs, but strictly limited to laws, treaties and agreements taking effect outside of the Commonwealth of Australian. This provision excludes any application affecting the internal affairs of the Australian Commonwealth. Any foreign treaty to which Australia is to become a participant must include provision for its review within a maximum period of ten years.

xxx. The acquisition of property on just terms and market valuation from any State or person for any purpose in respect of which the Commonwealth Parliament has the power to make laws:

xxxi. Conciliation and arbitration for the prevention and settlement of industrial disputes extending beyond the limits of any one State.

xxxii. Industrial relations in respect national safety standards and business practices in respect to employee/employer relationship, environmental concerns and competitive practices.

xxxiii. The control of railways to ensure access and transport of all branches of the armed forces when deemed necessary in relation to the nation's security and defence, and as appropriate.

xxxiv. The acquisition, with the consent of the people via a State referendum, of any railways of the State on terms arranged between the Commonwealth and the State.

xxxv. Railway construction and/or extension in any State with the consent and contractual agreement of the Parliament of that State.

xxxvi. Matters referred to the Federal Parliament by the Parliament of any State or States, but so that any resulting law shall extend only to the State or States by whose Parliaments raises the matters.

Any such law the applicable States choose to adopt must not create discrimination between the other States.

xxxvii. The management and control of the nation's waterways or rivers that pass through more than one State, but in coordination and agreement of each State involved.

xxxviii. The proper care, maintenance and efficient operation of all publicly owned Federal Government assets, including their sale or lease, if such is approved by the people, as the legitimate owners, at a Class 2 national referendum.

xxxix. The continued functioning of the Electoral Commission, as established on the adoption of this Constitution, but amended to comply with the conditions for candidature as set out in Chapter 2 Part 1 of this Constitution.

xl. The official registration of any recognised religious organisation wishing to formally practice in the Commonwealth. Every such organisation shall be classified in terms of the organisation's status, monetary and otherwise, and the activities to which it may be permitted to offer.

CHAPTER 3

PART 1

JUDICATURE

144. The ultimate judicial power shall reside in the High Court of Australia, as defined in Chapter 3 Part 2, but lesser judicial power shall reside in every other Federal Court, as created by the Parliament, and any other Court the Parliament invests with Federal jurisdiction.

145. The Federal judicature is responsible for the service and execution throughout the Commonwealth of the civil and criminal process as they relate to Commonwealth matters and Australian Federal law.

146. Subject to this Constitution, the laws, the public Acts and records, and the judicial proceedings of the States shall be recognised throughout the Commonwealth, but only when the Federal Parliament has prescribed the manner in which each such act, record, and/or proceedings shall be proved applicable to Federal law, and have an effect on Federal jurisdiction.

147. When the law of a State is inconsistent with a law of the Commonwealth, the latter shall prevail, if and when it is successfully challenged in a Federal Court. If found inconsistent, the State law shall be deemed invalid until amended, and the inconsistency addressed by the State Parliament. Retrospectivity shall not apply.

148. The Federal Parliament shall have the authority to create such other Federal Courts as deemed necessary, and to invest other Courts with Federal jurisdiction for specific functions and duration, and with a status, and/or designation, as deemed appropriate by the Parliament.

149. The Speaker of the House of Representatives and the President of the Senate shall create a Joint Select Committee of no more than four suitably qualified elected representatives from each House, to solicit recommendations for the appointment of judges to any Federal Court when appropriate, but excluding the High Court of Australia. The Committee's ultimate recommendation shall be submitted to Parliament for the formal approval and endorsement by the Australian Council. Any objection to the Committee's recommendation shall only be allowed on the basis of verifiable proof of unsuitability.

150. All Federal Judges, when appointed, may remain in office until reaching the maximum age of seventy years of age, or earlier retirement, and no Federal Judge shall be appointed who has attained that age.

151. A Federal Judge may resign the position by personally writing a letter of resignation addressed to the Head of State and subsequently acknowledged with the approval of the Australian Council.

152. A Federal Judge may be relieved of the position on the grounds of proven misbehaviour, but only after the impeachment procedure, as contained in Chapter 7 Part 2 of this Constitution. On the recommendation of the Select Committee, as per Section 149 above, a Federal Judge can be relieved of service by approval of the Australian Council, on the grounds of incapacity to perform the duties of office.

153. The joint select Committee shall also be responsible for recommending to Parliament, the respective remuneration packages for each level of Federal judicial appointments, including that of the High Court Justices. The approved remuneration package shall not be reduced during the term of office of any Judge, but may be reviewed by the Select Committee after an election.

154. No retired Federal Judge over the currently designated retirement age of seventy years shall be eligible to sit on any Federal Government Commission convened for a specific inquiry, or for any other purpose, except for a voluntary, non-remunerative, advisory capacity.

155. Parliament shall not make any laws preventing a citizen from proceeding against the Commonwealth, or a State, in matters within the control of the Commonwealth and/or its relationship with a State.

156. All trials, on indictment, or otherwise, whether State or Commonwealth, which include a penalty of more than one year's imprisonment, or a fine of more than five thousand dollars, shall offer the accused the following options. Either a trial by a jury of twelve peers, a hearing before a judge, or panel of judges, at the discretion of the accused. Every such trial shall be heard in the State or Territory where the offence is alleged to have occurred, but if the alleged offence occurred elsewhere the trial shall be held at a location within the Commonwealth, as agreed by the Defence, on behalf of the accused, and the Prosecutor. If agreement cannot be reached the Federal Attorney General shall decide the location of the trial.

157. Parliament shall make laws dealing specifically with the selection, empaneling and procedures relating to a jury and the function of a jury trial. No judge

shall be permitted to instruct a jury as to their findings, but when requested, shall advise the jury on elements of law in relation to the facts and evidence presented at the trial. All costs shall be attributed to the prosecution if an accused is found not guilty.

158. When the circumstances justify the benefit for having more than one judge involved, Parliament may prescribe the number of judges for any jurisdiction in any Federal Court, other than the High Court, but the minimum number shall be three judges.

CHAPTER 3

PART 2

THE HIGH COURT

159. With the adoption of this Constitution and the completion of the Transition period, the current High Court of Australia shall be reconstituted with seven judges made up of one judge nominated from each State and one judge to represent the Territories of Canberra and the Northern Territory.

160. The appropriate legal fraternity in each State, and the combined Territories, with the participation of all registered lawyers, shall nominate a candidate as their choice for the High Court position and present a detailed recommendation to the Parliament of the State or Territory concerned. The appointment of the chosen candidate must be endorsed by a two-thirds majority of the combined Houses of the State or Territory Parliament, as the case may be. Any objections to the recommendation must be based on provable allegations of unsuitability.

161. This State and Territory appointment process must be completed within six months from date set by the Australian Council for the initial change over. The same six-month provision shall apply for the replacement of any judge before the date of retiring from the High Court. In the event of any judge

leaving the High Court for reasons other than retirement, the State and/or Territory involved shall have a maximum of six months to nominate a replacement. Should there be any delay in appointing a suitable replacement, the High Court can continue to function provided there are at least five justices available.

162. All Justices of the High Court shall take the oath of office as administered by the Head of State and as per the Oath set out in Schedule 1.

163. The remuneration of all High Court Judges and costs associated with the functioning of the High Court shall be provided by the Federal Government, and all justices shall comply with the mandatory retiring age of seventy years.

164. Any current High Court Judge not subsequently reappointed under the revised appointment process shall be entitled to receive the current annual remuneration as calculated to the age of seventy years, plus applicable superannuation, but excluding any expense allowance related to the time not served.

165. At the first meeting of the seven appointees, they shall choose, by whatever process they mutually agree upon, one member to be the Chief Justice of the High Court.

166. The High Court of Australia shall be the supreme legal authority in determining the intent and interpretation of this Constitution, and any laws made by Parliament, but always in accordance with the principles and philosophy set out in the Preamble.

167. All decision of the High Court must be by unanimous agreement. If unanimity cannot be reached the Chief Justice is responsible for presenting a detailed report to Parliament outlining the reasons why unanimity

cannot be achieved, with or without recommendation as to what needs to be done to clarify the issues raised.

168. No Justice of the High Court shall be removed from office except on the grounds of proven misconduct or incapacity to serve, and only with the authority of the Head of State acting on the assessment of the Australian Council.

169. A High Court Judge shall only be relieved of the position on the grounds of proven misconduct, if so decided at an impeachment procedure, as contained in Chapter 7 Part 2 of this Constitution.

170. A High Court Judge may resign the position by personally writing a letter of resignation addressed to the Head of State and subsequently approved by the Australian Council.

171. The High Court shall have jurisdiction to hear and determine appeals from any judgements, decrees, orders and sentences from any other Federal Court, or Court exercising Federal jurisdiction. The High Court may also hear appeals from any State or Territory Court in the Commonwealth of Australia if granted by the State's or Territory's, Supreme Court.

172. The decision of the High Court shall be final in all cases, subject only to a review by the Australian Council if requested under Section 35(e) above.

173. The High Court shall have the authority to hear directly, without having being presented to a lower Court, any matters dealing with

(a) an international treaty that impacts on Australian law

(b) or affecting any official representatives of other countries

(c) in which the Commonwealth is a party to either suing or being sued by a person or any other entity.

(d) issues between States and/or residents of different States that cannot be resolved within the State's legal or political systems, but only if referred to the High Court by the Supreme Court of a State involved.

(e) A Writ of Mandamus, injunction, or prohibition is sought against an officer of the Commonwealth.

(f) Other matters which the Federal Parliament may determine to justify a direct hearing by the High Court.

174. The High Court shall have the authority to determine the number of judges appointed to a hearing, other than a case involving a Constitutional issue, which must always include the full bench of the High Court.

175. At no time shall Parliament prevent the High Court from hearing and determining an appeal from a Supreme Court of any State or Territory. Nor shall the High Court reject hearing such an appeal when granted by the State's or Territory's Supreme Court.

CHAPTER 4

PART 1

FINANCE

176. Section 143(i) gives the Commonwealth Parliament the exclusive power to control and manage the money supply required for the monetary sovereign nation of Australia. The Reserve Bank of Australia shall be re-constituted and re-named as the Bank of Australia and shall manage and administer Australia's total money supply.

177. As per Section 10 above, Parliament shall establish an independent Monetary Authority to be chaired by the Governor of the Bank of Australia, and consisting of a single, suitably qualified and nominated representative from within the following peak bodies in Australia

   a. The Business Community
   b. The Unions
   c. The Religious Community
   d. The Youth Community
   e. The Rural Community
   f. The Scientific Community
   g. The Aborigine Community
   h. The Military Community
   i. Retirees
   j. and a Government representative

The function of the Monetary Authority shall be to determine monetary policy with respect to the total annual money supply, taking into account population projections, employment, and the productive and consumption capacity of the nation. The Monetary Authority shall have access to any advice and data needed to determine their agreed proposals. The aim of the policy proposals is to benefit the people of Australia by supporting industry, maintaining employment, encouraging initiative, developing sustainable energy and developing Australian resources and infrastructure. The proposals shall be made public before being submitted to Parliament, with or without amendment, for ratification and translation into legislation covering the authorised programs.

178.	Section 143(ii) further provides for the Commonwealth Parliament to legislate for the control of national banking in Australia, which includes all aspects of retail and investment banking as currently carried out by the private banks, whether publicly, privately or foreign owned. The Bank of Australia shall be responsible for the sale of all credit access to the private retail banks and any publicly owned State banks, as proposed by the Monetary Authority and subsequently recommended for legislative approval by Parliament and authorisation by the Australian Council. The net proceeds of these sales shall be deposited in the Consolidated Revenue Account of the Government.

179.	The re-constituted Bank of Australia shall be the depository of all Federal Government revenue and the maintenance of the Federal Government's Consolidated Revenue Account.

180.	The Bank of Australia shall not function as a lender of last resort to the private banking sector, and no legislation or change in the Bank of Australia's Constitution shall be permitted to alter this restriction.

181. There shall be a separation of commercial retail banking from any form of investment banking, with the distinction that only majority Australian owned retail banks shall be allowed to access the Government approved credit facilities for advancing loans to their customers. These approved retail banks shall be required to take out adequate insurance to guarantee Government and/or shareholder approved levels of deposits as related to the bank's customers.

182. Any approved retail bank that is unable to arrange such insurance shall be in breach of its licensing requirements and shall be required to show cause why the bank should not have its licence revoked and/or be declared bankrupt.

183. All forms of investment banking shall take sole responsibility for any risk involved with their investment portfolio. The bank's management shall be entirely responsible to their shareholders, investors and clients in undertaking due diligence analysis of each and every investment, with the full knowledge that the Government of Australia will not support any investment bank in trouble.

184. Any foreign-owned bank licensed to operate in Australia shall comply with the applicable Australian regulations and prudential standards, and all foreign currency transactions shall be processed through the Impex system as detailed in Chapter 4 Part 2 of this Constitution.

185. The Bank of Australia shall establish a Department to be responsible for the creation of all physical currency

to be used in Australia, both in notes and coins, as well as printing any form of approved financial instruments, such as bond certificates, when appropriate.

186. Only the digital currency, as legislatively approved, will be sanctioned by the Bank of Australia and classified as legal tender, for acceptance in payment of any Commonwealth or State Government charges whatsoever.

187. Any contract, private or public that involves non-approved digital currency shall be unenforceable in any Court in Australia.

188. As per Section 143 (v) and 143(i) and (ii) the Parliament shall have the responsibility to provide sufficient annual revenue for the Government to discharge all the commitments and functions, which are approved in accordance with the five-year forward plan as per Chapter 2 Part 4, Section 135.

189. No money shall be drawn from the Consolidated Revenue Account unless approved by Parliamentary legislation, except for the provision allowed in Chapter 1 Section K during the transition period.

190. The cost, charges and expenses related to the collection and management of the Commonwealth Consolidated Revenue Account shall be defined and approved by Parliament and form the first charge against this account.

191. Under Section 143(i) which establishes the Commonwealth as a monetary sovereign nation, Parliament shall legislate for any and every proposed action related to the raising of revenue, including the sale of credit to the private and/or public retail banks in Australia, as per Section 178. In this latter case, the recommendations of the Monetary Authority should be adopted unless valid argument is raised to return

the recommendation to the Monetary Authority for amendment.

192. All Commonwealth revenue and expenditure shall be rigorously monitored and subject to an annual audit at the minimum, but more frequent audits can be made if deemed necessary. All audit reports shall be tabled in Parliament and made available to the public.

193. All Commonwealth Government expenditure shall be allocated on the basis of a Departmental budget for each project, or expense allocation, and approved by the Minister of the respective Department. The figures for every budget item shall be available to the public, without exception. The public service Department Head shall be directly responsible to ensure each allocation is appropriately managed. No approved allocated expenditure shall exceed the budget by more than fifteen percent without the Minister's approval.

    a. An additional function of the Monetary Authority shall be the creation of an independent Remuneration Committee of six personnel, as chosen by the Monetary Authority, to assess and recommend to the Australian Parliament the appropriate range of remuneration packages applying to the various levels of politicians and senior bureaucrats.

    b. These packages shall be reviewed on an annual basis in line with whatever appropriate criteria the Committee decides.

    c. The Minister responsible for a Government Department, together with the Department Head shall use their approved remuneration packages as the benchmark for establishing the levels of remuneration for the various grades of public servants employed within the Department concerned

d. The current remuneration packages applicable at the adoption of this Constitution shall form the benchmark for future reviews, but on the provision that no remuneration for any public servant shall exceed that payable to the Prime Minister.

CHAPTER 4

PART 2

TRADE AND COMMERCE

194. As per Chapter 2 Part 5 Section 143(v) the Bank of Australia is responsible for the management of Australia's foreign currency transaction by the Impex system as set out herein. Details for the operation of the Impex system shall be contained in legislation, but will conform to the following guidelines.

    i. All foreign currency transactions involving Australia's legal tender and/or financial instruments shall be conducted through the single Impex facility, set up as a Department of the Bank of Australia, and available through any branch of the Bank of Australia in Australia.

    ii. All foreign currency earned from exporting shall be converted to Australian currency at the going exchange rates, and the exporter issued with a certified Impex draft for the equivalent amount in Impex dollars.

    iii. The Impex Department of the Bank of Australia will manage the marketing of Impex dollars as the source of all foreign currency required by anyone wanting to acquire foreign goods or services. Depending on the availability of the foreign currency, the holder of an Impex draft could add a premium when selling their Impex dollars. This potential premium for exporters would provide an incentive to increase their export earnings, and at the same time, create a deterrent against foreign spending.

iv. The Impex Department of the Bank of Australia shall judiciously purchase Impex dollars to maintain a slightly positive exchange rate and thus encourage the exporters. The Impex Department could use their accumulated foreign currency to sell into the market for managing a high exchange rate, if necessary. Alternatively, the accumulated balance could be used to begin paying down the government share of the accrued foreign debt.

v. Any sale of Australian owned assets to foreign buyers shall be processed through the Impex system after receiving Commonwealth or State Government approval, as applicable.

vi. Any repatriation of Australian earnings converted to a foreign currency by a foreign entity of any description, from the sale of assets or the earnings from an investment, shall be processed through the Impex system.

vii. The sponsors of any Credit or Debit Card that allows foreign currency transactions shall be responsible for obtaining Impex dollars on behalf of their customers before finalising the transactions.

195. The Parliament shall not propose any legislation related to trade and commerce that gives preference to any State or Territory in comparison to the other States or Territory. Any existing legislation in conflict

to this provision shall be repealed and deemed invalid from the date proclaiming this Constitution, but no retrospective action shall be allowed in relation to any such prior legislation.

196. The Parliament shall not propose any legislation that deprives a State, or a resident of the State, from the reasonable use of the water of State inclusive rivers, as defined by State laws, for irrigation or other State approved purposes, except as provided for in Section 143(xxxv) dealing with national rivers, or waterways.

197. Parliament shall make laws covering the incorporation of all commercial enterprises, national or foreign, whose business operations extend beyond the borders of any one State or Territory. Those laws shall include the necessary and appropriate overseeing of ethical business practices for all federally registered commercial enterprises irrespective of the type of operation whether incorporated, a partnership, a charity, or any other arrangement whether in the private or public sector.

198. Parliament can make laws with respect to fair and honest trade and commerce practices that protect the general public from unethical and deliberate misrepresentation.

199. Parliament shall not make any laws that restrict the functioning of a free press to publish the facts and truth of any issue. Parliament shall be responsible to ensure the widest range of economically feasible forms of communication outlets are maintained and free from monopoly control. A communication monopoly shall be defined as ownership of more than two national communication outlets at the same time.

CHAPTER 5

PART 1

THE STATES AND TERRITORIES

200. The Constitutions of each State and Territory of the Commonwealth shall continue in force with the adoption of this Constitution. Until fully amended to remove all references to the monarchy and have such references replaced with the Australian Council and Vice President, as applicable; those monarchical references shall be read as meaning the Australian Council and/or the Vice President.

201. All powers vested in the States and Territories as at the adoption of this Constitution shall remain in place and shall apply until any conflict with this Federal Constitution renders those powers invalid from the date when a Federal Court proclaims its decision.

202. Every law in the States and Territories shall remain in force with the adoption of this Federal Constitution but shall become subject to this Constitution. Any law found to conflict with Federal law by a Federal, or State Court shall be deemed invalid from the date pronounced by the Court and until amended to conform to the Federal law. Any actions taken prior to invalidity being established shall be considered lawful. No retrospective actions are permitted in relation to an amended or repealed law.

203. As per Chapter 1 Part 2 Section 17, the State Governors shall formally announce their resignation to the Monarch and the State Parliaments shall initiate the provisions of this Constitution to select and appoint, or reappoint, a person to be the State Governor/ Vice President. In the event of the incumbent being replaced, they will be entitled to the remuneration due for the remainder of their term in office, but excluding any expense allowances, if applicable.

204. The Parliament of the State may arrange the transfer and due compensation of any part of the State to the Commonwealth, but only after gaining the approval of the people at a State referendum. If such a transfer is approved such part of the State shall come under the exclusive jurisdiction of the Commonwealth.

205. No State shall have the authority to raise any armed military force, whether navel, air or ground force, nor any armed militia, but shall not deny the Commonwealth from stationing military forces in any State, under agreed conditions, as part of the official defence of the nation.

206. No State shall impose a tax on Commonwealth property of any kind, nor shall the Commonwealth impose a tax on any publicly owned State Government property of any kind.

207. No State shall coin money as legal tender, but may establish a publicly owned State Government Bank as per Section 143(ii) and use State and Municipal revenue deposits as the reserve funds. Under Section 178 each State Bank could apply for credit access from the Bank of Australia, on the same basis as applies to privately owned retail banks.

208. The approved credit supply shall be represented as "digital" money and shall rank equally with the

"digital" money used by the privately owned banks. This State bank "digital" money can only be used for State Government infrastructure and other official State Government expenditure. The State Bank shall not go into retail banking in competition to the private banks but may partner with the private banks if there is a mutual benefit for the people of the State.

209. No State or Territory shall legislate to impose a deliberate disability, or discrimination on any resident, other than on the grounds of health and safety concerns.

210. The Commonwealth Defence forces shall protect every State and Territory from any invasion by foreign, hostile forces, but at no time shall the Commonwealth Defence Forces become involved in any civil disturbances within a State or Territory. The State Premier or Territory Administrator can request the assistance of the Defence Forces in the event of a natural disaster or natural emergency.

211. On application from a State Government or Territory Administration, the Federal Police can be called upon to assist the State's Police service.

212. Every State shall make provision, when requested by the Commonwealth Attorney General, for the detention and incarceration of any person accused, or convicted, of an offence against Federal laws.

213. Until such time as the State has established their own publicly owned State Bank, a State may request the Federal Government to take over all, or part, of any accumulated public debt of a State. A mutually agreed arrangement, as set out in Federal legislation, will detail the conditions as they apply to the lender and the borrower under Commonwealth laws.

214. All fermented, distilled, or other intoxicating liquids passing into any State or remaining therein for use, consumption, sale, or storage, shall be subject to the laws of' the State as if such liquids had been produced in the State.

CHAPTER 5

PART 2

NEW STATES OR TERRITORIES

215. The creation of any new State or Territory through the surrender of land of any existing State in the Commonwealth shall only proceed if approved at a Class 1 national referendum, as defined in Chapter 9 Part 1.

216. If a new Territory is created outside of the existing States and Territories, it too shall be subject to approval by a Class 1 national referendum before being recognised as part of the Commonwealth.

217. Any new State or Territory shall be treated on the same basis of the existing States and Territories in respect to Parliamentary representation. Any State surrendering part of their land to form the new State or Territory shall have their Federal representation in the House of Representatives adjusted in line with the formula in Section 76 and the diminished population figure.

218. Each new State or Territory shall have the same respective Senate representation as applies to the existing States and Territories.

CHAPTER 6

PART 1

ELECTIONS

219. Until otherwise altered via a Class 1 Referendum, as per Section 275 of this Constitution, registration with the Electoral Commission and voting shall be mandatory for every citizen in the Commonwealth over eighteen years of age or upon becoming citizens at an age above eighteen.

220. Until otherwise altered by a Class 1 Referendum, the counting system for voting of candidates for the House of Representatives shall be by optional preferential voting until one candidate achieves fifty per-cent plus one of the votes cast in each respective electorate.

    i. However, all votes cast, whether informal, or abstentions shall be counted, and if no candidate can achieve fifty percent, plus one, of the total votes cast, after distribution of preferences, all candidates shall be classed as unsuccessful for any given electorate.

    ii. A new election shall be called for the affected electorates, but no candidate from the failed election shall be eligible to stand for re-election.

    iii. If a third election attempt fails to elect a representative, the Electoral Commission is authorised to amend the electorate boundaries by absorbing the electorate into the adjoining electorates, as near as practical on a pro rata population basis.

221. Until otherwise altered by a Class 1 Referendum, voting for the Senate seats shall be by optional proportional representation according to the process currently in use at the adoption of this Constitution.

222. Every candidate for election to either Houses of Parliament is responsible for submitting a full and detailed account of all their electoral income and expenditure to the Electoral Commission for ratification and compliance before any candidate is announced as the official winner of the seat being contested. Any discrepancy in the account may lead to cancellation of the result for any individual candidate

223. Fund raising by, or on behalf of any candidate, is limited to ten thousand Australian dollars to any candidate at any one time. All funds donated, contributed, or in any way earned for the candidate, must be fully recorded and reported to the Electoral Commission as per Section 222.

224. The right to vote shall not be taken away from any citizen, especially if incarcerated. The Electoral Commission, on application, may provide for exemptions, but only on the grounds of mental or physical incapacity to cast a valid vote.

225. Votes shall be recorded on paper ballots, which shall be publicly counted with access for nominated scrutineers from any candidate for the electorate concerned. Electronic voting shall not be used unless this Section of the Constitution is amended at a Class

2 referendum and a fully accountable electronic system can be guaranteed.

226. This Constitution only recognises a citizen as a natural person, and no artificial entities, such as corporations, limited liability companies, and other entities, established by the laws of any State, or the Commonwealth, or any foreign country, shall be accorded the recognition as a natural person.

227. In the event of a media organised debate being arranged during an election campaign, whether Local, State or National, the organising party shall ensure all the candidates for the particular electorate are given an equal opportunity to participate.

228. Until amended by a Class 2 Referendum as per Section 276 of this Constitution, no candidate standing for election shall be entitled to any form of personal monetary, beneficial, or patronage compensation from the Government, a political party, or any other sponsor.

CHAPTER 6

PART 2

POLITICAL PARTIES

229. A political party shall be defined as any organisation with a verifiable membership of at least five hundred individual members that is established to nominate candidates for election to a State Parliament or the Federal Parliament. Any such organisation must be a registered business in any State where it contests an election, and in Canberra, if the organisation wishes to contest the Federal election. If the organisation fulfils the above requirements, it is then eligible for the compulsory registration with the Commonwealth Electoral Commission before it can nominate any candidate.

230. All political parties shall submit an annual audited set of accounts to the Commonwealth Electoral Commission within three months of the end of each financial year, showing the accurate amount of funds provided to, or raised by, each of the party's endorsed, or elected candidates, at any time during the related financial year. Failure to disclose accurate figures within the specified time frame shall result in de-registration of the political party.

231. A political party may choose to allocate some specific responsibilities to one or more of their

elected members, but that is an internal party decision and shall not impact on the agreed standard remuneration for the member. Nor shall there be any additional expense allowance related to the added responsibilities. The exception shall be the Prime Minister, and State Premiers, and any members sworn in as Ministers of a State, or Federal Government.

232. A professional lobbyist shall be described as any person, or organisation, who is paid to try and influence a political party candidate, or endorsed politician, by way of inducements, offering advice, or promoting any cause or issue. A lobbyist must be registered with the Commonwealth Electoral Commission in that official capacity, or face corruption charges.

233. No officially registered lobbyist, whether an individual or a member of a registered lobbying organisation, shall be eligible to nominate as a candidate for election to any Parliament as an individual, or as a member of any political party, on the grounds of vested interests on the part of the lobbyist.

234. No form of political literature, banners, photographs, whatsoever, shall be permitted to be displayed, or distributed, in relation to a polling station, or on the day designated for an election.

CHAPTER 7

PART 1

CITIZEN'S RECALL

235. The Citizen's recall process provided in this Constitution shall apply to all elected representatives in the Federal Parliament, as well as every public service appointee irrespective of their position or Federal Government Department involved.

236. A recall petition can be started by any citizen in the State, Territory, or electoral district, as applicable, and must detail the grounds for justifying the petition, and include evidentiary proof to support the claim. The petition must then be supported by the signatures, signing date, and addresses of the required percentage of registered voters, as applicable to the position of the person under potential recall.

237. All petitions must be compiled within six months from the date of the first signatory and comply with the conditions in Section 226 above.

238. If a petition aims at recalling a Senator from a State or Territory, the petition must contain at least eight percent of the total number of registered voters in the State or Territory, as applicable.

239. If the petition is aimed at a Member of The House of Representatives for a State or Territory the petition

must contain a minimum of eight percent of the registered voters in the Member's electoral district.

240. If the petition is aimed at a member of a Commonwealth Public Service Department, including the Defence Department, the petition must include endorsement by five percent of the adult population in the State or Territory where the Public Service employee is domicile.

241. A petition relating to a Senator shall be delivered to the President of the Senate within six months of the date of the first signature on the petition. The President of the Senate will then forward the petition to the Parliamentary Rules Committee to question the Senator who is the subject of the petition and assess the presented evidence. Depending on the nature of the alleged offence, whether a breach of the Parliamentary Rules or of the Constitution, the Committee shall determine the validity of the claim and recommend appropriate action including recommending impeachment proceedings to the Australian Council, as per Section 69 above.

242. A similar procedure shall apply in the case of a Member of the House of Representatives being reported, and in this case, the Speaker of the House shall refer the petition to the Parliamentary Rules Committee of the House to decide the appropriate action. After questioning the Member and assessing the evidence, as presented in the petition, the Committee shall decide what action should be recommended.

243. In the case of a Public Servant being the subject of a petition, the petition shall be presented to the Government Minister of the Department concerned, who shall then establish an independent committee of five people to question the person involved and to

assess the evidence presented with the petition. The Committee shall report to the Minister who will then decide on what action is appropriate.

244. On each occasion, the person or persons originating the petition shall be invited to attend and participate in the Committee hearings.

CHAPTER 7

PART 2

IMPEACHMENT PROCEDURES

245. Impeachment procedures can apply to any member of the Australian Council, the Federal Parliament, and the Government bureaucracy, from the Governor General/President down through the ranks. Every defendant shall have the right to legal counsel and the right to call witnesses. The procedures shall vary according to the position of the defendant, as detailed in this Chapter 7 Part 2 of the Constitution.

246. Governor General/President

Impeachment proceedings shall only be initiated against the Governor General/President on the basis of a unanimous agreement by the members of the Australian Council, as provided for in Chapter 1 Part 3 Section 50.

247. If the Council agrees to proceed with impeachment, the Governor General/President shall be offered the opportunity to resign with the loss of all benefits, entitlements and privileges. They may choose to defend their actions at a public hearing of the full bench of the High Court of Australia in response to the charges submitted by the Australian Council.

248. The High Court shall be required to render a unanimous decision on the charges, but if unanimity cannot be reached the majority shall propose whatever recommendations short of impeachment they consider appropriate, and those recommendations shall be adopted by the parties concerned.

249. No appeal shall be granted in this instance of impeachment charges.

250. If impeached, the Governor General/President shall be immediately dismissed from office and denied any entitlements or privileges otherwise applicable. The Governor General/President can also be open to civil charges if appropriate.

251. Members of the Australian Council
Each member of the Australian Council can be subject to impeachment proceedings if a documented and supported claim of misconduct, breach of Oath, or breach of this Constitution is formally submitted to the Head of State by any person, group, or organisation.

252. The Head of State shall determine if the breach is State-related or Commonwealth related. If State related the Member shall be suspended from the Australian Council until the issue is resolved by the appropriate State process. If Commonwealth related, the Member shall be offered the opportunity to resign with the loss of any accrued benefits, or to defend his/her actions at a public hearing of the full bench of the High Court of Australia.

253. Impeachment shall require a majority decision by the High Court and no appeal shall be permitted. If impeached, the Member shall be immediately dismissed from office and denied any entitlements or privileges otherwise applicable. The Member can also be open to civil charges if applicable.

254. Members of Parliament including the Prime Minister
Every elected representative to the Common wealth Parliament can be subject to impeachment proceedings resulting from claims of dishonouring their oath to the people of Australia, or for breaches of this Constitution.

255. In respect to elected Members of Parliament, all such claims have to be processed through the Citizen's Recall provisions contained in Chapter 7 Part 1. If a claim is deemed justified and supported by documented evidence, it would be submitted to a Tribunal of randomly selected High Court Judges to hear the arguments and decide on the merits of the claim. A unanimous decision of the Tribunal shall be final, but if unanimity cannot be reached that would be justification for an appeal.

256. If the elected Member is impeached, he/she shall immediately be dismissed from office and lose all benefits and entitlements applicable to their time in Parliament. The dismissed Member would also be barred from standing for any public Office for the next ten years.

257. The dismissed Member of Parliament can also be open to any civil charges that may arise from their actions while in office.

258. A High Court Judge.
If evidence is presented to the Australian Council charging a High Court Judge with misconduct, or other inappropriate behaviour, while serving on the bench, the Council shall determine if he or she shall be subject to an impeachment process in front of the full membership of the Australian Council. The Council shall allow the judge to defend the charge

and face the accuser, but if the evidence is found valid by a unanimous decision of the Council, the judge shall be relieved of office and lose all entitlements.

259. The Council shall also determine if any other action might be appropriate against the judge.

260. If unanimity cannot be reached within the Council the charge will be deemed lost, but the judge, if he or she so chooses, shall be allowed to retire on full benefits, as applicable to the date of retirement.

261. **Commonwealth Government employees**
The Citizen's Recall provisions allow for claims against any public servant employed by the Commonwealth Government, irrespective of their level of employment. All such claims shall be processed through the Citizen's Recall procedures and supported by documentary evidence of either a breach of this Constitution or of dishonouring their oath to the people of Australia.

262. If the claim is deemed justified by the Minister of the Federal Government Department concerned, it shall proceed to a hearing by a High Court or Supreme Court Judge, to be appointed by the Chief Justice of the Court in the State or Territory where the Public Servant is domicile. The Judge shall adjudicate to decide whether impeachment is warranted, or some other disciplinary action should be taken

263. The Judge's decision shall be final, and no appeal shall be allowed as the defendant will be able to argue the case at the proceedings.

264. If a Public Servant is impeached under this Section of the Constitution they shall immediately be dismissed from their position and lose all entitlements or benefits otherwise applicable to that position. They

shall also be barred from any future Commonwealth Government employment for seven years. The dismissed public servant can also be open to any civil charges that may arise from their actions while employed.

CHAPTER 8

PART 1

A PERIODIC CONSTITUTIONAL REVIEW PROCESS

265. Parliament shall establish a periodic Constitutional Review Process that will be entirely independent of the Government and political party control. It is to be open to any interested person, group, or organisation, to submit proposals for amending the Constitution. The intent and purpose is to keep this Constitution relevant and up to date.

266. Parliament shall set a date for initiating the process within five to seven years from the date proclaiming this Constitution.

267. Parliament shall include a provision for setting up independent Constitutional Committees in each State and Territory to allow maximum public participation. These Committees shall be under the auspices of the State Governor/Vice President, or an eminent Territorian outside of the Administration. (Guidelines for these Committees are contained in Schedule 4 below)

268. Parliament shall also provide for a National Constitutional Convention to be convened within one year from the commencement of the Process and consisting of Constitutional Committee

representatives from each State and Territory. The purpose of the Convention is to arrive at a selected list of amendments from the recommendations made by the respective States and Territories. The full proceedings of the Convention shall be open to the public at all times.

269. The Convention shall be responsible for drafting the final wording of the selected proposed amendments, as it is to be inserted in the Constitution, along with the argument for their adoption.

270. It shall be mandatory for the Government to arrange a Class 1 National Referendum, in conjunction with the next general election, to put the selected amendments to the people for their consideration. Where the amendments impact on the system of Government, the Government and/or the political parties, or other interested parties, shall have the right to submit a counter argument to the proposals for presentation at the Referendum.

271. The result of the Referendum shall be final, and the approved amendments to the Constitution shall become effective from a date within three months after the final counting of the referendum results. Three months will be sufficient time to implement any appropriate action that might be related to the amendments, but no retrospective action of any type will be allowed as a result of the amendments coming into force.

272. Nothing in this process shall prevent the Federal Parliament from proposing amendments to this Constitution at any time outside of the Review process, should such urgency be deemed necessary. The one exception being a bill to nullify the Review process in any way.

273. To develop an informed public with the knowledge and ability to constructively participate in this review process, this Constitution shall be a permanent and compulsory curriculum subject for all High School students in the Commonwealth of Australia.

CHAPTER 9

PART 1

AMENDING THE CONSTITUTION

274. This Constitution shall only be amended, added to, or altered, by a Class 1 national referendum, as described in Section 275, except for the few limited provisions herein that will allow Parliament to update those specific Sections when applicable.

275. The Class 1 Referendum shall be mandatory for any issue that applies to altering this Constitution and/or any issue that involves one or more of the States and Territories in relation to any other State or Territory. This Class 1 Referendum shall require a majority of the eligible voters of the nation to approve the change, as well as a majority of the States. The Territories are to be included with respect to the majority of the eligible voters, but shall not be included in respect to the majority of the States.

276. The Class 2 Referendum shall apply to any national issue that requires the approval of the eligible voters of the nation but does not involve altering this Constitution, or the relationship between the States, or the relationship between the States and the Commonwealth. A simple majority of the votes cast shall represent approval of the issue involved.

277. In the case of any Referendum where the issue involves changing the wording of the Constitution, or legislation, it shall be mandatory that the proposed changes, and/or law are made available to the public in its complete and unalterable form, at least thirty days prior to the date set for the referendum. A printed copy of the changes and/or the proposed law shall be made available at every polling station for the referendum. The merits, or otherwise, shall be addressed in the published arguments for and against the proposal going to referendum. The actual referendum proposal can consist of a simple question to be answered Yes or No, but on the understanding that the unalterable proposed changes and/or law are to be used, or rejected.

278. There shall be a period of not less than thirty days from the day a Referendum is announced and to the nominated day when the Referendum is to be held to allow open discussion on the pros and cons of the proposal being put to the nation.

279. All proposals that emanate from the Periodic Constitutional Review Process, as defined in Chapter 8 Part 1, shall be put to the people according to the timing set out in Section 270.

280. Parliament has the authority to initiate either a Class 1 or a Class 2 Referendum at any time and independently of the Periodic Constitutional Review Process, but any such Parliamentary proposals shall require the same majority approval from both Houses as applies to legislative bills before a referendum can proceed.

281. The Head of State shall give consent to the result of any successful referendum and Parliament shall forthwith proceed to implement the outcome within the time frame as stipulated in Section 271.

SCHEDULE 1

OATH OF OFFICE

Governor General/President

Sworn before the Chief Justice of the High Court of Australia

On behalf of the people of Australia, I .... do hereby promise to discharge my responsibilities as Governor General/ President in an honest and unbiased manner, to the best of my ability, and in compliance with their Constitution.

Special Oath for Vice Presidents/State Governors

To be used initially by the Acting Head of State and subsequently by the formal Head of State

On behalf of the people of Australia, I .... do hereby promise to discharge my responsibilities as the Vice President/ Governor of the State of ...., and as a Member of the Australian Council, in an honest and unbiased manner, to the best of my ability, and in compliance with the State Constitution, as amended, and the people's Constitution for an independent Australia.

All elected representatives of the Commonwealth Parliament

Sworn before the Australian Head of State

On behalf of the people of Australia, I .... do hereby promise to discharge my responsibilities as an elected representative of my constituents, in an honest and unbiased manner and in compliance with their Constitution.

It is a condition of this Constitution that all elected representatives shall take the above Oath of Office, which by virtue of their compliance with the Australian Constitution, means their sole allegiance to the Australian people and the nation.

The Prime Minister and the appointed Ministers of Government Departments shall be required to take an additional public Oath to include upholding the people's Constitution of Australia and acknowledge their wider responsibility to the people of the Australian nation in addition to the constituents of their electorate.

The Prime Minister of Australia

Sworn before the Australian Head of State at a public ceremony

As the elected Prime Minister of Australia, I .... do hereby promise to uphold and comply with the people's Constitution of Australia. I further promise to discharge my responsibilities to the Australian people without bias, and with fairness and honesty for the benefit of our Australian nation.

The Appointed Ministers of Federal Government Departments

Sworn before the Australian Head of State at a public ceremony

As the appointed Minister of the .... Department of the Australian Government, I .... do hereby promise to uphold and comply with the people's Constitution of Australia, and to discharge my responsibilities without bias, and with fairness and honesty for the benefit of our Australian nation.

All appointed officers of the Commonwealth Government

To be sworn before a Member of the Australian Council in the applicable State

On behalf of the people of Australia, I .... do hereby promise to discharge my responsibilities as an appointed officer of the Commonwealth Government in an honest and unbiased manner and in compliance with their Constitution.

In the case of Commonwealth Government officers appointed in the Territories, the Oath can be taken before the most convenient Council Member, or by a witnessed and recorded Oath using electronic technology before an appropriate Council Member.

SCHEDULE 2

POWERS, PRIVILEGES AND IMMUNITIES

The "powers" given to the politicians are spelt out in this Constitution, as are the "powers" they are prohibited from using. Any "power" not specifically referred to shall remain the property of the people, but should it be deemed necessary for a Government to have access to such a "power" the Government must ask for the people's permission through a Class 1 Referendum.

As career politics is no longer an option under this Constitution all privileges granted the elected representatives shall cease on leaving office. As this Constitution prohibits retrospective action, the arrangements applying to currently retired, or retiring politicians on the adoption of this Constitution, shall remain in place. All subsequent privileges shall conform to the same standards as are applied to the general population. In particular regarding superannuation, travel and expense allowances, and accommodation provisions, in as far as such standards apply and are not exorbitant.

All future privileges shall be determined by the Australian Council on written request from the Speaker of the House of Representatives and/or the President of the Senate. Such requests shall be published in the Government Gazette and made available for public comment. If approved by the Australian Council, the agreed privilege shall be recorded in the Government Gazette.

The practice of providing immunity for statements made in Parliament shall continue to be observed, but any other issues related to immunity for elected representatives shall not apply.

SCHEDULE 3

Geographical Description of Australia

The territory of Australia is defined as including:
a. The island continent and the continental lands between Latitudes 9°12' South & 40°30' South and Longitudes 113° East & 154° East.
b. The island of Tasmania
c. Norfolk Island at Lat 29° 02' S and Long 167° 57' E
d. Lord Howe Island at Lat 31° 33' 8.89" S and Long 159° 04' 52.38" E
e. Christmas Island at Lat 10° 30' S and Long 105° 40' E
f. Cocos (Keeling) Islands at Lat 12° 10' S Long 96° 50' E
g. Macquarie Island at Lat 54° 61' S and Long 158° 85' E
h. Heard Island at Lat 53° 05' S and Long 73° 30' E
i. That area of the Antarctic delineated as the Australian Antarctic Territory.
j. The continental shelf of the territory of Australia
k. The 200 nautical mile Economic Zone surrounding the above except where the midpoint between neighbour nations has been agreed and accepted by treaty and ratified by the People of Australia at referendum.

l. The special economic zone of ocean and ocean floor granted to Australia by the United Nations in 2008.

m. The air space above the territory of Australia

SCHEDULE 4

A PROPOSAL
for a
PERIODIC CONSTITUTIONAL
REVIEW PROCESS
First created in June 1998

Updated Draft No. 9 14/11/17

CONTENTS

INTRODUCTION

This Schedule 4 describes a suggested type of Constitutional Review Process in relation to the Australian Constitution.

The aim is to create the opportunity for every interested Australian citizen to become involved in formulating changes to *their* Constitution.

This concept embraces a fundamental philosophy that must apply in our Democracy - this philosophy is -

The Constitution of Australia is the exclusive property of the citizens of Australia - it is *never* the property of the Parliament.

It is rejected that the Commonwealth Parliament has the sole right to propose amendments to the Constitution, despite that being the practice in the past.

This Constitution requires Parliament to write the legislation for initiating a fully independent Review Process, a process that will be open to any interested person.

The key to making the Review process as independent as possible from the Parliament, the Government, and the legal fraternity, lies in selecting the members for the State and Territory Review Committees. Members of these Committees need to be open-minded and unbiased people, able to vet the submissions as objectively as possible.

1. THE PROPOSAL

It should be a fundamental truth that the Australian Constitution is the basic means by which the people of Australia can control and limit their Government and its instrumentalities.

Obviously, that has never been the case with the British Act, and no Australian Citizen has ever had the right, or opportunity, to propose amendments to what should be their Constitution. Only political parties have had that opportunity even though the British Act never gave them that "right."

The primary objective of a periodic review process is to give people the opportunity to voice their concerns about the Constitution and propose changes. But there a number of other aims a review process can fulfil - such as

- Maintaining Australia's status as a true and proper independent nation as declared by this Constitution.
- Updating the protection of Individual Rights
- Reviewing the principles of Rule of Law and the way it has developed between the review periods.
- Where necessary, reinforcing the principles of the Democratic system of Government to protect the nation against tyranny.
- Strengthening the hand of the people to ensure the Government and the High Court remain institutions that are there for the benefit of the people and not institutions beyond the control of the people.

Our Society does not remain static - we are in a state of ever-changing flux - what may have been appropriate even five years ago may become less appropriate today.

Because of this continual state of change, there is a very real need to ensure that 'our' Constitution remains relevant.

Although the fundamental principles of honesty, ethics and fairness will not alter significantly over time, they are always tested, and the people need to ensure the Government and the High Court are constantly monitored to maintain those principles.

This Constitutional Review Process is based on the above reasoning and supported by the belief that Constitutional change must always be motivated and driven from the perspective of the 'people'.

The Periodic Review process becomes an integral part of this new Constitution that creates Australia as a true and proper independent nation.

Every Constitution requires a rational and independent periodic review to keep it current and up to date.

2. THE CONSTITUTIONAL REVIEW PROCESS

A Constitutional Review Process aims to achieve a number of goals.

- It is suggested that the Review periods should be at a minimum of five years and a maximum of ten-year intervals. An eight-year interval is possibly a good compromise, as it avoids delays for any nominated amendments to go to referendum at the next election.
- The ultimate aim of the process is to arrive at a set of proposed amendments for presentation to the Federal Parliament.
- *One of the key factors in this overall Review Process is that it then becomes obligatory on the part of the Federal Government to hold a referendum within six months of receiving the National Review Committee's proposals.*
- Another goal is to provide an opportunity for any interested citizen of Australia to participate in the Review Process. This includes any organisation, group or interested body, including the Local, State and Federal Governments.
- The third goal is to establish a formal system to undertake such a review on a nationwide basis, and over a reasonable time frame of, say, one year.
- A fourth goal is to make the Review process as independent as possible from the Government, from political parties, and legal or academic domination.

- Separate State and Territory Constitutional Review Committees are established at the outset of each Review period. These Committees are under the auspice of the respective Governors/Vice Presidents of each State, or in the case of the Territories, an eminent person independent of the Territory Governments.
- Each State and Territory Review Committee will have nine months to promote the review process, hold Regional forums, canvass proposals for amendments, and then analyse and assess these proposals.
- This is followed by a three month period where a core of Representatives from each of the State and Territory Review Committees convene a National Committee Meeting. The purpose of this National meeting will be to debate and assess the proposals originating from the initial nine-month Review period. The responsibility of the National Committee is to decide on the set of Amendments to be put to Referendum through the Federal Government.
- A Class 1 referendum would be held in accordance with the provisions laid down in the Constitution, a majority vote and a majority of the States agreeing.
- Both State and Federal Governments can use this process to submit proposals. All such proposals would be treated in the same manner as any other Submission.
- It is not intended that this process be the only avenue available to the Federal Government. The Government remains free to organise referendums at any time between the nominated Review periods **if** the urgency arose for such a course of action.

3. DETAILS OF THE REVIEW PROCESS

- The easiest way to maximise public participation is to have each State and Territory conduct separate campaigns for seeking amendment proposals
- Depending on the timing of the Review Process, each State Review Committee will be jointly funded by Federal and State Governments, for the reason that any amendment to the Commonwealth Constitution will impact on both Governments.
- The Federal Government will fund the cost of the National Review Committee for the three months, or less, of its duration.
- The publication of the Reports and conclusions will be a joint State and Federal funded project.

It is believed that the best way to obtain the degree of independence needed for the process is to have it conducted under the auspice of the Governor/Vice President of each State, and an eminent person from each of the Territories.

The actual mechanics of the Process would be in Stages as outlined below.

Stage 1. - Advance publicity

The Electoral Commission in each State and Territory can develop a publicity campaign for one to three months before the starting date of the Review Process.

The purpose would be to alert anyone interested that Submissions will be officially called for at a nominated date in the near future.

This publicity would provide a basic outline of the Review Process and a contact where interested parties may obtain further information.

Stage 2. - Administration

An important feature of the process is the appointment of an Administration Manager, or Consultant, to cover each State and Territory.

This appointment would be for a term of twelve to fifteen months.

The Administrator would set up a Computer database to handle the cataloguing, sorting and statistical reporting of Amendment Submissions.

Stage 3. - State Review Committees

- The Governor/Vice President of each State, and the Chief Administrators of each Territory, shall be responsible for selecting whatever number of Review Committee members they deem appropriate, according to the General Guidelines listed below. These Committees shall consist of a minimum of seven members, but no more than twenty members.
- The selected members shall come from the general community and reflect a range of occupations and the different areas of the State, or Territory. They must confirm their willingness to act in an unbiased and open-minded manner.
- The initial task of the Review Committee will be to select their Chairperson and arrange an appropriate

program for encouraging submissions from the public.

- They will liaison with the Administrator for the implementation of their agreed program for soliciting and reviewing submissions.
- Depending on the available expertise of the Committee members, various areas of particular interest might be allocated to those members.
- The advertising campaign seeking Submissions will be ongoing for a further period beyond the initial three months, or so, if deemed appropriate by the Committee.

Stage 4. - Summing up

The goal of the Committee is to arrive at a set of significant and agreed proposals, which will be taken to the National Committee Meeting.

The Administrator will provide relevant statistical information on the makeup and frequency of submissions and their relationship to respective areas of the Constitution.

The Committee itself will largely determine the type and quality of data they will need to short-list and what they consider to be the more pertinent submissions.

One of the criteria that will need to be taken into account is the possible level of success any Amendment proposal would have in passing a Referendum.

There is not much point in putting up a proposal if it is expected to fail at a Referendum.

The program calls for the Review Committee to select five members to act as Representatives to the National Review Committee Meeting to finalise the set of Amendments to be put to the Federal Government.

Stage 5. - National Review Committee

The National Review Committee Meetings forms the penultimate Stage of the overall Review Process. It is expected to take place over a two month period.

This National Committee would comprise of forty delegates, and ideally, would be held under the auspice of the Governor General/President or the relevant State Governors/Vice Presidents if the Meeting is held in a State.

The National Meeting will operate with a fair degree of flexibility, but records of its deliberations shall be kept for public access.

The National Committee can form Sub-Committees to review and assess proposals in respect to specific sections of the Constitution.

The aim of the National Meeting is to agree on an appropriate number of the most relevant Amendment proposals for presenting to the Federal Government.

Stage 6. – Referendum

This is the final Stage of the process where the selected proposals are handed over to the Federal Government.

As these proposals are the direct expression of the will of the people, the Government and the Parliament will have the opportunity to express their views on the proposals when the referendum is announced.

The Government has six months to arrange the Referendum and put the proposals to the people.

The National Committee shall provide the reasons and justification for each of the proposed Amendments when handing the list to the Government.

These explanations would then form the arguments for adopting the Amendments when put to the Referendum.

The last part of this final Stage is the publishing of the Summary Reports from each State and Territory Review Committee and the National Committee, together with a listing of all the Submissions received throughout the process.

4. GUIDELINES FOR REVIEW COMMITTEE APPOINTMENTS

There are a number of guidelines that need to be taken into account when determining the final composition of the Review Committees.

These guidelines should not be construed as implying the need for any bias in the selection process. They are simply factors that should be weighed up and considered as part of a logical assessment of potential members.

1. It would seem obvious and logical that all the selected Members should have a reasonably sound knowledge of the Australian Constitution.

2. All members ought to be able to demonstrate an interest and concern for the way the Australian Constitution functions.

3. This does not mean that applicants need a background in Constitutional Law - the Constitution is, or ought to be, about people hence the Legal aspects should not be a primary requirement in the appointment of Members. By the same token a background in Law, Constitutional or otherwise, would not preclude the selection of any applicant.

4. All other things being equal, the final composition of the Review Committees should strive to achieve a reasonable representation of the population.

This is meant to imply that, provided the initial guidelines are met, there ought to be a reasonable gender balance as well as a reasonable attempt to cover the age spectrum.

Regarding the number of Members on the Review Committee, this would probably vary according to the size and population of the States and Territories.

5. It can be reasonably assumed that candidates will become from a wide range of interests, and hence, one of the factors that will need to be taken into account is the person's ability to work with other people.

All selected Members must appreciate that they are there to represent the Community's views on changes to the Constitution. They are not there to push their particular view point, no matter what it may be or how passionate they may believe in it.

5. GUIDELINES FOR SUBMISSIONS

The Legislation setting up a Constitutional Review Process must not try to spell out rigid or specific rules about how the Committees must assess Amendment Proposals.

It must be left up to each Committee to develop their own guidelines and process.

There are a number of possible principles that could be used to help in the evaluation of Submissions. It must be left up to each Committee to arrive at their own set of guidelines and priorities, but with an ultimate aim of establishing some form of consistency in their deliberations.

Amongst these principle issues (without conferring any priority) could be:

1. Frequency of similar types of Submissions
2. Constitutional ownership issues.
3. Distribution of 'powers' and their limits or control.
4. Involvement of individual Rights and freedoms.
5. Levels and areas of concern expressed by different groups of respondents.
6. A realistic appraisal of the chances of the Amendment being successful at a Referendum. (There would seem little point in putting up a proposal for Referendum if it is expected to fail)
7. Being open-minded and trying to be impartial in assessing submissions.

8. Keeping Party Political issues out of Committee deliberations.

9. Not to reject any proposal on the sole basis of the number of like submissions. It may well be that some good ideas and valid reasoning may be associated with infrequent proposals.

10. Addressing the future needs of Society, and how the proposals for Constitutional change might best contribute to this.

11. The importance of making the Constitution pertinent by saying what it means.

12. The legal impact of certain amendments must be considered, as too, the issue of retrospectively.

13. There must be no restrictions placed on the initiation of any amendment proposals regarding who is permitted to make a submission.

14. A formal submission procedure would need to be set up, but this must be kept as straightforward and simple as possible.

15. Each submission should deal with only one specific aspect of the Constitution at a time.

16. Each Submission would need to provide a reference to the Chapter, Section and/or Clause to which the proposed amendment relates.

17. Each submission should include an outline of the reasons, purpose and desired objective of the proposed amendment. This may, but not necessarily, include the specific wording of the proposal, although the wording would be subject to change in the light of other related proposals.

18. All submissions must be acknowledged by the Administrator.

19. The Review Process should become the conventional vehicle for both the State and Federal Governments

to make submissions. It would be anticipated that the bulk of such submissions will deal with the division of powers between these two entities.

It is not intended that the Review Process would be the only way for Governments to propose Amendments. Governments would retain the right to propose Amendments at any time should the urgency for such action arise.

There would also be nothing to stop the Government from adding their proposals to the final submissions put forward by the National Review Committee.

As the Process develops, other issues of prominence will come to light. It will then become the responsibility of each Committee to take these issues into account and weight them according to their perceived levels of importance.

6. FUNCTIONS OF
THE ADMINISTRATION PROCESS

There will be a considerable amount of Administration associated with the Review Process itself.

Because of this obvious workload, and the limited duration of the Review, it is believed that the appointment of a contract Administrator would best serve the process.

Appointment

Probably the fairest and simplest method of seeking a suitably independent Administrator would be to have the Government arrange a tender for the contract. The Administration will be a wide-ranging commission and should include all necessary Computer Services, compilation and printing of reports, and the ability to bring in short-term Staff, as appropriate.

Timing

The appointment of the Administrator or Consultant should be made approximately three months prior to the commencement of the Review Process itself.

This will allow the Administrator to organise the appropriate procedures to assist the orderly functioning of the Review Committees.

Advertising

The Administrator will liaise with the Electoral Commission on the initial publicity campaign to announce and promote the Review Process.

This campaign would require advertising throughout each State and Territory via both major newspapers and Regional papers.

The level of TV advertising would need to be determined from the budget that would be allocated to the overall Review Process by the respective State and Federal Governments.

Subsequent advertising will be coordinated with the respective Review Committees as appropriate,

Setting Up An Information Service

Because the concept of a People's Constitutional Review Process is quite new to the Australian political scene, it is expected there will be a need to establish a formal Information Service.

This Service would consist of both published material and an Information phone Service.

There would also need to be a proper Internet link set up which will require periodic up-dating as patterns develop in the more frequently asked questions.

Classifying And Cataloguing Proposals

The classifying and cataloguing of the amendment submissions will be a significant and important function of the Administrators duties.

1. This will involve sorting all the submissions under the specific Chapter and Section of the Constitution to which they relate.

This cataloguing will also include cross-referencing as well as defining new additions to the Constitution compared to changes in the existing wording.

2. As the process develops other forms of sorting and classifying will probably be requested hence it is essential that an adequate Data Base system is used. There are a number of suitable, proven, systems available in the market which obviates the need to consider any customised software for this exercise.

Statistical Analysis

As the sorting and classifying process can be done on a normal computer Data Base program it will be readily possible to extract a set of Statistics.

One of the principle statistics that will be utilised is the frequency of proposals in relation to specific areas of the Constitution. Obviously, this would indicate the areas of most concern from a State to State basis and also from a National point of view.

It will be the responsibility of the Administrator to provide such Statistical analysis as might be requested by the Review Committees.

Furthermore, the State/Territory Administrators will be required to liaise to produce a coordinated set of statistics for the National Review Committee near the end of the various State/Territory programs.

7. OVERVIEW

As the Constitutional Review Process is an entirely new concept it is impossible to anticipate the level of response that might be achieved in Amendment proposals.

What is possible though is to project some of the broad categories of proposals that are likely to result. This does not imply that there is any question of 'right' or 'wrong' about any form of submission.

This Overview is simply an indication of the type and extent of proposals that logically would be expected to be raised.

In essence, the categories would be as follows: -

1. <u>Technical and Legal</u>

   It is almost certain that there will be a number of technical and/or legal proposals received, which, while having merit, may need careful presentation to relate to the broad population.

2. <u>Legislative</u>

   It is also highly likely that there will be a number of proposals that will overlap or encroach into the area of Legislation. It will need careful assessment to determine whether such proposals are proper for a Constitution or whether they are better dealt with through Legislation.

3. <u>Philosophic</u>

There will most likely be a number of submissions dealing with the Philosophic approach to the Constitution.

In essence, such proposals would involve defining matters of principle crucial to the whole question of interpretation of the Constitution.

The Constitution should be viewed as the 'home of principles' rather than the place to expound detailed Law. Sometimes there is a necessary stage between pronouncing a 'principle' and making sure the intent and purpose is clear.

Where such explanations are deemed necessary, to avoid misinterpretation, they should be included in the Constitution.

4. <u>Single Issues</u>

It is almost certain there will be a number of proposals promoting Single Issue items that are obviously considered very important to the groups, or individuals, submitting.

Part of the advantage of the Review Process is that it allows the Constitution to be assessed in its entirety. The Review Committee can evaluate Single Issue items in the context of the overall Constitution and also in the context of society's concerns at the time.

5. <u>Subtle Amendments</u>

One would expect a number of Amendment Proposals suggesting minor changes to either the Constitution itself or to the wording of certain Sections.

Some of these proposals may involve quite profound changes in Legal interpretation when fully analysed.

It will be in situations such as this that the accompanying explanation of the proposer's purpose and intent of the amendment will help in assessing the importance and effectiveness of the change.

6. <u>Frivolous Proposals</u>

Very likely, there will be a percentage of irrelevant and/or frivolous proposals submitted. Depending on the extent of supporting argument that may or may not accompany the proposals, the Review Committee should be able to assess whether there is any foundation in the submission.

7. <u>Major and Significant Proposals</u>

It is guaranteed that there will be some submissions proposing major and significant changes to the Constitution.

The Review Process should be able to evaluate these proposals on their merits.

In most cases it would be expected that these submissions would be accompanied by properly argued supporting documentation.

These proposals will require a considerable amount of discussion and evaluation to determine their value, importance and likely success.

8. CONCLUSION

It is obvious that the Constitutional Review Process will open up the Constitution to a wide-ranging and thorough scrutiny. This will be achieved in a way that has never been done previously. What is more important is that the final outcome of the Process will be translated into definite action. Of equal importance is the fact that the people of Australia will be the ones driving the changes, and not the Government.

The People will be in a position to claim ownership of the Constitution, which from now on will always been theirs. The further benefit of the Review Process is that it will develop a thorough and systematic evaluation of the relevance of the Constitution to current and future conditions. This type of evaluation will be done from the People's perspective and not from the vested interests of the Government.

Another very pertinent benefit will be the message passed on to the High Court of Australia. The High Court has tended, on many occasions, and particularly of late, to spuriously assume an insight into so called "public opinion". These assumptions have been made without any supporting evidence to back them up. The deliberations, submissions and results of the ongoing Constitutional Review Process will now give the High Court a much truer picture of "public opinion" as far as the people's perceptions of the Australian Constitution are concerned.

Review Requested:

If you loved this book, would you please provide
a review at Amazon.com?